Ambient Stories in Practice and Research

Bloomsbury Studies in Digital Cultures

Series Editors
Anthony Mandal and Jenny Kidd

This series responds to a rapidly changing digital world, one which permeates both our everyday lives and the broader philosophical challenges that accrue in its wake. It is inter- and trans-disciplinary, situated at the meeting points of the digital humanities, digital media and cultural studies, and research into digital ethics.
While the series will tackle the 'digital humanities' in its broadest sense, its ambition is to broaden focus beyond areas typically associated with the digital humanities to encompass a range of approaches to the digital, whether these be digital humanities, digital media studies or digital arts practice.

Titles in the series
The Trouble With Big Data, Jennifer Edmond, Nicola Horsley, Jörg Lehmann and Mike Priddy
Digital Humanities and the Cyberspace Decade 1990–2001, Claire Warwick
Queer Data, Kevin Guyan
Hacking in the Humanities, Aaron Mauro
Herman Melville and the Digital Humanities, Christopher Ohge and Dennis Mischke
The Language of Cyber Attacks, Aaron Mauro
Investigating Google's Search Engine, Rosie Graham
Reading Audio Readers, Karl Berglund
Metamodernism and the Postdigital in the Contemporary Novel, Spencer Jordan

Forthcoming titles
Listening In, Toby Heys, David Jackson and Marsha Courneya
People Like You, Sophie Day, Celia Lury and Helen Ward

Ambient Stories in Practice and Research

Digital Writing in Place

Edited by Amy Spencer

BLOOMSBURY ACADEMIC
LONDON • NEW YORK • OXFORD • NEW DELHI • SYDNEY

BLOOMSBURY ACADEMIC
Bloomsbury Publishing Plc
50 Bedford Square, London, WC1B 3DP, UK
1385 Broadway, New York, NY 10018, USA
29 Earlsfort Terrace, Dublin 2, Ireland

BLOOMSBURY, BLOOMSBURY ACADEMIC and the Diana logo are
trademarks of Bloomsbury Publishing Plc

First published in Great Britain 2025

Series design by Rebecca Heselton
Cover image © Iaroslava Kaliuzhna/ iStock

A catalogue record for this book is available from the British Library.

Library of Congress Cataloging-in-Publication Data
Names: Spencer, Amy, editor.
Title: Ambient stories in practice and research : digital writing
in place / edited by Amy Spencer.
Description: London ; New York : Bloomsbury Academic, 2024. |
Series: Bloomsbury studies in digital cultures ; vol 9 | Includes bibliographical references.
Identifiers: LCCN 2024035703 (print) | LCCN 2024035704 (ebook) |
ISBN 9781350234130 (hardback) | ISBN 9781350234178 (paperback) |
ISBN 9781350234147 (pdf) | ISBN 9781350234154 (ebook)
Subjects: LCSH: Experimental fiction, English–History and criticism. |
Authorship–Technological innovations. | Ambient Literature Project (2016–2018) |
LCGFT: Literary criticism. | Essays.
Classification: LCC PR890.E982 A43 2024 (print) | LCC PR890.E982 (ebook) |
DDC 823.00901–dc23/eng/20240812
LC record available at https://lccn.loc.gov/2024035703
LC ebook record available at https://lccn.loc.gov/2024035704

ISBN: HB: 978-1-3502-3413-0
ePDF: 978-1-3502-3414-7
eBook: 978-1-3502-3415-4

Series: Bloomsbury Studies in Digital Cultures

Typeset by Integra Software Services Pvt. Ltd.

To find out more about our authors and books visit www.bloomsbury.com
and sign up for our newsletters.

Contents

Figures

Contributors

Tom Abba is a specialist in the convergence of narrative, books and future platforms for storytelling and design. A practising artist for thirty years, he has developed world-leading processes and techniques exploring interdependencies within digital and physical arts fields. From 2016, his digital storytelling practice formed the core of the AHRC funded Ambient Literature Project, and he was named in 2018 as one of the *Booksellers* '40 Most Disruptive Innovators in Publishing'. He is the Director of the Digital Cultures Research Centre (DCRC) and is Associate Professor in Art & Design at UWE Bristol.

Richard A. Carter is a Senior Lecturer in Digital Culture at the University of York. Carter's academic practice investigates the more-than-human as it manifests across technical activities, objects and environments.

Claire Dean is a writer and independent scholar living in the north of England. Her short stories are widely published and have been selected for anthologies including *The Best British Short Stories* (edited by Nicholas Royle). Her first collection is titled *The Museum of Shadows and Reflections* (2016). Dean's PhD focused on materials and technologies for environmental story-making (2018), and she continues to explore materials and sustainability as an early career conservator.

Ben Gwalchmai is a Lecturer in Digital Innovation at the University of South Wales. His research interests are extended reality in public space, borders, open data in digital innovation, eviation and Welsh poetry. His most recent book is *swimming in locks // kites over marches* (2019).

Donna Hancox is Professor at Queensland University of Technology in the School of Creative Practice. Her research interests are the social impact of arts and culture in under-served communities, amplified storytelling and creative data gathering. She has published widely on these topics. She was a 2021 Fulbright Senior Scholar.

Malcolm McCullough is Professor of Architecture at the University of Michigan. A pioneer of digital design culture in architecture in the 1990s, his more recent work has focused on hyperlocal media at street level, particularly for resilience. His most recent book is *Downtime on the Microgrid–Architecture, Electricity, and Smart City Islands* (2020). His most widely read book is *Digital Ground–Architecture, Pervasive Computing, and Environmental Knowing* (2003).

Lee Miller is a UK-born practitioner-scholar whose research lies in the space between bodies in performance, with a specific focus on the affective gap between audience and performer. He is Professor of Performance at Falmouth University, where he is also the lead for the Centre for Blended Realities and Head of Postgraduate Research. He has published widely about practice as research and audience–performer interaction, while his recent research expanded to digital performance exchanges.

Agnieszka Przybyszewska is Assistant Professor at the University of Łódź, Poland, co-creator of a programme of creative writing studies, promotor and translator of electronic literature. Her research interests focus on electronic literature and textual materialism in the context of the modern evolution in conceptualizing categories such as the book, the act of reading, literature and literariness. She has published several dozen articles in peer-reviewed journals and joint academic publications (in Polish, English and Spanish). Her most recent book is *Liberackość dzieła literackiego* (*Liberariness of Literary Work*, 2015), and her new monograph *Kate Pullinger and Innovation in Digital Writing* will be published by Bloomsbury.

Phil Smith is a performance-maker, writer and academic researcher, specializing in work around walking, site-specificity and mythogeographies. He is an Associate Professor (reader) at the University of Plymouth and most recently the author of *Albion's Eco-Eerie: TV and Movies of the Haunted Generations* (2024) and *Goblin Queens and Qualia Knights* (2024). With visual artist Helen Billinghurst, he is one half of Crab & Bee, publishing *The Pattern* (2020). He is also the author of *Making Site-Specific Theatre and Performance* (Methuen Drama, 2020). Since 1980, Smith has been company dramaturg for TNT Theatre (Munich); his and TNT's artistic director Paul Stebbings' book about the history and aesthetics of the company, *TNT: The New Theatre*, was published in 2020.

Amy Spencer is a writer and postdoctoral researcher based in the Centre for Cultural and Creative Industries at Bath Spa University. She works as part of MyWorld, researching the future of creative technology innovation. Previously, she was a postdoctoral researcher working at UWE Bristol as part of the Ambient Literature project. Her previous books include *DIY: The Rise of Lo-Fi Culture*. She holds a PhD in Cultural Studies from Goldsmiths.

Joanne 'Bob' Whalley is an artist, dramaturg and acupuncturist, who focuses on radical kinship and politics of care. She is Director of Doctoral Training and Development at University of the Arts London. Her book *Between Us: Audiences, Affect and the In-Between* (2017) celebrates spaces which cause an affecting, and bodies affected.

Acknowledgements

My thanks go to all the writers who contributed their knowledge of and visions for the future of ambient modes of storytelling to this collection. Thanks go to the Ambient Literature Project team: Kate Pullinger, Jon Dovey, Tom Abba, Ian Gadd, Matt Hayler, Michael Marcinkowski, Emma Whittaker, James Attlee, Duncan Speakman and Nick Triggs. You are pioneers in the field and this work is inspired by your contributions. Thanks also go to my wonderful colleagues at Bath Spa University, especially everyone in the Centre for Cultural and Creative Industries.

Introduction: Ambient stories – embodied, authored and unpredictable

Amy Spencer

Imagine creating a story that uses the intimate and technological relationship that your reader has with their smartphone, their 'personalized, indispensable and irreplaceable companion' (Kuzmičová, Schilhab and Burke 2020: 337), and the data all around them to evoke a unique, immersive experience that responds to their location to position them within the story as an active participant. Over the past decades, pervasive and ubiquitous technologies have led to changes in user behaviours as people have become increasingly untethered to technologies within the home, such as the desktop computer (Farman 2015). Building on traditions of locative storytelling (Hight 2006), these mobile technologies can be put to creative use to tell ambient stories that play with a range of ambient materials in the physical world, such as those drawn from a phone's APIs (application programming interfaces). These materials can include, for example, location, time, weather and proximity to specific objects and places as well as audio, images and text. Ambient stories may also include elements of the physical, such as printed materials that may take the form of a book or other artefacts, which augment the digital. The kinds of ambient stories that can be told are endless, for instance, historical tales, literary works resembling the novel, political and social commentaries, ghost stories, travel writing and so on.

Ambient stories, rooted in place and accessed using a smartphone, are not only told through the authored words that are presented to a reader through text on the screen of a smartphone or through elements of audio listened to through headphones but also the language found in the world around them, which can also be read. These may include the physical landscape, for example the architectural features of the city street, elements of the natural world or other people passing by. It is not an encounter with a static story but rather one that is in flux (Dovey 2016) as the reader remains part of the physical world with its multitude of moving elements.

I have been inspired by this emerging form of storytelling, the experience it offers readers and the ways in which writers and technologists have embraced the new narrative possibilities it brings. The chapters in this collection take both academic and practice-led perspectives to explore how such situated reading experiences, which are embodied, authored and often unpredictable, shared through text, audio and sensor-based delivery, offer distinctive new forms of reading and listening and lay the groundwork for a new poetics of situated writing practices.

The Ambient Literature Project

The term 'ambient literature' (Dovey 2016; Abba, Dovey and Pullinger 2021) emerged from a two-year research project, the Ambient Literature Project, led by Jonathan Dovey and funded by the Arts and Humanities Research Council (AHRC), which ran from 2016 to 2018, and as part of which I worked as a postdoctoral research fellow. The project was a collaboration between three universities in the United Kingdom (UWE Bristol, Bath Spa University and the University of Birmingham), and we defined this emerging digital literary form as: 'situated literary experiences delivered by pervasive computing platforms, responding to the presence of a reader to deliver story' (Ambient Literature Project n.d.). In this form, the ambient is both in the background and the foreground (Eno 1978; Schmidt 2013) as a reader's attention is drawn both to a story and to the world around them and back again, becoming an integral part of a literary form.

The project centred on a practice-led approach to research, and three writers, Kate Pullinger, James Attlee and Duncan Speakman, were commissioned to develop ambient literature projects to help us to explore and understand the concept of this emerging literary form. Each work could be experienced using a smartphone, was rooted in the notion of place, made use of ubiquitous forms of data and needed a reader to be present to engage with the story through a process of embodied reading. This engagement involved movement, both through physical spaces and through a physical engagement with technology. These three literary works helped us to question the relationship between readers and smartphones as well as the technological potential for storytelling, and they can be used to reflect on three key features that are present within works of ambient storytelling: embodied reading, reading unpredictability and authored movement (Abba and Spencer 2021).

The first commissioned work was *It Must Have Been Dark by Then*, by Duncan Speakman. This work, 'somewhere between a travel journal and a poetic reflection on connection, progress and memory' (Ambient Literature Project n.d.), includes a printed book and app-based audio experience. It uses music, narration and field recordings to reveal stories of environments that are changing and disappearing, predominantly due to climate change: from the swamplands of Louisiana to empty Latvian villages and the edge of the Tunisian Sahara. An audio experience prompts a reader to walk to locations, carrying an accompanying printed book with them, but there is no preset route, rather, a unique map is built for each person's experience, and they are asked to follow it. There is an interplay between the printed word in the book that the reader carries, the stories told to the reader through audio and the physical locations around them. There is a boundary that the reader needs to cross between the work and the physical world to engage with the experience. This resembles Roquet's (2016) understanding of ambient aesthetics as providing affordances for reflective drift as a reader is promoted to explore place in an almost meditative state.

The reader must be present in a physical location to experience the work, but this does not need to be the same location for each reader. However, this is a part of the narrative that the writer cannot fully control. It is part of their authorial territory but, as they might not know exactly what the reader sees in front of them, uncontrollable elements may become unexpected features of the story. A reader actually navigating the physical space in a piece of digitally situated literature is not always controllable and cannot always be directed by an author in the same way as in a printed book. The narrative is not, like a book, bound by a material form. Without such a framing device, and with its position embedded in the physical world, the boundaries of this narrative form are often in flux, and the boundaries between reader and text become more porous. The experience for the reader is as though there are stories in the air waiting to be discovered. These stories have a temporal rather than a physical frame; they appear and then they disappear. They might be authored, or they might be elements that a reader experiences for themselves during an encounter with a place. Adriana De Souza e Silva (2006) argues that in such an experience, pervasive computing, on which ambient literature relies, offers an opportunity for us to be connected to our environment, not just immersed in an electronic device.

The second commissioned work was *The Cartographer's Confession* by James Attlee. This exploration of London, based on the personal history of Attlee's own family, 'combines fiction and non-fiction, imagined and real locations, to create a story of migration, loss, betrayal, and retribution that builds to a savage denouement' (Ambient Literature Project n.d.). A reader is asked to follow a preset route across London and experience real locations, which are each tied to an unfolding story. As they follow, their attention is directed to what they see around them, and they are shown photographs of the same sites taken at different times on their phone. Some elements of the city will be recognizable but others have vanished into history. Through this approach to incorporating real locations, the reader experiences a sense of blurring reality and of experiencing several time periods at once.

The use of physical, authored movement shapes the reading experience of this work, although it must be noted that not all works of ambient literature rely on the physical act of walking to deliver a story. There is a long history of literary walking that can be drawn on to understand this process, including the figure of Walter Benjamin's *Flaneur* (2002) and Guy Debord's *Society of the Spectacle* (1992) experience of the *dérive*. However, these are enactments of a particular kind of walking – a celebration of wandering and of moving through space. In an ambient story, a reader is physically situated in a place and a writer is able to draw deep connections to context and time. For example, this may be achieved through an audio piece told to the reader through headphones as they walk and the experience of someone telling them a story connects them directly to the narrative. This experience of moving through space is mediated and authored. Michel de Certeau (1984) writes that, 'walking in the city is an acting out of place' as both walking and language are creative acts, which you can improvise, make connections with and make your own decisions about. And, as Merlin Coverly (2022) explains, the act of walking with its bodily rhythms leads to thoughts taking the shape of a coherent narrative.

The third work commissioned by the Ambient Literature Project was *Breathe* by Kate Pullinger, developed with Editions at Play (a collaboration between Google Creative Lab Sydney and London-based publisher Visual Editions). The work is a literary ghost story told through accessing a website using a smartphone, designed to be experienced anywhere in the world. The reader experiences the story through the character of Flo, a young woman who is haunted by ghosts, by technology and by her phone. The use of APIs evokes a sense of the uncanny as the story is personalized with details relating to the location, time and weather that are unique to each reader. Juan Álvarez-Umbarila (2022) recognizes that this customized reading experience involves the 'triangulation' of story, technology and environment. This work does not involve a reader being physically present in a location. The way in which a reader physically interacts with the story is through their interaction with their smartphone in the form of movement and gesture, for example by swiping the screen and by moving the phone to reveal hidden sections of text.

Each of these three ambient works offers unique ways to understand storytelling that relies on the coming together of reader, technology and place. They reveal how literary experiences can be created, personalized and consumed, and provide a framework for understanding new and immersive opportunities for readers and authors.

Ambient storytelling

This collection of essays critically examines the ecology of ambient storytelling from a range of perspectives, broadening the scope of ambient literature to examine stories that focus on more than a literary experience. The ambient story not only offers a reader an encounter with place that is mediated by ubiquitous, familiar technology, which draws their attention to place and a recognition that their presence is necessary for their interaction with the story, but also offers a lens through which we can understand storytelling more broadly. The collection recognizes that ambient storytelling is not a fixed genre or a particular way of writing, so the concept of ambient literature is expanded. For example, works may engage with place and technology to make visible hidden processes or political and social issues.

In an interview, Duncan Speakman (in Hancox 2021) explains that ambient storytelling is a way to understand types of stories and story-making that use technologies rather than being a specific genre. Kate Pullinger (in Hancox 2021) adds that the concept can be used to reflect upon and begin to understand the presence of ubiquitous computing. It 'reflects what is already occurring in people's relationships to their mobile devices and their environments, rather than a form of storytelling that directs or disrupts the relationship with technology' (Hancox 2021).

Addressing the recognition that the ambient story offers a lens through which to examine our relationship with technology and the world around us, this collection includes a wide range of academic and practitioner perspectives. Researchers and practitioners working in diverse fields, such as architecture, performance, literary studies and creative writing look towards the emerging field of ambient storytelling and draw on their own background, interests and experiences. Such interests include examining how embodiment and architecture can provide an active approach to experiencing text in the city; looking at ambulatory arts and site-specific performances; exploring engagements with ecological and climatic challenges; investigating critical and creative cartographies; and understanding the metaphorical work of ambient as a form embedded in the social, technological and political spheres. Critical attention is paid to the concept of ambient literature and the wider concept of the ambient story is examined. The collection includes several practice-based chapters from writers, artists and practitioners on topics such as the use of data to construct poetry and the position of the writer as maker. I hope that the following chapters will shed light on the poetics, politics and context of ambient storytelling and build on the history of ambient literature to help us to understand the immersive, situated experiences this approach can offer readers. They are intended to prompt reflection on our relationships with the pervasive and ubiquitous technologies that we carry with us and the creative opportunities that ambient storytelling can offer practitioners.

Chapter overview

This collection begins with chapters that explore a close examination of ambient stories in various forms through accounts of the process of their making. This offers us a unique understanding of how such stories operate, how they are written and experienced. In 'On Writing Instability: How Ambient Literature Reconfigures the Reader/Writer Relationship in Situated Storytelling', Tom Abba revisits the set of ambient poetics that emerged from the Ambient Literature Project (Abba and Spencer 2021) and sets out to reach a comprehensive definition of the form. The chapter offers a reflection on a new work, *From Bitter Ground*, 'a haunted house story, a journey through the twentieth century and an exploration and examination of the grammars of ambient storytelling'. This is an in-depth account of developing an ambient work that plays with time and place as well as the interplay between the physical and the digital and will serve to help us understand both the authoring and reading processes of the ambient story.

'*Persephone's Footsteps*: Story Making on Foot' by Claire Dean recounts the process of developing *Persephone's Footsteps*, a tactile story with ecological roots that must be walked into existence by its reader through the contemporary city, which is transformed into a 'book-space'. Framing the making of this work as an investigation into an ambient form, Dean explores how the work leaves room for the reader to uncover physical spaces as well as narrative elements as it is 'made and remade through walking'. The chapter reflects on how developments in technology bring new opportunities to write story into place and offers insights to writers as well as, what Dean terms, 'walking readers'. It offers an insight into the writing and making process, a sharing of the joy of experimentation and a meditation on emerging possibilities for writers to experiment and make. In exploring these processes, Dean touches on issues of accessibility and access to technologies, which is crucial for the development of the ambient form to flourish and reach its readers.

In '*Waveform*: Writing across Ocean, Air and Algorithms', Richard A. Carter provides an in-depth exploration of *Waveform*, a speculative digital writing project that converts visual data into poetry as a form of technically mediated sense-making. Carter outlines the key themes that form the conceptual and aesthetic locus of the project, including machine sensing, the politics and aesthetic potentials of ocean and atmosphere, and how they can be expressed and experienced through generative writing. The project involves co-authorship with natural environments and highlights the potential of the data-driven ambient story to bring about radical environmental change. The work discussed here focuses on the use of data more broadly and expands on what we consider ambient storytelling, highlighting the expansive nature of the emerging field.

The chapters that follow address modes of interaction between audience and performance and reader and text. In 'Dear Reader, Can I Borrow Your Body to Tell a Story? On Ambient Interactional Metalepsis, Sylleptic Readers and Palimpsestuous Embedded Reading', Agnieszka Przybyszewska offers a close reading of several works of ambient literature, including *Breathe* by Kate Pullinger (2019) and Semyon Polyakovskiy's *Maginary* (2018), through the lens of palimpsest, metalepsis and syllepsis. By positioning ambient literature in a broader research and creative context, Przybyszewska offers an in-depth understanding of the narrative form used to create such specifically literary experiences. In particular, she pays critical attention to the second-person narrative, an enhanced form of a spoken monologue and an emerging feature of ambient literary poetics, and to the relationship this intimacy evokes between author and reader. The chapter offers a broad sweep of research in the field, uncovers some intriguing features of the ambient story and places them in a wider context.

In 'At the Edges: A Question of Audience Invisibility, Disappearance and Failure', Joanne 'Bob' Whalley and Lee Miller address the performative aspect of the ambient story through an autobiographical exploration of their mishap-filled experience of encountering Blast Theory's *Uncle Roy All Around You* (2003). Blending the real and the fictional through a large-scale performance, this work involves the audience using problem-solving and cooperation skills and adhering to a series of predetermined rules, which structures their participation. However, as Whalley and Miller explain, there is the potential for ambient failure through an encounter with unpredictability as part of such an immersive experience. The chapter offers a detailed understanding of what can go wrong in an experience that is often porous and unpredictable and its impact on an audience of an ambient work.

Ben Gwalchmai's chapter '*Here. Now. Ours*: Interrogating the Use of Situated Augmented Reality' addresses the process of story-making through a reflection on a practice-led research project on aspects of embodiment and touch in a situated work. This chapter prompts us to question the politics of public and private space and ask who controls the stories that are consumed in the physical world, how do we read them and how are they mediated. It raises issues of playing and playfulness in the immersive experience and asks how these can be used as a form of resistance in the smart city.

The final chapters of this collection examine how ambient stories can engage with built environments, how the street can become a site of performance, how the solid and the virtual can overlap through narrative, and how the reader can be prompted to reflect on social and political issues. In 'Retrospect on the New Epigraphy: Walking, Reading and Marking the City', Malcolm McCullough reflects on the experience of moving through the built environment and how this experience is structured through architecture, with the city being a fertile ground for story to emerge through an engagement with ambient informational surroundings. Through looking at a range of projects, such as Yellow Arrow by Brian House and Jesse Shapin (2003–07), McCullough examines the heritage of annotations on city spaces as early forms of ambient story to offer a look at the roots of the form.

Donna Hancox's 'Ambient Activism: Place, People and Process' recognizes the lineage of forms of ambient storytelling in tactical or guerrilla media, and the work of the Situationist International and the DIY aesthetic of the 1980s and 1990s. This is place-based tactical storytelling that relies on the intersection of technology and attention to provide visceral experiences. This chapter examines the nature and elements of ambience and the ways they have shaped contemporary political and social activism.

In 'Ambient Writing in a Terrain of Threatened Subjectivity: Unfolding Codes, Tainted Models and Holey Spaces' by Phil Smith, we are offered a meditative exploration of the possible roots of ambient literature in psychogeography and the methodology of the *derive*, and a multitude of ways to navigate a city space. Smith examines the performance of everyday life, which can be harnessed as inspiration for stories, through an examination of the position of the situated reader who holds an agency equivalent to that of the ambulatory artist with their engagement with space resembling the interaction with a live art performance. This rich practice-led approach gives us a framework for understanding the emerging field of the ambient story both as writers and readers.

Conclusion

Emerging from ambient literature, and rooted in an understanding of this situated, literary form, I hope that the concept of ambient storytelling will broaden the field and prompt us to consider our relationships with ubiquitous and pervasive technologies and our interactions with data through telling and interacting with stories. The ambient story challenges the concept of an authored form as it requires its authors to let go of some authorial control, provides readers with an embodied and situated reading experience that involves an element of authored movement, and incorporates the unpredictability of both the physical world and technologies. Such situated experiences mean that the reader is positioned inside and outside both the physical world and the story, offering a space to reflect, question and imagine.

References

Abba, T. and A. Spencer. (2021), 'Writing Ambient Literature', in T. Abba, J. Dovey and K. Pullinger, eds, *Ambient Literature: Towards a New Poetics of Situated Writing and Reading Practices*, 275–318, London: Palgrave Macmillan.

Abba, T., J. Dovey and K. Pullinger, eds. (2021), *Ambient Literature: Towards a New Poetics of Situated Writing and Reading Practices*, London: Palgrave Macmillan.

Ambient Literature Project. (n.d.), 'Ambient Literature.' Available online: https://research.ambientlit.com (accessed 10 November 2022).

Coverley, M. (2022), *The Act of Wandering*, Harpenden: Oldcastle Books.
de Certeau, M. (1984), *The Practice of Everyday Life*, Berkeley: University of California Press.
de Souza e Silva, A. (2006), 'From Cyber to Hybrid: Mobile Technologies as Interfaces of Hybrid Spaces', *Space and Culture*, 9(3), 261–78.
Dovey, J. (2016), 'Ambient Literature: Writing Probability', in U. Ekman, J. D. Bolter, L. Diaz, M. Søndergaard and M. Engberg, eds, *Ubiquitous Computing, Complexity and Culture*, 141–54, London: Routledge.
Eno, B. (1978), 'Ambient Music from Liner Notes Music for Airports/ Ambient 11'. Available online: http://music.hyperreal.org/artists/brian_eno/MFA-txt.html (accessed 10 November 2022).
Farman, J. (2015), 'The Materiality of Locative Media: On the Invisible Infrastructure of Mobile Networks', in A. Herman, J. Hadlaw and T. Swiss, eds, *Theories of the Mobile Internet: Materialities and Imaginaries*, 45–59, New York: Routledge.
Hancox, D. (2021), *The Revolution in Transmedia Storytelling through Place: Pervasive, Ambient and Situated*, London: Routledge.
Hight, J. (2006), 'Views from Above: Locative Narrative and the Landscape', *Leonardo*, 14(8), 1–10. Available online: https://www.leoalmanac.org/wp-content/uploads/2012/09/09_JHight.pdf (accessed 10 November 2022).
Kuzmičová, A., T. Schilhab and M. Burke. (2020), 'm-Reading: Fiction Reading from Mobile Phones', *Convergence: The International Journal of Research into New Media Technology*, 26(2), 333–49.
Roquet, P. (2016), *Ambient Media: Japanese Atmospheres of Self*, Minneapolis: University of Minnesota Press.
Schmidt, U. (2013), 'Ambience and Ubiquity,' in U. Ekman, ed., *Throughout: Art and Culture Emerging with Ubiquitous Computing*, 175–87, Cambridge, MA: MIT Press.
Umbarila, J. A. (2022), 'Breathe: The Spatial Triangulation of Everyday Literary Experiences in Ambient Literature and m-Reading', *Perífrasis. Revista de Literatura, Teoría y Crítica*, 13(26), 123–41.

1

On writing instability: How ambient literature reconfigures the reader/writer relationship in situated storytelling

Tom Abba

Part one: Affective registration

At the close of the Ambient Literature Project (2016–18), the accompanying book (Abba, Dovey and Pullinger 2021) undertook an exploration of the manners of writing work in this form. Specifically, the project proposed a set of *Ambient Poetics* by which writers and designers looking to compose works of ambient literature might approach the specific registers and tones afforded by literary experiences of this nature. What was not offered, though, was any guidance as to 'how' to write for an ambient form. We were, it should be acknowledged, justifiably nervous about dictating a set of overarching principles by which work in this form *had* to be written. Such a diktat, we felt, would stifle an emerging form, as much as if the paperback novel or the short story had been prescribed in this manner at the outset of its inception.[1]

[1] Michael Chabon delivers a withering broadside on this theme in '*Trickster in a Suit of Lights*' in *Maps and Legends* (2008), as follows: 'Imagine that, sometime about 1950, it had been decided, collectively, informally, a little at a time, but with finality, to proscribe every kind of novel but the nurse romance from the canon of the future. Not merely from the critical canon, but from the store racks and library shelves as well. Nobody could be paid, published, lionized, or cherished among the gods of literature for writing any kind of fiction other than nurse romances. Now, because of my faith and pride in the diverse and rigorous brilliance of American writers of the last half century, I do believe that from this bizarre decision, in this theoretical America, a dozen or more authentic masterpieces would have emerged. Thomas Pynchon's *Blitz Nurse*, for example, and Cynthia Ozick's *Ruth Puttermesser, R.N.* One imagines, however, that this particular genre – that any genre, even one far less circumscribed in its elements and possibilities than the nurse romance – would have paled somewhat by now. In that oddly diminished world, somebody, somewhere, is laying down his copy of *Dr. Kavalier & Nurse Clay* with a weary sigh. Instead of "the novel" and "the nurse romance," try this little thought experiment with "jazz" and "the bossanova," or with "cinema" and "fish-out-of-water comedies." Now go ahead and try it with "short fiction" and "the contemporary, quotidian, plotless, moment-of-truth revelatory story." Suddenly you find yourself sitting right back in your very own universe.'

That nervous disposition notwithstanding, it is helpful, I think, to offer some thoughts on what ambient literature offers a writer, in terms of the relationship between reader and writer, form and content, and embodied experience.

In the chapter 'Writing Ambient Literature' (Abba, Dovey and Pullinger 2021; Abba and Spencer 2021), we posited that:

> Ambient Literature is in its general conception a mode of embodiment. A reader of an Ambient work is present within the text to a different degree than a conventional text allows. The works themselves seek to respond to the presence of their reader, manipulating aspects of that presence in order to reinforce the physicality of a reader's situation. These responses might correspond to a direct address to the reader's bodily presence (as they move through space, or respond to external stimuli), or a reflection on the connections between that presence and the world around them. That the reader is embodied within the textual object places their perceptions of the story, their interpretation of events and sequences, as central to their understanding.

That grounding allowed us to conceive of a series of manners by which ambient literature could be positioned as distinct from situated storytelling and locative narrative. The interplay between presence, embodiment, data and technology affords a means to consider work that moved around a spectrum of seven poetic qualities. Each work considered demonstrated a varying degree of intensity as regards how it employed these, and the suite of poetics were offered as guiding principles by which to construct and consider ambient work. Summaries are presented here:

Embodied reading

The specific register afforded by an ambient work asks its reader to reflect on their presence as a participant within the overall frame of the project. Operating on both spatial and temporal axes, the reader is placed within an emergent narrative as an object within a larger continuum. The physical world around them, as architecture, sensation and location, places them as figures within a present ground.

Movement

An ambient work will, in response to its reader's physical presence moving through the piece, ask them to make use of that moment to progress the narrative. Moving through space, they will embody the narrative as a participant, through time as an agent of story causality.

Performance

That ambient works are often described in temporal terms is not accidental. The experience of listening to music, and composing music, is akin to experiencing an ambient story. The music flows around the listener, slipping into their understanding of the space they are in, and offering a profoundly affective response to the world. Participants in ambient works do not perform as we might understand a theatrical performance, or free-form role-playing, rather, they occupy a temporal space that asks them to interact with their location for a time, responding as themselves rather than a character.

Textual space

The site within which an ambient work is experienced is necessarily co-opted by the work into the frame of the overall story. That the reader is physically present, and reads or participates in response to their environment, offers a scale of engagement with this textual space, marking the physical locale as significant to the ground of the composed work.

Unpredictability

At the heart of many digital experiences is a relinquishing of authorial control over textual fixity, such that readers have more agency within a work where their presence is a foundational element in the construction of a cohesive narrative. This, though, is not without difficulty, and ambient literature, much as experimental arts and performance does, considers methods to offer agency whilst retaining authorial responsibility. The fabric of the physical world becomes a factor here, in that environmental considerations might appear to be out of the author's control but can be incorporated into the experience in a number of ways.

Temporality

In addition to the compositional nature of writing ambient works, the removal of a material object (book, film, stage) as a primary platform allows writers the opportunity to explore temporal registers outside of conventional media forms.

Building on Gérard Genette's (1980) proposition that 'story time' points to the 'chronological sequence of the events and incidents in a story' and 'narrative time' refers to the 'pseudo-temporal order of the incidents and their arrangement in the narrative' (35), ambient literature offers ways to manipulate the reader's perception of time as it occurs within the narrative itself. Their relative unfamiliarity with the form – as it emerges in canon – blurs the liminal space between story and real world, in turn fogging the degree to which fixed temporal presence can be understood.

Reflexive technology

That the purpose of many media forms is to disappear from the frame of the reader's experience, and the means of engagement in ambient works (to date) has been the smartphone, or an equivalent device, the presence of that device as an arbiter of experience is more problematic than with other media forms. A smartphone is not a neutral carrier of story in the way a printed book is – it provides a sonic and geolocated way of navigating an accompanying printed text, or it's a carrier for data, or it stands in for a 'book' – but however that role is unpacked in relation to the reader and the story, the device(s) employed have a more foregrounded role to play. The frame demands consideration,[2] and the answers to that consideration are potentially part of the overall experience.

This chapter argues that by taking a (careful) step further into the process of authoring ambient literature, these poetics afford an applied series of 'mechanics', or grammars, of ambient storytelling. It will examine aspects of existing works that occupy an extended canon of ambient literature – *A Hollow Body* (Circumstance 2014), *These Pages Fall Like Ash* (Circumstance 2012/2020), *Breathe* (Pullinger 2018) – then provide a detailed exploration of the writing strategies employed in creating *From Bitter Ground* (Abba 2023), consolidating ideas presented earlier.

In order to satisfactorily explore the ways in which ambient works provide an affective register, it is helpful to consider ambient narratives in the light of three questions:

1. What is it?
2. What is happening?
3. How is the trick being done?

[2] It's worth remembering that the novel moved through a number of registers before settling (if it ever did) on the form we understand today.

Writing is, in part, the illusion of control. Control of the narrative as it becomes story, of the reaction of the reader as they are propelled through it, and control of the form of the story itself as it manipulates the affordances of its presentational medium. That summary is necessarily short, provocative and hugely incomplete, but nevertheless provides a structure within which to proceed.[3] We are also bound to consider the role of affect. If we begin with Miall's approach to affect as it responds to story, then the means by which character is construed as being informed primarily by the concerns of the self and motivated by the *anticipatory* function of affect is a firm starting point (Miall and Quicken 1988). Affect is also a pretextual mode, in which an emotional response to a situation is prompted by the reader's relationship to the narrative *as it speaks to them*. John Clute (2006) further elaborates on affect (as it relates to horror), suggesting that, as Stephen King makes explicit in his study of horror literature as a writing enterprise, *Danse Macabre* (1981), the job of the writer (of horror) is to make the reader experience powerful emotions. Furthermore, within an ambient work, we double down on affect's anticipatory function, in that the role of the reader as *present*, as embodying the story as much as reading it, compounds their affective experience.

Accepting that ambient literature comprises an embodied narrative experience, the first question to answer is whose body are we considering, and what are the limits of that reification? Ambient works (to date) place the reader as an active participant in the text; their presence activates the experience, which prior to that presence, comprises a set of media objects or sequence of predetermined events. This is our first significant difference – in that a book (bound, printed and purchased) presents a completed object (albeit 'triggered' by the act of being read) that cannot be subsequently altered by the author; an ambient work, drawing from the poetics described above, is wholly incomplete prior to its activation. Each element is predetermined, but the synthesis of the whole is unknown to the writer.

As proposed by Samuel Beckett (1988):

> Then I went back into the house and wrote, It is midnight. The rain is beating on the windows. It was not midnight. It was not raining.

[3] *Ambient Literature: Towards a New Poetics of Situated Writing and Reading Practices* (2021) drew on those works published under the aegis of the research project – *It Must Have Been Dark by Then*, *The Cartographer's Confession*, and *Breathe*, and two additional commissions: *Yesterday You're Still Dreaming* (2017) and *Words We Never Wrote* (2018). The canon was expanded with inclusion and reference to a large range of works made prior to the research project and by authors unconnected to the funded work. This chapter also draws on *These Pages Fall Like Ash* (2020) and *From Bitter Ground* (2023) to make its case.

Within the reception of an ambient work, it is entirely possible that midnight and rain are both present at the point of reading. Whilst it is also true that a reader of Beckett's might encounter the same serendipity, the conventional text is not contingent on the time of day and weather in the same way as an ambient work might afford. Kate Pullinger's *Breathe* manipulates this moment synthetically, in that the API data gathered by the web app is inserted into the text, placing the reader *within* the descriptive space of the story. This technique is dealt with in the chapter 'Writing Ambient Literature' (Abba and Spencer 2021) as an example of embodied reading; however, it is worth dwelling on the affective nature of the text too. Pullinger employs affect to underscore the 'haunting' present in her work – the incursion of time and weather responsive text provides a foundation for more overt incursions from the ghost voices within the work. Her reader will, one suspects, not notice the foundational API work that provides a means by which their presence within the text is established. Whilst Italo Calvino's (1981) address to his reader at the start of *If on a winter's night a traveller* purports to describe events happening to the reader themselves, as a means to dissolve the relationship between reader and text (a technique whose efficacy falls away during the novel), *Breathe* dissolves the physical distance between Pullinger's authorial voice and her reader in order to provoke an *affective response* specific to the ambient medium. The limitations of the print format (despite the best intentions of the Oulipo movement) are laid bare by Calvino's attempt to break down the space between his pen and his reader,[4] what Pullinger achieves though, with a digital device, is commensurate with Clute's recognition that terror precedes horror (terror announces the horror to come – which is the atrocity that breaks you). The affect here produces a counterfactual moment – that which has not taken place is underscored by something that patently has.

Before we dive down a data-driven and API-orchestrated rabbit hole, we should ask the most important question of a writer's technique.

Why?

What I want to stress is that *why* is the key to writing *into* any medium. Our suite of poetics describes a set of qualities that ambient works possess; the means to employ them successfully are unlocked by understanding and honestly addressing why any affect is attempted. Firstly, what presence and embodiment afford is control over the reader as an individual, as a *human being*, in a manner

[4] David Mitchell (2004) notes that 'however breathtakingly inventive a book is, it is only breathtakingly inventive once. But once is better than never.'

distinct from other storytelling media. The potential affects offered by digital enhancement supplement that presence, providing experiences specific to an ambient work. The hinge here is *why*, and why demands an understanding of materiality as it applies to story and form. The material form of a text – as book, film, aural story – impacts on the ways in which the story is told; it informs those specific grammars of story structure dictated by the medium it is told in. Film has the 180-degree rule, the camera as a third-person perspective; the book has chapters, physical movement through pages; aural storytelling the instability of accurate rendition. These pertain to the grammatical 'rules' their media afford. Secondly, unlike most conventional media, the function of the frame of an ambient work is to remain visible, and not disappear. Immersion within a book is described as forgetting time, such that the physicality of the pages fall away. An immersed television or film experience suspends temporality; the duration of the work becoming invisible. These media share a status as imitations of reality – all the way back to Aristotle – whereas ambient literature positions itself as an *embodiment* of that reality. The frame of an embodied work – both as the world in which it manifests and the device that mediates it – remains as a reminder, a set of semiotic signals to ground the reader. The work, transmitted through the phone in your hand, is about the world, and the world remains framed around a liquid crystal display in a metal and plastic case.

To understand what this means for storytelling in a medium, we will turn to the materiality of an intangible media. Ambient works, despite their transitory, experiential nature, afford an experience examinable through new materialism as it pertains to our performative relationship with the world. Matthew Hayler's proposition that 'ambient literature reveals all reading as entangled' (Abba, Dovey and Pullinger 2021: 80) and that these works ask us 'to pay attention to the substrate of a work and note the ways in which all texts bring medium into meaning' (81) requires that we consider the interrelationships between design, meaning, platform and text as critical to creating work.

Furthermore, N. Katherine Hayles (2002) offers *Technotexts* as her shorthand for those literary works that interrogate the inscription technologies that produce them and in doing so provide a way to unlock the relationship between construction and material practice. Ambient materiality, as required by Hayler's desire to address the substrate of a work, can be understood as a metaphor, a stand-in for a hybrid of embodied reading and reflexive technology. Hayles expresses her *why* as an insistent reminder that materiality is expressed by each medium differently, emerging from the 'interactions between physical properties and a work's artistic strategies' (33). In turn, ambient materiality, we propose, finds itself in the interplay between presence and space, between performance and technology. The *why* for writing in this medium is an appreciation of those tensions and a desire to provoke an emotional response from them.

To understand what this means in practice, we'll go to the drawing board. Literally.

Although not falling into the production portfolio for the Ambient Literature Project, *These Pages Fall Like Ash* (2020) represents a proto-ambient work, in that the genesis of the whole project began with the development of *These Pages Fall Like Ash* in 2013, and continued through the body of work developed by Circumstance during 2014 to 2016. Reconfiguring the software guiding each reader was undertaken in 2020, two years after the formal conclusion of the Ambient Literature Project and subsequent to the completion of the book accompanying the project. As a work itself, *These Pages Fall Like Ash* demonstrates much of the poetics described above and stands as an attempt to address the presence/space/performance/technology interplay we proposed. The specific properties of the work are relatively simple – two platforms, that is, a physical book describing an imagined city set obversely against a meditation on your own physical surroundings and a series of digital texts made visible as readers walk a mapped space they construct in an opening chapter, and rewalk throughout the work. Reading the digital text requires participation in a guided experience and familiarity with the contents of the physical text, neither providing a cohesive experience without its counterpart. The software underpinning the work records locations tied to the reader's phone (and linked to a unique email login), providing a stable reading experience (Figure 1.1).

The other major touchstone for the development of Ambient Literature is Circumstance's *A Hollow Body* (2014). A cinematic walk for two people around the City of London, it was originally commissioned by the Museum of London as part of their Sherlock Holmes season and was inspired by the mythology of Conan Doyle's great detective. The pre-install guide specifically identifies it as:

> not a typical history walk or tourist guide. Imagine walking through a film where you are the main characters; the streets and narrow alleys of London acting as your cinematic backdrop.[5]

The participant is the central character, mise-en-scène is provided by the environment and the narrative language of cinema is purposely referenced to provide a ground for the work to respond to. *A Hollow Body* is a work for two

[5] https://duncanspeakman.net/projects/ahb/.

participants, evoking the London of Sherlock Holmes as a walk through around St Paul's Cathedral, Barbican and the City of London.

Amongst the elements not included in the final cut of *A Hollow Body* were two story beats illustrating an affective interplay. Both took place in Guildhall Yard on the City of London's Square Mile. The first comprised a phone call to the participant as they reached the centre of the square. *A Hollow Body* is designed around challenges to trust; in that participants generally come with someone they know well, the work questions who can be trusted to know anyone and the ramifications of that on the London evoked by each interpretation of Holmes since Conan Doyle's original stories. The call, whilst consistent with the theme of being surveilled, tracked and observed (by your partner and, unseen, other agencies) was ultimately felt to risk a break in the rhythm of the work – removing the participant from an experience sustained by an orchestral score and changing the nature of their engagement at a critical moment. It would have offered an *affective* moment though, situating the listener squarely within the Holmesian setting, and given certain knowledge of their participant's location, could reference lines of sight, windows, data points and other mechanisms of the surveilled city.

The second was more ambitious, and if achieved, it would reinforce the counter themes of trust and mistrust running through the piece. In rehearsal[6] it became clear that on arrival in Guildhall Yard, 10–15 seconds ahead of your partner, it is possible to walk briskly to a partially covered, pillared section at the south-east corner of the square, leaving your partner alone in an open, 100-square-metre space, effectively vanishing into thin air. The purpose – aside from a Holmesian flourish[7] – was to disorient the second participant as to what would happen next. A work hitherto relying on partnership and static collaboration between partners would be rendered otherwise, disrupting the expected 'flow' of narrative in an experiential work. The 'reveal', although presenting both surprise and shock, was not taken forward. Too many factors risked its success – the instruction to find the correct pillar had to work on exact timing, with little margin for error. An unanticipated pedestrian gathering, or hesitation on the part of the first participant, would render it unavailable and ruin the moment, throwing both participants out of the flow of their experience. In development

6 All of Circumstance's works are run, rerun and rehearsed to respond to the site in which they are set. *A Hollow Body* was no exception, and probably included 30–40 miles of walking during this stage. Each member of Circumstance knows their quality footwear.

7 Conan Doyle makes use of impossible vanishings (often via locked-room mysteries) in *The Speckled Band*, *The Adventure of the Empty House* and others.

though, and as a piece of media-specific storytelling grammar, it is an idea to return to and as such bears discussing.

If then, a quality of ambient literary works is the subversion of expectation (from a conventional story 'norm'), our saturation in filmic, written or theatrical narrative form serves to both unintentionally 'blinker' our assumptions about how a story situation will play out and simultaneously maintain an 'on-rails' aspect to the overall storytelling grammar, that, nevertheless, can be carefully manipulated.

Part two: Writing within a medium

From Bitter Ground (2023) is both a follow-up work to *These Pages Fall Like Ash* (*TPFLA*), and a stand-alone piece of ambient literature. It succeeds *TPFLA* in that it employs the same underlying technical mechanism as its predecessor – each participant self-selects a series of locations as prompted by a poetic 'guide', which then form the basis for an emergent, site-responsive story experience. *TPFLA* asked each reader to identify a series of points – a cafe, a visible clock face, higher ground – which were then used to provide the 'map' for a personal mediated experience that locked to those locations as its locative framework. As such, their Movement (above) formed the basis for the Textual Space they created with the work. *From Bitter Ground* is not a sequel to *TPFLA*, rather, it was conceived as the answer to a set of questions arising from the re-release of that work, and the time elapsing between the end of the Ambient Literature Project in 2018 and the germ of an idea in late 2020.

From Bitter Ground

From Bitter Ground is a haunted house story, a journey through the twentieth century, and an exploration and examination of the grammars of ambient storytelling. Materially, it takes the form of a set of three books, provided to two 'paired' readers (identified prior to the experience commencing and linked to each other), which (see Figure 1.1) provide no straightforward route into or through the overarching story, rather, proposing a larger frame for the work to emerge through. The two books 'contained' within the concertina sections – the *book of entrances* and the *book of exits* – suggest a sequence; the former opening out akin to an analogue Ordnance Survey Map, the latter a saddle stitched section; the concertina itself reading both *forward* and *backward*, the covers

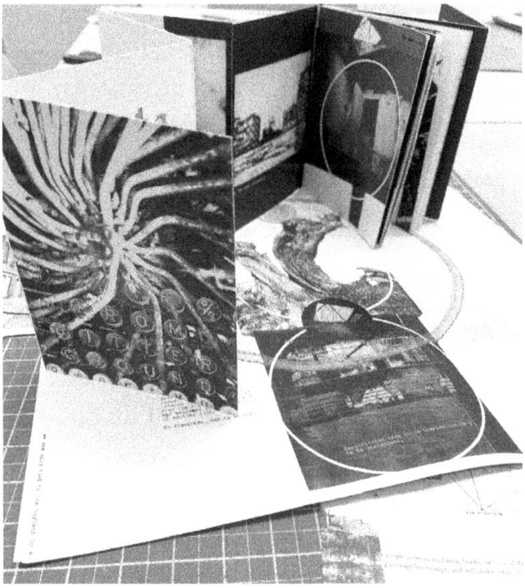

Figure 1.1 *From Bitter Ground.* Courtesy of Tom Abba.

each leading to a sequence of images accompanied by ambiguous title phrases. The overall effect is designed to induce a disorientation in the reader – the first question ought to be 'how do I actually read this?', rather than identifying a starting point.

From the writer's perspective, this strategy is deliberate. The *book of exits* contains a series of transparent pages; the only conventional textual element offered. Four 'introductory' texts run through the book, offering a sequential order in which to read *something* prior to the experience proper. Other texts are contained within the folded-out 'maps' in the book of entrances and buried into the illustrations in the *book of exits*. Taken together, the work is deliberately, opaquely unreadable.

Briefly then, to explain the frame of the work.

Each paired reader reads a different digital work. An identical prologue ('onboarding' both to the manner in which the work operates) is read on location, identifying each reader's chosen location – they are asked to choose a site as follows:

> I'd like you to find somewhere. Somewhere specific, and it should be a place you can revisit, that you'll find again, and feel is familiar. It's not a specific place, that we can predetermine, but rather a kind of location.

> It's a place, somewhere near where you are now, that might have been a home. Or could have been. It might be abandoned, a burned out shell, an unfinished building, it might be a zone that's marked off in some way. What's important is that it is yours, in that you feel you belong there somehow. There isn't an absolutely right place, either, just the right one for you.
>
> Think of it as your un-house.
>
> (Abba 2023: location 0, prologue)

The purpose of the prologue is twofold.

1. The reader 'maps' a series of sites around their un-house, the relationship between each described as points by which to divide the space. At completion, five such points are mapped, four of which form a cross bisecting the un-house, containing it within a 'zone'.
2. The prologue introduces a discussion of architectural philosophy, framed through examination of figure/ground, legibility, negative and positive space, and subjectivity, each of which makes reference to the texts within the books of *entrance* and *exit*, permitting the reader to recognize the connections between physical and digital reading platforms.

The prologue, then, is an enacted exercise in using movement to construct textual space, under an umbrella of embodied reading. Each point selected is guided by a direct address to the reader, suggesting the qualities each should embody – a point no more than a minute's walk away; a place where resting is permitted, or possible; directly in front of an imagined 'entrance' to the un-house itself – inviting an imagined construction of the house itself through motifs familiar to each observer. These points, and the zone they create, are given to be 'real' within the frame of the work, and reference is made to the placement of imagined boundaries as they relate to physical obstacles, walls and access to the ground upon which the textual space is being brought into being.

The inclusion of architectural design as an arbiter by which to select points is also deliberate, and it draws upon the Anarchitecture project (1974 and subsequent) and broader canon of Gordon Matta-Clark's practice to hint towards a further-than-Euclidean geometry at work within the identified textual space. This was a key ambition when writing *From Bitter Ground*; that while the act of embodied reading asks each participant in an ambient work to 'to increase their engagement with their immediate environment' (Speakman quoted in Abba, Dovey and Pullinger 2021: 285), the potential of combining embodied reading with textual space as a key motif[8] within an ambient work might allow the work to provide the scaffold for an imagined space existing beyond the confines of physical reality. How to do that, specifically speaking, demanded the employment of extra-physical geometry as a present metaphor for the interplay between imagination and reality the ambient lens affords. Matta-Clark's approach to Anarchitecture, at times elusive, contradictory (and subsequently hijacked by scholars and practitioners following Matta-Clark's death in 1978), is nevertheless a genuinely held perspective on the limits of conventional architectural practice. As James Attlee (2007) remarks:

> Whatever its origin, the term Anarchitecture, expressing as it does a creative tension between Apollonian and Dionysian opposites, has come to summarise many of the concerns explored by Matta-Clark during his brief career.

Indeed, it becomes evident as the reader progresses through the prologue that *From Bitter Ground* also takes Matta-Clark's ideas very seriously indeed.

Both Matta-Clark and Le Corbusier shared a fascination with the way buildings act on human consciousness – the interplay, perhaps, between the elements Barthes identified within architecture of function and dream – and also in the attitudes that might give rise to new building types (Attlee 2007).

Invoking Matta-Clark's employment of the cut, semi-situates each reader at a position removed from conventional geometry, as described here:

> he told Lisa Béar, his 'normal sense of gravity was subverted by the experience. In fact when you got to the top floor and looked down through an elliptical section through the floor that was cut out, you would look down through the fragments of a normal apartment space, but I had never seen anything like it. It looked like … almost as though it were a pool. That is, it has a reflective quality to it and a surface – but the surface was just the accumulation of images of the spaces below it.'
>
> (Moure 2006: 268)

The invitation to see each cut they have made around their un-house:

> There is an invisible line here. It runs between the point you already chose and this one. If you look back now, can you see it out of the corner of your eye? A shimmer in the air, a refraction of the light that shouldn't exist, but nevertheless does. A line between who you were then and who you are now.
>
> (Abba 2023: Location 2)

[8] Deliberately going further than the construction of imagined space in *It Must Have Been Dark by Then*, *The Cartographer's Confession* or *Words We Never Wrote* (Abba, Dovey and Pullinger 2021: 312–16).

In accordance with the relationship between their temporal presence within the experience and prior to it, this is the first direct connection between the reader as they are now and the suggestion that temporality will become significant in the work they are reading.

After the prologue is completed, the digital experience unfolds over four days, with each participant's progress partly determined by their partner (both are required to complete the prologue before day 1 commences, and then day 1 before day 2; however, each can subsequently complete the remaining 3 days at their own pace). This structure affords a degree of certainty for each reader, in that whilst the entire sequence of days is invisible to them in the interface, the concertina indicates (the only place where numerals are included) a 1–4 series. Narratively, too, the details of the reading screen guide a degree of increasing complexity, suggesting that, in fact, this is not an open-ended narrative progression but instead is leading *somewhere*.

Significant to the construction of a complex temporal experience (narratively, as opposed to conditionally or experientially), as suggested by Abba and Spencer (2021: 302), *From Bitter Ground* is narrated by a consistent address to the reader. This 'voice' speaks as an individual, apparently personally familiar with reader, and reflective of an entity observing the experience, whilst unseen as a participant in the unfolding story. This voice grounds their experience, both serving as an instructional address (guiding the section of each 'point' in the prologue and providing the structural frame within which the whole participatory story is 'told') and speaking to the reader as the story progresses. This was a further deliberate choice – there is a tension in ambient works between the necessity to 'onboard' the reader in the mechanistic grammar of the work itself and the 'poetic' voice within the story as it unfolds. At no point has this been mandated as necessary in order to adopt any single strategy, rather, recognizing that the tension exists is a design prompt to which a solution should be found, so that the overall tone of the story is served by the tenor of the medium. This calls to Clement Greenberg's argument that painting found its way to medium specificity through looking to music; not to imitate it, but to understand how it operated.[9] Understanding how an ambient work operates in this regard is an appreciation of the experience itself, as perceived by the reader. Do they understand their position within the work as a 'bookish' experience, as 'filmic' or 'theatrical'? Careful employment of paratextual components guides their understanding, but

[9] Music, Greenberg contended, is inherently pure and abstract because it cannot be described in terms of any other media.

ultimately, if a work is constructed as attending to literary conventions, its reader will incorporate those into their perceptions, similarly if filmic language is used, they will see themselves as a participant in an emerging drama – with accordant expectations of *how* film works and how narrative in film is usually employed. Grammars, then, are critical to positioning the reader as present and as an *agent* in the work to come.

Here too, it is helpful to consider the role of Charles Olson's (1950) proposition that, in the case of Projective Verse:

> ONE PERCEPTION MUST IMMEDIATELY AND DIRECTLY LEAD TO A FURTHER PERCEPTION. (2)

Harnessing poet Robert Creeley's assertion that 'form is never more than an extension of content' and Edward Dahlberg's belief that 'one perception must immediately and directly lead to a further perception', Olson argues that the breath should be a poet's central concern, rather than rhyme, metre and sense. To listen closely to breath, Olson suggests, 'is to engage speech where it is least careless – and least logical'.

Olson's concern with the relationship between the breath and the ear – that is, as a poet breathes, the listener is breathing the work alongside the poet, anticipating the next line and incorporating that into their own experience of hearing a poetry performed aloud – is especially useful for an ambient work because Olson's subject is also experienced as a dialogue (i.e. an emergent verse not confined to the printed page) – both are removed from the confines of print, film stock or the stage. Ambient works find common ground with projective verse, that is, each speaks to a reader who has had their material referent removed, only voice anchors and moves them forward. An ambient reader – in a work that leans into a performative mode – is reliant on the flow of narrative to appreciate the structure of the work and to perceive themselves as working with the narrative towards a conclusion.

Structurally speaking, each 'day' of *From Bitter Ground* presents a story of its own, imparted to the reader as a series of short sections delivered at each point selected in the prologue. These chapters are narrated to the reader by the consistent voice described above. This voice, narratorially speaking, does not accurately perceive the reader's physical reality. Instead, it speaks from a position apparently confident as to temporally *where* in the work the reader is and that their relationship to the un-house is determined by the overall sequence of the story; however, this narrator has not been permitted knowledge of the precise details of the physical space the reader has chosen for *their* zone. They occupy an unstable point of view that permits the variance in location each reader has agency over. The narrator can be certain that there is an un-house, that the reader has mapped each point, and that they are negotiating their journey around and in respect of these certainties. Nothing more is prescribed, therefore, the precise nature of the reader's engagement with the space is mediated by a combination of ambiguity and generality in terms of descriptive language. For example:

> There was once a tree here. If there is one now then it might be the offspring of those boughs. The tree stood as high as the tallest building here, its canopy covering the sky above, and its roots burrowed into the earth, extending out and touching the boundaries of the zone you're standing in.

The author of the work cannot know for sure whether a tree is present in the location the reader has selected. It is likely, given the preponderance of trees in both urban and rural sites across the world, but necessarily the narrator cannot be certain either, hence the relative statements above. 'If there is one now' obviously operates in relation to the statement that 'there was once a tree here'. These instances are written into the text to create moments where the world breaks in,[10] such that composing enough of them into a work guarantees the presence of at least a few that resonate specifically for a reader in their physical environment.

Taken purely as a structural model, *From Bitter Ground* constitutes a mapping of user-defined space (prologue) followed by successive walks around the same space (days 1–4). A second part to the story (part 2) unlocks three months after the conclusion of day 4, requiring each reader to return to the same space and rewalk their zone. This structure, though, belies the narrative complexity of the story as it unfolds as a participatory, ambient experience. Returning successively to the same site affords an opportunity to deepen the reader's engagement with the textual space they construct and builds on a similar motif in *TPFLA* in which each reader walked the route they had identified in Episode I[11] of that work, but in a different order, and adding an additional location in Episode II. Additionally, the narratorial 'voice' present alongside their own changed in each episode – Episode I featured a female voice, relating events in the 'other city',[12]

[10] Courtesy of Duncan Speakman, to whom thanks is given.

[11] Each Episode in *These Pages Fall Like Ash* comprised five locations, at each of which a series of short texts were available.

[12] *These Pages Fall Like Ash's* 'about' text was: 'Imagine a world that sits alongside your own. Full of people, with wants and fears and desires just like yours. With history and culture that are very different though. This city is invisible, and it can't be touched. It hides in plain sight, and you'd never know it was there.' The other city – overlaid over the reader's own, was purely imaginary.

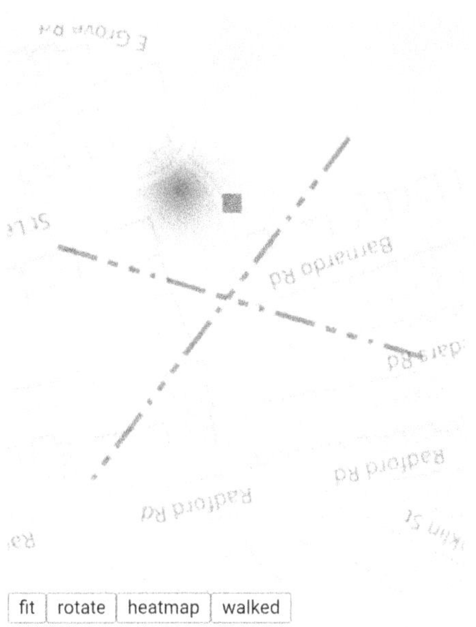

Figure 1.2 The map has rotated from day 2 to 3.
Courtesy of Tom Abba.

Episode II's voice was that of her missing husband, present in the reader's reality, and in Episode III both voices acted as counterpoint to each other, with the reader a conduit between them. The design of *From Bitter Ground* presented an opportunity to explore new solutions to the same design problem – how to use the space a reader identifies as their 'own' as textual space, whilst avoiding instilling a sense of needless repetition during the experiential narrative.

Addressing these two facets as a unified whole provides the solution to the primary problem. Narratively speaking, the story the reader is told (as reader 1 or 2) on day 1 ends abruptly, and apparently without resolution. These two opening chapters describe encounters with an un-house much like the reader's own – one following the conclusion of the First World War, and the other in a more contemporary but unspecified time period. The second day commences narratively with no regard to the abrupt ending the day before, describing the dreams of a homeless child living in this physical space some fifty years prior, and the experience of denizens of the un-house as they witness the world outside.

Notably though, the reader's access to the work has changed since day 1. Their digital map (Figure 1.2) of the site, with points and cuts marked on it as per the prologue, has rotated relative to their actual position by 30+ degrees.

This displacement exists for several reasons:

1. The abrupt end to the first day masks a narrative event only made evident by the end of day 4. Considered within a temporal frame, the reader's experiential temporality has been extended and then removed. Narratively (not physically), they both entered their un-house after the abrupt cut and made their way inside, to a point where they were killed by forces within the house. With those (traumatic) memories removed, they have been returned to the start of the experience on day 2. The rotation of the map signifies their displaced status.[13]
2. The reader's return and rewalk of the same site (see above) is now made more complex (see below).
3. Matta-Clark's desire to subvert normal experience, alongside the ambition of the work 'to increase … engagement with their immediate environment' (Speakman quoted in Abba, Dovey and Pullinger 2021: 285) is realized through the alteration of a familiar digital trope. A digital map, always pointing north when opened on a mobile device, and understood to be a reliable arbiter of the surrounding physical space, is rendered uncanny (specifically un-homelike) by this action.

The map still functions as a *map*, though. Travelling north in the real world might appear to be moving the reader along a trajectory 30 degrees to the west of north; however, relational navigation still holds true. The locations chosen in the prologue have moved too but are stable – for that day – in their new positions. What the alteration to the interface between digital and physical spaces is designed to do is twofold:

1. To re-engage the reader's relationship with the physical space they have mapped. That points have moved around a rotated point (the centre of rotation is the un-house) requires each reader to reconsider their original choices in the light of a series of uncontrolled circumstances. A site originally chosen to provide a space for resting, for leaning against, might now be placed in the open and visible to the un-house. That each point was directed relative to the un-house is significant too. The software moving each point does not mediate around buildings or other obstacles,

[13] Yes, they're in a Choose Your Own Adventure book and have just died and turned back to the beginning. The irony that I designed this mechanism without first realizing that is not lost on me.

so a request to 'put buildings between you and it' or 'keep the house in sight if you can' are equally likely to now produce an opposite effect.
2. To ask a fundamental question at the beginning of day 2 (as expressed earlier in this chapter) – 'what is happening and *why*?' Writing in any medium is frequently a matter of surprising one's audience, whether that be in narrative terms or through more formal, structural manners. If two days into an experience that appears to be 'on rails' those rails suddenly alter, the question as to what else might change and how stable the reading experience actually is becomes a pertinent concern.

The reader's demise, and ongoing rebirths, provide an implicit subtextual structure for the remaining three days of part 1 of *From Bitter Ground*. At the close of day 2, the story of the child/inhabitants of the un-house ends just as abruptly as day 1 did, although in this, second, instance the unexpected stop is rendered less sudden by anticipation (by the reader, and reminded, obliquely, of such by the narrator). What becomes apparent is that during day 2, a portion of the journey past the door on day 1 is recalled, similarly for day 2's stricken memories on day 3. It is significant that this precise mode of storytelling (an overtly unreliable textual space composed through embodied reading, movement and temporality) operates this way within an ambient work. That is, the reader is physically present and, themselves, is the structural scaffold for this story; if the same story were told as a film, or in a conventional book, then that scaffold would necessarily be constructed differently. The poetics of ambient literature, described as guiding principles above, provide the means by which to construct that scaffold within *this* writing medium. To summarize:

- Each reader has a relationship with the site they chose and are asked to return to it over a period of days.
- Their presence within that material frame provides the narrative momentum for the whole work – unlike other media, which can arrive fully formed (a book is complete as *an object* before it is opened, as is a film, although theatre, we acknowledge, operates differently), ambient works, viewed as *objects*, exist as a collection of media, moments and temporal scores activated by their readers through the specific combination of ambient poetics being employed by the author.

To date, the corpus of ambient works is too narrow to prescribe a complete or in any way extensive overview of the relationship between form and content as it pertains to genre, but we can demonstrate with some certainty that ambient works lean towards those stories that unsettle the world. Kate Pullinger's *Breathe* is overtly a ghost story, albeit with a primary concern to the migrant crisis of 2017; Duncan Speakman's *It Must Have Been Dark by Then* disrupts the reader's relationship with their ecological present and their sense of geography within the immediate environment; James Attlee's *The Cartographer's Confession* ostensibly relates a story about migration and family connections but does so through temporal hauntings between time zones and locations in the city of London. My own *Words We Never Wrote, These Pages Fall Like Ash* (with Duncan Speakman) and *Yesterday You're Still Dreaming* (2017) each find themselves telling stories that blur real and imagined worlds, situating their readers as participants in liminal spaces and telling the stories that are found there. Reality, and the subversion of it, then, is potentially a common factor in ambient work to date. Unlike a fully virtual space, the reader of an ambient work is engaged in the world and directed to pay attention to it, and the work presented to them adopts a strategy responsive to that attention. As befits the first work completely composed since the release of *Ambient Literature* (Abba, Dovey and Pullinger 2021), *From Bitter Ground* more directly addresses the relevance of genre in ambient works. The un-house is constructed as a *thing* that haunts the reader – it is evidently present in their reality, and its significance becomes material when the reader experiences the work across each day. Cuts that are made through it do not, of course, exist in the real world, but they are described as occupying an *imagined* real to underscore the structure's incursion into the world. The reader's repeated death and rebirth at the apparent whim of the un-house traps them in a circular narrative, denied closure once the first day has been realized, within which they are reborn, make the same 'mistakes' over again and are subsequently reborn the next morning to repeat this sequence. Theirs is a Sisyphean fate, and as such, the genre of the overall story can be identified as horror. Furthermore, on completing the fourth day, two final things are revealed to each reader:

1. It is explicitly demonstrated that they have 'died' each day, and that their relationship to the rotated map is the result of this is made clear.

   I watched you walk through the door. My steps were hesitant, and you took in the state of the floor, the ladder going down, the ragged hole it stood in. I descended nevertheless, each step made in the certain knowledge that the rung on which you stood would shatter under my weight, that this was the wrong choice to make. Finally, standing in front of the hook on the wall, we died. You died. I was left behind. I am still here.

2. The nature of the narratorial voice is revealed. The work has, as outlined above, been narrated by a voice familiar with the reader but not able to articulate anything of detail about where the reader is, aside from their point in the story so far. This second narrator *is the voice* of the reader, addressing them as an echo of themselves after each day has been completed. Notably, the narrator on day 1 is speaking after day 1, and only remembers the prologue and the events of day 1. For day 2, day 1 is remembered in detail. Day 3, day 2; and day 4, day 3. Despite occupying a relatively omnipotent position as a third-person narrator, the narratorial voice also has no knowledge of how the experience will finally end – from their perspective, the reader has died on day 3, and day 4 is still incomplete, is still in flux, with events unfinished. Their guidance is, rather than continuing to revisit the house, to stop. Breaking the loop of entry–death–rebirth is the only way the narrator can be in any way sure that there won't be a narrator on a fifth day. The reader must end the experience themselves, finding closure as a *participant* rather than a *reader* might choosing to stop reading rather than reaching the end.
3. The narratorial voice is, diegetically, the reader's doppelgänger, in that a doppelgänger is identified as a double who is being followed,[14] in this instance the reader is doubled through the accompanying narrator and by the existence of their previous selves who entered the house, each locked into a circuitous relationship with the others.

It is here that the physical books that accompany the work become clearer in their intent and purpose. There is, deliberately, no clear way to coherently read them as textual objects – none of them affords a route through the work until the reader is *inside* the entirety of it and able to perceive the whole work. Once this is achieved, the set of books – a concertina *looping* continuously back on itself; a book of *Entrances* mapping an imagined space dominated by a fragmented house; and a book of *Exits* exploring the environs of such a building – begins to offer some structural sense. Each reader is trapped within a work that has no route back to its beginning. The first 'version' of the reader is gone, removed on day 1, and what remains is only ever a copy, looping over and over again. These are tropes familiar to readers of horror, but that this is a work composed within the framework of an ambient literary experience, the reader is present within the

[14] Doppelgangers being explicitly tied to the notion of haunting, or pursuit of such. The ur-doppelganger relationship – that of Jekyll and Hyde – ties the two identities together in a dance of death.

story rather than at a safe distance,[15] and appreciating such, *From Bitter Ground* goes further than a conventional horror story,[16] stepping into a space occupied by an increasingly vertiginous terror; a cosmic horror of the self.

The only way to escape the structure of the story is to step away from it. The accompanying voice – the reader's own voice – urges this course of action as day 4 concludes.

> The pilgrim stood here too, and they knew there was no way forward. There was no route that did not end in disaster, and their death. What they chose we will never see, and cannot know. Their story is contained within these walls, but the end is incomplete. Your conclusion is clear. I am the last echo of you that can be; I am the end of our line. What has happened before must not happen again, or we will be stood here day upon day upon day, reciting these lines, rehearsing this call and response.
>
> Step away.
>
> Go home.

The last act of agency, then, on the part of the reader of *From Bitter Ground*, is to close the book and go home. The final affective moment in the story is to make the work itself tangible, to manifest it as an object and to complete it. *From Bitter Ground* frames itself as book-like in its scaffolding – each day is titled as a chapter, the work contains books as part of its material composition – and proposes a conclusion that reifies its status as an object conforming to bookish motifs, ultimately containing a beginning, middle and end. The work finally becomes the visible object it denied the reader access to at its outset.

Whilst the guiding poetics outlined earlier are a useful means by which to write within an ambient register – indeed, we hope that the detailed exploration of *From Bitter Ground* explains how reference to them can be critical in ensuring that work in this medium produces a genuinely affective response – they remain a guide and should not prescribe design, writing or intention. We can reliably observe them in operation in works considered part of an ambient canon, but these are principles, rather than rails. They are ways to describe the thing you're writing, not the thing itself. *From Bitter Ground*, though, serves to reinforce some aspects of ambient works:

15 The barrier-breaking narrative techniques of *The Blair Witch Project* (1999) – which positions its viewer as a participant within the narrative by denying the safety of a third-person camera perspective – come to mind too.

16 Owing to the nature of the medium it is being told in, it cannot embrace body horror, jump scares or visual elements of suspenseful surprise.

- The experience – for the writer as much as the reader – is unstable. A writer in any medium cannot completely know their audience. For an ambient work, external factors come into play – location, weather, access – and internal ones too.
- Managing those internal factors requires attention to the medium itself. It's not sufficient to approach an ambient work as a direct transposition of authorial intent as it might exist in literature or film – the medium makes its own demands on the shape of the text, the responsibility of the reader and the nature of their agency. Media can imitate each other   indeed, they begin by assuming the tropes and forms of older media – but if ambient literature can be said to have an agenda, then that agenda is to be true to itself and to explore how stories are told *in* this medium, rather than manifesting as ghosts of other forms.
- The reader cannot understand the work until they are inside it. This does not undermine an appreciation of an ambient work prior to its beginning, but the specific frame of these works require presence and participation. What happens can be described to a participant prior to the work beginning, but their experience is incomplete at that stage and politely asks for the work to commence before being understood.
- Inside the work, an architecture will be visible to the reader. Much as a physical, conventional book possesses an architectural form – pages collected as chapters bound into a case containing these elements, and other paratextual parts – tacitly understood by the reader to mark the boundaries of the work as an object, an ambient work might have a temporal structure that dictates the reader's anticipatory experience. They might see their embodiment in the story within an architectural scaffolding – how they are being asked to respond to the work as it emerges, for example. Architecture, and the recognition of such, is inherently present in ambient works.
- Recognizing that the perception of architecture – however it is understood – is foundational to reading a work in this medium, offers a way to respond, authorially, to the reader's expectations. Much as reading widely and writing often affords an understanding the orthodoxy of the book, permitting a writer to push back against the confines of that form, perceiving the underlying shape of an ambient work offers a writer equivalent opportunity to surprise the reader and subvert their expectations of what that architecture will produce.

If the purpose of this chapter was to explore the mechanical language of immersion, as it manifests in ambient literature, then the pages might shine a light on how weaving between formal construction and poetic devices illustrates the ways ambient immersion can be constructed. It remains, though, a work in progress and an exploration of the relationship between form and content that should be tested with each iteration of the medium.

References

Abba, T. (2017), *Yesterday You're Still Dreaming*. Available online: https://people.uwe.ac.uk/Person/TomAbba.

Abba, T. (2018), *Words We Never Wrote*. Available online: https://people.uwe.ac.uk/Person/TomAbba.

Abba, T. (2023), *From Bitter Ground*. Available online: https://people.uwe.ac.uk/Person/TomAbba.

Abba, T. and A. Spencer. (2021), 'Writing Ambient Literature', in T. Abba, J. Dovey and K. Pullinger, eds, *Ambient Literature: Towards a New Poetics of Situated Writing and Reading Practices*, 275–318, London: Palgrave Macmillan.

Abba, T., J. Dovey and K. Pullinger, eds. (2021), *Ambient Literature: Towards a New Poetics of Situated Writing and Reading Practices*, London: Palgrave Macmillan.

Abba, T., D. Speakman and E. Grenier. (2013/2020), *These Pages Fall Like Ash*. Circumstance. Available online: www.wearecircumstance.com (accessed 6 June 2024).

Attlee, J. (2007), 'Towards Anarchitecture: Gordon Matta-Clark and Le Corbusier', *Tate Papers*. Available online: https://www.tate.org.uk/research/tate-papers/07/towards-anarchitecture-gordon-matta-clark-and-le-corbusier (accessed 12 November 2023).

Beckett, S. (1988), *Molloy, Malone Dies, The Unnamable*, New York: Chelsea House Publishers.

Calvino, I. (1981), *If on a Winter's Night a Traveller*, London: Everyman.

Chabon, M. (2008), *Maps and Legends*, San Francisco: McSweeney's.

Circumstance. (2012/2020), *These Bodies Fall Like Ash*.

Circumstance. (2014), *A Hollow Body*. Available online: https://duncanspeakman.net/projects/ahb/ (accessed 6 June 2024).

Clute, J. (2006), *The Darkening Garden: A Short Lexicon of Horror*, Cauheegan, WI: Payseur & Schmidt.

Genette, G. (1980), *Narrative Discourse*, trans J. E. Lewin, Oxford: Basil Blackwell.

Hayles, N. K. (2002), *Writing Machines*, Cambridge, MA: MIT Press.

King, S. (1981), *Danse Macabre*, New York: Berkley.

Miall, D. S. and D. Kuiken. (1998), 'The Form of Reading: Empirical Studies of Literariness', *Poetics*, 25(6), 327–41.

Mitchell, D. (2004), 'Enter the Maze', *The Guardian*, 22 May, Available online: https://www.theguardian.com/books/2004/may/22/fiction.italocalvino (accessed 1 December 2022).

Moure, G., ed. (2006), *Gordon Matta-Clark: Works and Collected Writings*, Barcelona: Ediciones Poligrafa/Museo Nacional Centro de Arte Reina Sofia.

Olson, C. (1950), *Projective Verse*. Available online: https://www.angelfire.com/poetry/jarnot/olson.html (accessed 6 June 2024).

Olson, C. (1959), *Projective Verse*, New York: Totem Press.

Pullinger, K. (2018), *Breathe*. Available online: https://breathe-story.com/ (accessed 6 June 2024).

Speakman, D. (2017), *It Must Have Been Dark by Then*. Available online: https://research.ambientlit.com/index.php/it-must-have-been-dark-by-then/ (accessed 6 June 2024).

2

Persephone's Footsteps: Story making on foot

Claire Dean

The story and the city

In every city there are streets thick with stories, and writers have walked them, gathering, recounting and inscribing, for hundreds of years, but the development of mobile digital technologies has brought with it new ways to write story into place. Ambient literature can be understood as a lens through which a range of situated works explore narrative experience, place and their entangling in myriad new ways. These works take advantage of digital technologies, the reinvigoration of analogue forms and the hybrid manifestations between them. In 1923, anticipating the emergence of the 'electro-library' and calling for the 'book-space' to be reset to 'correspond to the tensions and pressures of content', El Lissitzky wrote, 'The new book demands the new writer' (cited in Tullet 2010). When the city becomes the book-space, new possibilities for content unfurl. For writers, ambient literature expands practice; a reader's experience of place and digital technologies become additional materials to be worked with in the creation of a story.

This chapter considers the methods and materials used to develop *Persephone's Footsteps*, a work of altitude-responsive ambient literature, and offers insights from the story-making journey. *Persephone's Footsteps* is a contemporary reimagining of the Persephone myth, a response to escalating carbon emissions and a map that can be used to explore any city. As Persephone climbs higher – first to escape the underworld and then to escape the polluted streets of the city – the reader must climb higher to hear more of her story. The technology is carried inside a hand-drawn box map (see Figure 2.1). An Arduino microcontroller with MP3 shield uses an altitude sensor, to trigger different sections of the story at different altitudes, so the listener must keep walking upwards to hear the next part of the story.

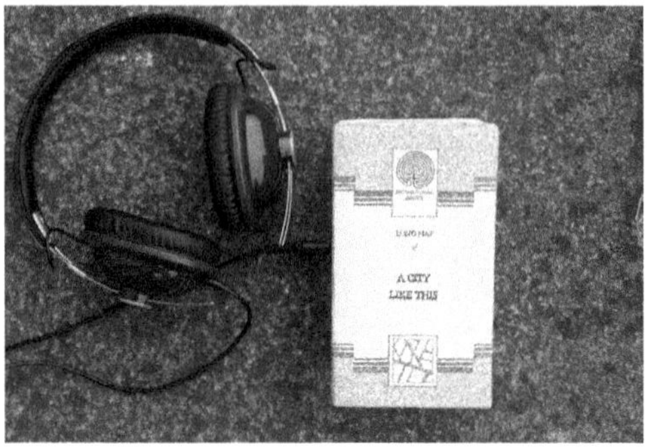

Figure 2.1 *Persephone's Footsteps* map box. Courtesy of Claire Dean.

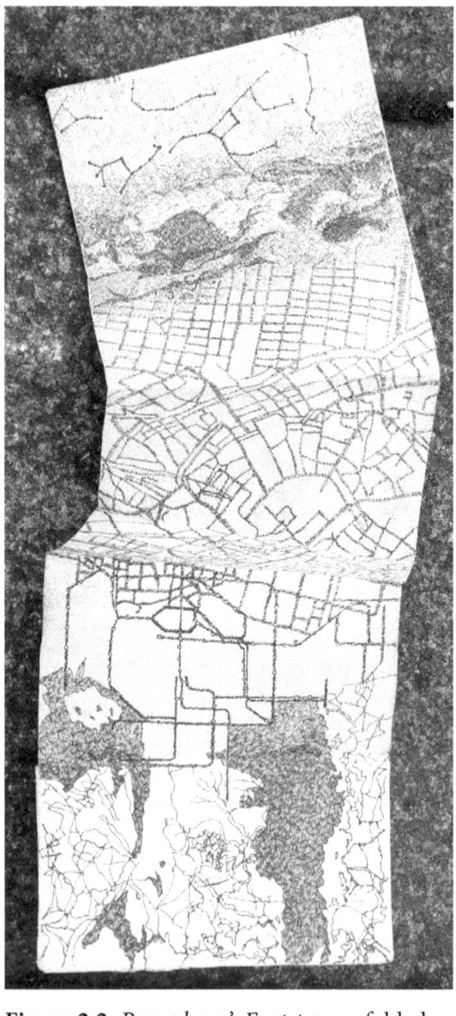

Figure 2.2 *Persephone's Footsteps* unfolded map. Courtesy of Claire Dean.

It's not possible for a writer to approach their work as literary critic and analyse it from the outside, but writers can share insights from the inside out, reflecting on the making of a work and capturing the 'thinking in the act' that characterizes creative practice (Manning and Massumi 2014: vii). *Persephone's Footsteps* is a work conceived, made and remade through walking. This chapter can also be considered as a walk through the intricacies of process that traces the path taken to develop the work so far. As Persephone walks upwards in extracts from the work, you are invited to follow, through the variegated strata of practice, theory and place.

The understory

The Underworld isn't far beneath your feet. If you crouch and place your fingertips against the hooded skin of the earth, you're almost there. It doesn't take much to slip through a crack or fall down a rabbit hole …

Stories can have their beginnings in a scrap of overheard conversation, a chance encounter or a lingering image, or they may grow from a much older story. Many contemporary writers reimagine traditional tales, and it has been central to my work for many years. Acknowledging the practice, Sara Maitland notes, 'a tale which has been around for centuries is highly likely to be a better than one I just made up yesterday' (2012: 12). She retells fairy tales because she feels, 'they can tell more truth, more economically, than slices of social realism' (12). I knew I wanted to reimagine an old story with ecological roots into the contemporary city, but I didn't know which one. Initially, my search for a story to work with was deskbound. The only paths taken were between bookshelves and along virtual trails, and no story I came across felt right. In the end, the story I needed came to me by chance. I was reading David Almond's *Skellig* to my sons at bedtime and there Persephone was, 'struggling her way towards us. She squeezed through black tunnels. She took wrong turnings, banged her head against the rocks' (2013: 166).

Persephone's is a story that has been told and retold for at least 3,000 years by poets, artists and storytellers (Downing 1994). Her emergence from the Underworld each year brings with it the beginnings of spring. Once discovered, I started seeing Persephone everywhere as I walked. She was with the Lesser Celandines that crept out at the edges of pavements. She was with the swallows that skimmed the football pitch in the park. The more attention I paid to the arrival of spring in the city, the more curious I became, and learning the names of wildflowers made them visible to me where I hadn't seen them before. *Persephone's Footsteps* had its beginnings outside rather than at my desk. I began to imagine the story into the cracks of the city as I walked, following a goddess's footsteps through its streets. Like most writers, I am a creature of habit and may have been tempted to return to my desk to write the story if I hadn't broken two fingers, leaving me unable to write for two months. And so, I had to find ways to walk the story into existence.

Story walking

> *The paths up are ever shifting. Persephone read the way in worm castings and the beat of rain, in bell-song and boot-clack. And as she climbed she wondered at what people bury and forget just beneath their feet.*

There is a long history of writers who walk. Many left traces of their journeys in writing, they haunt our future footsteps, meaning we never have to set out alone. Rebecca Solnit describes most modern writers as 'deskbound, indoor creatures', noting, 'nothing more than outline and ideas can be achieved elsewhere' (2014: 113). She contrasts this to William Wordsworth's techniques of composition on Lakeland walks where, '[h]is steps seem to have beat out a steady rhythm for the poetry, like the metronome of a composer' (13–14). For Wordsworth, walking and writing were part of the same process. Other writers have recounted their walks on their return home, so we can shed the 'shell-like covering our souls have excreted to house themselves' and plunge into the winter dusk with Virginia Woolf as she sets out to buy a pencil (Woolf 2005: 2), or shadow Charles Dickens as he finds brief company in the clock chimes on a night walk (Dickens 2010: 9). With surrealist writer Louis Aragon, a stroll through a Paris passageway becomes a journey into the marvellous. His proclamation that 'New myths spring up beneath each step we take' (Aragon 1994: 10) was at the forefront of my mind when I set out to walk with the Persephone myth.

We might consider the walking reader to have a shorter lineage, imagining their existence to be tied to advances in mobile technologies, but if we think about storytelling rather than writing and listening, rather than reading, we are taken much further back in human history. From the many oral traditions that locate story in landscape; 'an alliance so thorough that the speaker must pace his stories or songs to match the speed with which he moves through the terrain' (Abram 2017: 174), to the long-lived folk truth that telling stories will shorten a journey, fictions have accompanied our footsteps. In the 1990s, Janet Cardiff began making storied walks, describing them she says, '[m]y voice gives directions but also relates thoughts and narrative elements, which instil in the listener a desire to continue and finish the walk' (Schaub 2005: 15). Cardiff's work combines pre-recorded sound effects, and sometimes photographs and video, to make vivid the layering of time in specific landscapes.

Thanks to the ubiquity of mobile phones, literary experiments are now being walked in cities around the world. These works often take advantage of combinatory smartphone functions to mediate the relationship between reader, story and city. Current examples in the United Kingdom include *The Cartographer's Confession* (2017), by James Attlee and the Ambient Literature Project, which uses GPS to reveal story elements; *Talking Statues*, a project which uses NFC tags to trigger the transfer of story to your phone (Sing London 2014–17); and *The Walk* (2013) by Naomi Alderman and Six to Start, which links narrative delivery to a pedometer as part of a health initiative. Describing new forms of locative media, Jeremy Hight writes, '[p]ublication can be signal, air, a spot of land. It can be on maps, and it can only be transcribed by a person as they move' (2010: 322). The experience of making *Persephone's Footsteps* has convinced me that to fully exploit these diverse new possibilities for publication we first need to engage with the narrative possibilities uncovered when we walk the city as writers.

Revealing the city: Writer as cartographer

> *Is there anything growing where you are now? There's always something growing. A dandelion, a shadow, a block of flats, a goddess sprouting between tarmac and curb, bringing spring out of step, out of time, out into the city streets.*

I walked a long way to make *Persephone's Footsteps.* Some walks were part of my everyday routine. Others I undertook with a particular focus or intent. The everyday walks contributed an accretion of imaginative detail and helped me to play with the idea of walking as writing, but it was two of the focused walks that provided me with the space to develop the bones of the story. In Lancaster, the city where I live, I set out to explore as far as I could using only alleyways, ginnels and passages. A small northern English city, with Georgian architecture, millworkers terraces and the remains of docks that make visible its history as a major port for the slave trade in the eighteenth century, my walk took me through both run-down and more affluent areas. I wandered close to the quays, by post-industrial ruins, through housing estates and shopping areas. Undertaking the walk in the spirit of what Donna Haraway describes as a curious practice (Haraway 2016: 126–34), I took the character Persephone with me. I walked 'holding open the possibility that surprises are in store, that something interesting is about to happen' (127). Using only alleyways was an attempt to render my own city unfamiliar to me, as the surface would be unfamiliar to Persephone when she emerged from the Underworld each spring.

As I walked, I gathered materials from what I saw, smelled, heard and imagined. Abandoned things, such as a sewing machine and a mattress, and growing things, for instance tangles of weeds and wildflowers, all became part of the story. I was particularly drawn to the collisions between human and non-human lives – fag ends and petals curled together in the gutter, crows eating crisps – and to the marks left by others – peeling layers of posters, claw marks in mud, graffiti on old stone walls. Occasionally, I crossed tracks with one of my own memories and remembered Paul Auster's assertion that, 'if in some sense the world imprints itself on our minds, it is equally true that our experiences are imprinted on the world' (1989: 166). In the overgrown hush of a ginnel, where voices and traffic noises were the only company encountered, I sensed that the city I knew was both nearby and very far away.

The challenges of Persephone's journey upwards were in my mind when I set out to walk from the lowest point I could reach in a city to the highest. I selected Liverpool, a large northern maritime city. I began in Liverpool James Street, one of the oldest underground stations in the world, and was trying to get to the top of the city's cathedral, which sits on a rise 500 feet above sea level. The act of writing in all its dimensions can be understood as a process of discovery. Tim Ingold discusses writing as a gathering process, asserting that ideas are not projected fully formed from the mind to the page but uncovered through the physical act of writing (Ingold 2011: 178–9). Here, they were uncovered through writing as walking. Describing the process in my practice journal, I wrote:

> Walking with the character
> Writing with footsteps
> Making story in the world

I paid attention to things as Persephone might and this brought chance encounters and surprises, such as the realization that many of the city's neoclassical statues were her family members. Up a back alley, I found a polished steel sign that said Elysian Fields. I worked in fragments of story, drawing insights, ideas and scraps into an interweaving of real and imaginative space. I started to imagine how a reader might walk with Persephone. As Walter Ong writes, '[h]uman communication is never one-way. Always, it not only calls for response but is shaped in its very content and form by anticipated response' (2002: 173). The reader became my shadow companion whose footsteps I began to anticipate.

The first draft of the story remained in those walks, and I found I could recollect it through real or remembered movement. By this point I could write again for short periods of time, and I decided to write the story down. Yet, literally writing it down the page felt wrong. My fingers resisted, so instead I wrote from the bottom, following the story in its constant journey upwards.

Exploring technologies: Writer as maker

Persephone made false blooms from sharp-toothed glass, slivered brick, porcelain limbs, and bent nails. Her garden would be rust-thick and plastic-wrapped. She forced a new spring out through a crack in the pavement of a city like this.

In contemporary publishing, most writers make content for books that are published by others. Ingold writes that the role of writer as content-maker has been prevalent since writers became separated from the design and production of their work following the development of the printing press (Ingold 2016: 27). My PhD research was rooted in an open approach to practice, where the way a story will be shared is not predetermined at the outset. Recognizing that technologies shape and are shaped by stories (Zipes 2012: 21–2), I am interested in finding out how the methods and materials I use to make a story impact the development of its content, form and medium.

After setting up the Visible Language Workshop at the Massachusetts Institute of Technology (MIT) in the 1970s, Muriel Cooper predicted that, 'the line between reproduction tools and design would blur when information became electronic and that the lines between designer and artist, author and designer, professional and amateur would also dissolve' (cited in Reinfurt 2007: 15). Cooper's courses treated writing as a material practice and 'integrated the reproduction tools as part of the thinking process and reduced the gap between process and product' (7). Despite continued advances in technologies this approach remains rare. As a practitioner, it can feel like there are very few digital writer-makers compared to the vast number of writers working on manuscripts with the aim of print publication.

There are many possible barriers to writers engaging with digital making, including being daunted by code, the speed of technological change and the threat of obsolescence. I was drawn to experimenting with microcontrollers and sensors such as the Arduino and Raspberry Pi as they are small-scale, longer-lasting, reusable and not prohibitively expensive. Access to technologies is an important issue that can prevent both readers and writers from engaging with digital literature. Publishers aim to produce exciting work at the limits of what the technology can do, but this excludes people for whom those devices are not affordable or accessible. As a low-income writer, I have been frustrated by my inability to afford a phone on which many digital literature apps can be used, and this has motivated me to make digital stories that don't rely on the reader to own a specific device. Working with Arduino, an open-source platform, I was able to take advantage of the huge amount of support material and resources provided by online maker communities. I learned to solder, build circuits, code in C++ and Python, and began to explore the ways in which sensors can locate a reader in space and reveal parts of the story in response to their physical movements.

GPS modules can be used to link story elements to specific locations in a city, but I didn't want to geographically limit the work in this way. Compass, gyroscope or accelerometer sensors would have given me a reader's orientation or localized movement to work with, but an altitude sensor was the best way of working with the upward drive of the story that was emerging from my walks. Initially my attempts at using the sensor would give me altitude readings but I was unable to get the audio files to trigger. I was fortunate to be able to seek face-to-face advice from a colleague in computing and working through the code with him was an invaluable learning experience. I was surprised to realize his approach to coding was a creative process not very far removed from writing a story. We started out with pen and paper, working through what I wanted to happen in note form, using natural language rather than code at first to create a loose structure. In this way, I was able to make the logic work and then write the code. This felt akin to the satisfaction of feeling a plot click whilst making notes before writing out a full story.

The process-oriented approach I've taken to practice as research means traces of the making are embedded in every aspect of the work. Ingold writes that printed text 'bears no witness to the activity of those whose labours brought it into being, appearing rather as a pre-composed artefact, a work' (2016: 260). I have not tried to hide the work's making and the processes involved, but rather I have embraced them. Readers of *Persephone's Footsteps* have commented on its pleasing tactility. Karen O'Rourke has described locative media 'as real-world answer to "decorporealized, screen-based experience of net art"' (2013: 125). My work brings the materiality of the story object, which must be carried as the reader walks, to the fore.

Paradoxically, working with digital materials brought me into contact with a wide variety of other materials and earlier technologies of communication, including bookbinding, drawing and map-making, and so the work bridges an uncertain space between digital literature and artist's book. This chimes with Helen Clarke's assertion that, '[t]he recent resurgence of interest in (and the use of) the artist's book as a form may be perceived as a reaction to the digitisation of reading and the anxiety about the future-proofing of digital archives' (Clarke and Kivland 2017: 11). In my case, though, it was making with digital technologies as a material practice that took me to other forms of making and the result is a hybrid work.

Revisioning with the city

> *Are you high enough? When you look down from above you can make toys of a city. It's easier up here to be a god. With one breath Persephone felt she could rearrange the city as she chose.*

Revision is an essential part of the creative writing process and can be understood as a creative act in itself. As a draft, *Persephone's Footsteps* existed in upwardly handwritten and typed form, as an oral composition, in a collection of drawings and remembered fragments of walks, and as various paper and digital prototypes. Just as the work couldn't have been written at a desk, it also couldn't just be revised at a desk; it needed to be taken back into the city. The redrafting involved more than words. I was redrafting the design of the experience as I walked and focusing more and more on how I could shape the gaps that would be needed for the reader's experience of the story. Walking with an early mock-up of the vertical map that used capacitive touch sensing in addition to the altitude sensor I realized it was impossible to carry the work and activate touch sensors. As I noted in my practice journal:

> I can't create digital stories as fictional things and work on them only in that form. They have to become material things as early as possible or I will go wandering way off from what is possible.

From this point on, there was a constant backwards and forwards movement, a tug and push, between making and writing. When something wasn't working with either technology or story it had to be fixed, which directly impacted the other, and more changes would have to be made. There was tension in this but also opportunity, and as the work became more solid, so did my sense of the reader.

The imagined reader becomes more solid

> *Persephone asked the signs for help, but they couldn't speak for themselves. She asked the shadows for help, but they were too weak and too few in the bleached city night. Finally, she approached the statues ...*

Working on any piece of writing that is intended to be shared requires an imagined reader, but with ambient literature it is not only reader but also their experience of reading that has to be imagined. Of course, writers are also readers, and engaging with ambient and locative works in a variety of settings has enabled me to develop a sense of what I enjoy as a reader. I know the feeling of delight when a work chimes unexpectedly with my present surroundings, and I have been equally delighted by visceral dissonance. I want to enjoy a work's palimpsestic qualities by reading it into a space.

As we walk a work, even if it is audio based, I think we are still readers. In English, the word read has its roots in reasoning and counsel, but most other languages have a word for read that relates to a gathering up (Online Etymology Dictionary n.d.). With ambient literature, the reader is gathering the rest of the materials for the story; they are gathering associations between the work and the environment, and they are gathering meaning from the entanglement of both. All reading involves interaction with an environment in a present moment, and there are considerations of reading, which while referring to the printed book, can be usefully applied to ambient literature. Roland Barthes described reading with his head lifted (Scott 2012: 60), writing that a text 'produces, in me, the best pleasure if it manages to make itself heard indirectly; if in reading it, I am led to look up often, to listen to something else' (Barthes 1975: 24). Janet Cardiff compares the experience to Proust's notion of 'the miracle of an analogy ... an unexpected merger of something from a long time ago with something that is being experienced in the present' (Schaub 2005: 17). This is the spontaneous creative work of the reader. As Umberto Eco notes, '[w]hen a work is finished, a dialogue is established between the text and its readers (the author is excluded)' (1985: 47). With works of ambient literature, from this point onwards the dialogue is between the text, the reader and the place.

The city interrupts

Do you know the paths of the city? They're always shifting whatever the map might say.

Working on *Persephone's Footsteps* in more than one city helped me counter the temptation to tie narrative details to specific experiences in exact locations. At times I felt bewildered by writing in an anticipatory mode for unknown urban environments, aware of the non-exhaustive potential for syntony, dissonance, interruption and disruption. This was where having a simple storyline and a well-defined structure helped. Naomi Alderman (2018) has spoken of the need for clarity when writing for people who are on the move and whose progress through the story may be interrupted at any time. Along with clarity, there are other characteristics found within the oral tradition that help listeners hold on to a story that I think may be usefully employed in making ambient literature. These include considered use of celerity, rhythm and repetition, and working with what Ong describes as 'heavy characters ... persons whose deeds are monumental, memorable and commonly public' (2002: 69). Working from myth enabled me to bring such a 'heavy' character into the everyday city.

Every experience of *Persephone's Footsteps* will be different, and the story from which people's multitudinous readings begin is itself not a fixed work. The code can be adapted to suit urban environments with different altitudinal spreads. There is potential for sections of the story to be changed and re-recorded, or for new layers of story to be added. The technologies used to share the story are easily accessed and adapted. The paper map the reader carries is unmarked and made in a spirit of transformed cartography, employed by the situationists to invite exploration of one city using a map of another (Debord quoted in McDonough 2009: 62). Geology, carbon emission and constellation charts are combined with underground and surface maps from some of the most polluting cities in the world to make a skeletal city that can flesh out into the space where it is taken.

Reaching a staging post

Look up ... Persephone sits in the sky. Just above the city, just beneath the stars, just where the spume and jetsam of human life comes to rest in the air ...

Persephone's Footsteps currently exists as a single work. There is potential for the work to be reproduced, for it to be developed further to make the digital elements more robust, to give the reader more control over audio functions and improve accessibility to the work. So far, the work has been tested on a small scale and more explorations are needed to uncover the work's potential in different cities. A single work in which momentary experience, narrative and physical materials are so intertwined cannot be shared via other media, meaning its audience will always be tiny compared to that of a print, or more widely available, digital publication. For me, though, there is a small beauty in a work passed from one person's hands to another. It is the learning from the process of making the work that I feel more compelled to share with a larger audience.

In response to El Lissitzky, I don't think the new book needs a new writer, but it does need a new approach to writing. There are many possibilities for writers to explore in domains they may not have anticipated entering, and the benefits of jumping in can be manifold. Working with digital technologies has also taken me towards writing as a material practice in many forms. Working on ambient literature has helped me to consider the gaps I leave for the reader in all the stories I write. There is a widening of process rather than a narrowing – an opening up where before there was only a predetermined route to conventional publication. Whether working individually or in collaboration, writers can utilize their narrative skills in every aspect of making a work of digital fiction. Playing with different sites of composition and exploring different methods of production feels essential when stories are increasingly received in so many different ways as part of what Kate Pullinger (2016) has called digital literature's quiet revolution of form and content.

On returning from her journey, an early reader of *Persephone's Footsteps* said, '[t]here's nothing between me and the story and the place I'm listening to the story in'. As we read these works in the city, our footsteps 'weave places together' (Certeau 1988: 97). Ambient Literature offers not only a new journey of discovery for readers but the beginning of one for writers too.

Acknowledgements

This work was funded by the Digital Economy programme (RCUK Grant EP/G037582/1), which supports the HighWire Centre for Doctoral Training at Lancaster University (http://highwire.lancs.ac.uk).

References

Abram, D. (2017), *The Spell of the Sensuous*, New York: Vintage.

Alderman, N. (2018), Naomi Alderman's Podcast, Listeners Walk Into The Story. *NCPR*. Available online: https://www.northcountrypublicradio.org/news/npr/596443185/in-naomi-alderman-s-podcast-listeners-walk-into-the-story (accessed 12 November 2022).

Alderman, N., and Six to Start. (2013), *The Walk*. Available online: https://play.google.com/store/apps/details?id=com.sixtostart.thewalk2 (accessed 10 November 2022).

Almond, D. (2013), *Skellig: 15th Anniversary Edition*, London: Hodder Children's Books.

Aragon, L. (1994), *Paris Peasant*, Boston: Exact Change.

Attlee, J. (2017), *The Cartographer's Confession*. Available online: https://research.ambientlit.com/cartographersconfession (accessed 6 June 2024).

Auster, P. (1989), *The Invention of Solitude*, London: Faber and Faber.

Barthes, R. (1975), *The Pleasure of the Text*, New York: Hill and Wang.

Certeau, M. de. (1988), *The Practice of Everyday Life*, Berkeley: University of California Press.

Clarke, H. and S. Kivland, eds. (2017), *The Lost Diagrams of Walter Benjamin*, London: Ma Bibliothèque.

Dickens, C. (2010), *Night Walks*, London: Penguin.

Downing, C., ed. (1994), *The Long Journey Home: Re-visioning the Myth of Demeter and Persephone for Our Time*, Boston: Shambhala.

Eco, U. (1985), *Reflections on the Name of the Rose*, London: Secker & Warburg.

Haraway, D. (2016), *Staying with the Trouble*, Durham, NC: Duke University Press.

Hight, J. (2010), 'Locative Narrative, Literature and Form', in J. Schäfer and P. Gendolla, eds. *Beyond the Screen: Transformations of Literary Structures, Interfaces and Genres*, 317–30, Piscataway, NJ: Transactions Publishers.

Ingold, T. (2011), *Being Alive: Essays on Movement, Knowledge and Description*, Abingdon: Routledge.

Ingold, T. (2016), *Lines*, Abingdon: Routledge.

Maitland, S. (2012), *Gossip from the Forest: The Tangled Roots of Our Forests and Fairy Tale*, London: Granta.

Manning, E. and B. Massumi. (2014), *Thought in the Act: Passages in the Ecology of Experience*, Minneapolis: University of Minnesota Press.
McDonough, T. (2009), *The Situationists and the City*, London: Verso.
Ong, W. (2002), *Orality and Literacy*, London: Routledge.
Online Etymological Dictionary. (n.d.), s.v. 'read'. Available online: https://www.etymonline.com/word/read (accessed 10 November 2022).
O'Rourke, K. (2013), *Walking and Mapping: Artists as Cartographers*, Cambridge, MA: MIT Press.
Pullinger, K. (2016), 'Introducing the Next Generation of Ambient Literature', *The Bookseller*. Available online: https://www.thebookseller.com/futurebook/introducing-next-generation-ambient-literature-338141 (accessed 12 November 2022).
Reinfurt, D. (2007), *This Stands as a Sketch for the Future*. Available online: http://www.dextersinister.org/MEDIA/PDF/Thisstandsasasketchforthefuture.pdf (accessed 1 October 2022).
Schaub, M. (2005), *Janet Cardiff: The Walk Book*, Vienna: Thyssen-Bornemisza Art Contemporary.
Scott, C. (2012), *Literary Translation and the Rediscovery of Reading*, Cambridge: Cambridge University Press.
Sing London. (2014–17), *Talking Statues*. Available online: http://www.talkingstatues.co.uk (accessed 12 November 2022).
Solnit, R. (2014), *Wanderlust*, London: Granta.
Tullet, B. (2010), 'Electro-Library Dreams', *Eye Magazine*. Available online: http://www.eyemagazine.com/blog/post/electro-library-dreams (accessed 10 November 2022).
Woolf, V. (2005), *Street Haunting*, London: Penguin.
Zipes, J. (2012), *The Irresistible Fairy Tale*, Princeton, NJ: Princeton University Press.

3

Waveform: Writing across ocean, air and algorithms

Richard A. Carter

Waveform is a speculative digital writing project that commenced in the spring of 2017. The project is characterized by its use of a camera drone as part of an apparatus for generating poetry. Initially, the drone is used to photograph different patterns of incoming ocean waves above remote coastal shorelines. The visual data gathered is then processed using a simple machine vision algorithm that scans and detects the varied contrasts of each scene, before attempting to draw a border where it determines the divide between land and ocean to reside. The data points that constitute this nebulous frontier are then parsed by another algorithm that generates poem-like texts – its stored vocabularies, and subsequent outputs, being curated to engage themes concerning the coast, climate change and the scientific measurement of both.

This project was conceived as an apparatus for entangling different concepts, artefacts, processes and representations concerning electronic environmental sensing, seeking to mobilize alternative dialogues that cut across discursive and disciplinary thresholds. The project is concerned especially with enacting the potentials of creative, speculative modes of sensing and sense-making in an age of precipitous ecological decline – highlighting the historical contexts, technical schemas and incommensurate values that escape the attuned thresholds of the contemporary, data-driven episteme, but which are foundational to the experiences of negotiating a rapidly changing ecology.

This chapter will examine in detail the critical contexts and key themes that form the conceptual and aesthetic locus of the project. For this end, it will discuss in turn the key elements that constitute *Waveform* as a material and theoretical assemblage, considering the varied entanglements that draw together machine sensing, the politics and aesthetic potentials of ocean and atmosphere, and their expression through generative writing.

On ambience

Before proceeding into the core of the discussion, it is worth spending a moment of reflection on the topic of ambience and the literary. *Waveform* has been presented in numerous different formats and interpreted in various ways over recent years (see Carter 2023), and this chapter renders it in the context of a book exploring instances of ambient literature. This has been defined by Jonathan Dovey, Tom Abba and Kate Pullinger as '*situated writing practices in which text is able to respond to the site of reading*' (2021: 5; original emphasis). Practically stated, this encompasses an emergent body of works, digitally embedded, that employ sensory devices, or locative technologies, or even provide simple cues for action, to create a reading encounter that acknowledges its situated contexts, harnessing these to shape how it is experienced and interpreted. Crucially, as Dovey, Abba and Pullinger highlight, whilst the resulting enactments are 'temporary, ambiguous, and unpredictable in their meaning … unlike the theatre, the gallery, or the cinema, they take place in the everyday shared world' (2) – a world that is saturated by GPS, Cellular and Wi-Fi signals, ever-present social media and web data, augmented and mixed realities, as well as multimodal surveillance.

Initially, this definition would appear to favour works that are prepared for variable unfolding at the specific moment of the reading encounter – structured around carefully predefined channels of variability in response to set operational cues – rather than incorporating ambient inputs to guide their *initial* composition by the author, which is the case with *Waveform*. Indeed, some theorists have previously dismissed the very possibility of more-than-human forces as having any viable hand in shaping the composition of expressive texts, with Knapp and Michaels (1982) interrogating the image of a poem written by the action of rolling waves on the shoreline and declaring that, without the guiding contexts of authorial intent, such markings would always, ultimately, be meaningless.

In their exploration of how ambient literature is authored, Abba and Spencer consider that the 'ambient work is an event produced by the intersection of complex systems, [and so] the process of conceiving and writing it requires an understanding of the complexity of those systems precisely as they intersect at the moment of enactment' (2021: 276). They go on to remark that ambient texts involve the writer 'deliberately manipulating and employing aspects of [the reader's] situation in order to generate *affect*' (276; original emphasis). Once more, this definition appears to explicitly favour the real time of the reading encounter, whereas *Waveform* presents the traces made after the contingent moment of what can be defined as the *writing* encounter. However, Abba and Spencer emphasize their wariness in laying down specific, unyielding rules by which ambient works can be understood to operate. Moreover, they acknowledge that 'a reader of an ambient literary work does not only embody a narrative through place or enact it through walking. The experience is also one built of data, which is experienced through narrative … as the literary equivalent of certain kinds of data visualisation' (305). Here, they cite the work of J. R. Carpenter's *This is a Picture of the Wind* (2016), which remixes its constituent text using live weather data, and so meditating reflexively on these aspects, technical and metrological, as they circulate throughout the contemporary environment – more on this text later in the chapter.

While *Waveform* is not restructured in real time, it nevertheless, like Carpenter's work, draws attention to the affective capacities of wider ambient contexts and forces that form part of our worldly being, granting them a direct role in shaping the text that is ultimately delivered to the reader – and, from this, rejecting Knapp and Michael's minimization of their expressive powers. Each output that makes up *Waveform* works to make explicit their origins in one particular set of material entanglements and resonances that, nevertheless, are inexhaustible in their potential becoming, never set or stable. The markings formed at the moment of inscription are thus less significant in themselves than the contexts and processes from which they emerged and are framed, and *Waveform* aims to interrogate these reflexively through its very status as a sensing and writing apparatus, made up of diverse components. Ultimately, *Waveform*'s gesture towards the immanent and the ambient is in its enactment through, and representations of an always lively, always more-than-human world that forever exceeds our framings at any given moment, granting opportunities for experience, knowing and meaning that are irreducible to any one act of writing or reading.

Speculative sensing

This chapter was written originally in the week marking the fiftieth anniversary of the Apollo 11 lunar landings, with the varied commemorations being the culmination of many months of reflection on the historic milestones that made this mission possible. Most prominent among these in popular coverage was the Apollo 8 lunar circumnavigation, on 24 December 1968, with a particular focus on the imagery it generated. It was on this flight that the three crew members, orbiting high above the lunar surface, first observed a waxing Earth rising serenely above its cratered horizon. Scrabbling around in their cramped and cluttered spacecraft, each of the crew took a series of images in both colour and black and white – of which one, AS8-14-2383, has become known officially as 'Earth Rise', depicting a radiant Earth set above the monochrome hamada below.

Many such 'Earth Rise' photographs were taken on each of the subsequent Apollo missions to the lunar surface, but it was on the last mission, Apollo 17, that another noteworthy portrait was produced, the so-called 'Blue Marble', AS17-148-22727, on 7 December 1972. At the time, it was one of the first such images depicting a fully illuminated Earth, with the sun being directly behind the spacecraft at the point of capture. After being cleaned, cropped and rotated so that the North Pole faced upwards, it proliferated across a range of media channels and has been characterized as one of the most reproduced photographs in history.

Although the Apollo programme did not produce the very first such images of the 'whole Earth' from an orbital vantage – these came courtesy of the military DODGE and civilian ATS-3 satellites in 1967 – they emerged into the popular consciousness at a time of growing concern regarding the state of the environment and human society more broadly. Early campaigners such as Stewart Brand advocated the dissemination of whole Earth imagery, presenting it 'as an island, surrounded by a lot of inhospitable space … this little blue, white, green and brown jewel-like icon amongst a quite featureless black vacuum' in order to orient the prevailing imaginary towards a new mode of reflecting on the Earth and its ecology – as profoundly singular and precious, amidst the howling darkness around it ('Stewart Brand Interview' 2003). Brand himself had the earlier ATS-3 satellite image emblazoned on the cover of the first *Whole Earth Catalogue*, which he had published in 1968 – listing myriad books, tools, materials and expertise necessary for making experimental inroads towards an alternative way of living and being. The covers of subsequent catalogues would employ numerous images from Apollo of the whole Earth, and in preparation for the first Earth Day, on 22 April 1970, its founder John McConnell designed what he termed 'The Authentic Earth Flag' to provide it with a rallying symbol – the design being a dark blue field with a charge consisting of a stylized image of the whole Earth, which was replaced later on with the 'Blue Marble' photograph of 1972.

There are many published academic works charting the influence of whole Earth imagery upon the nascent environmental movement (see e.g. Henry and Taylor 2009). However, at the present time of writing, with the planet in the grip of a particularly terrible, and quite likely terminal moment of ecological decline, we can note how our detailed knowledge of this situation has been made largely possible not through the circumferential gaze of Apollo's eye, but through the datafied Earth that was also coming to the fore during the 1960s and 1970s. The ATS-3 satellite was among the very first deployed for conducting Earth observations, of any description, and as the decades have gone by, its sophisticated descendants, notably the GOES and Landsat series, are now as critical to climactic and ecological monitoring as localized, manual measurements of land, air and ocean. Even these are now heavily augmented by a proliferating array of automated weather stations, surveillance radars, monitoring buoys, and sounding probes, all feeding into innumerable data relays that are, to varying degrees, linked to the internet.

It is through these global infrastructures, whose acquisitional capacities reach far beyond the thresholds of the human sensorium, that scientists have recorded and measured rapid transformations in the Earth's climate and ecology over recent decades. So extensive are these transformations, indeed irreversible, they have been hypothesized as marking the beginnings of a new, geo-climatic epoch, the Anthropocene, which proclaims the profound impact of human collective agency upon every aspect of the Earth as a planetary entity (see Crutzen and Stoermer 2000).

Nevertheless, despite its undoubted scientific efficacy, this data driven aesthetic has not been without its critics. Gabrys (2018) has noted that, '[i]t is now not uncommon for the planetary to be invoked in discussions of technology … Technology is seen to overrun and command the planetary', presenting to us an Earth that is held in a space of complete data capture and enclosure, that is, an Earth that can be more effectively bent to human agency, an Earth that can be programmed. Following this, Gabrys notes how these totalizing planetary discourses have their deep origins in colonial histories of spatial enclosure and control, which is a point made also by Cosgrove:

> Mapping the globes climates and physiography into 'natural' regions [naturalized] patterns of control and strategy among the imperial powers … the distribution of lands and seas, of landforms, natural resources, or 'races' … had to be exploited if a state was to survive, compete, and prosper.
>
> (2001: 243)

It is in this context that Gabrys (2018) enquires as to whether such modalities of planetary observation and computation are in fact reducing 'the possibilities of what the planetary is or might become – of being planetary as praxis'.

She asks whether it might 'be possible not to remake the pretensions of globality and globalisation through planetary media projects, but rather begin to unsettle figures of totality and regulation in order to attend to the incommensurate, the unjust, and the yet to be recognized?'

Gabrys herself has long examined the ways in which sensory systems form part of the processes of individuation by which environments, entities and affectivities are crystallized. That is, of the ways in which sensory practices function not as a window onto the world, but as an assemblage through which it is performed in a variety of different ways. It is this that suggests a path of exploratory enquiry, where new entities and environments form within the intersection of computational and distributed sensors. It is on this point that Gabrys leaves us with this consideration, '[i]nstead of remaining firmly embedded within the utensil-problem space, where environmental sensors facilitate increasingly regimented and automated ways of life, another approach might be to consider how environmental computational practices open into experimentation, expanded experiences, and speculative adventures' (2016: 270). Following Whitehead, she observes:

> [A] speculative project is most interesting when it is involved in 'bringing adventures into existence.' Rather than demystifying, mapping out, and nailing down everything in a grand gesture of rationalism, adventure seeks to create conditions for both hope and change. A speculative adventure is then an approach invested in experimenting worlds.
>
> (Gabrys 2016: 272)

Engelmann and Thomson (2016a, b) raise a similar possibility in their account of the more rarefied scientific concern of detecting neutrino decay. They describe how an entire array of technical devices, geological formations and disciplinary structures become entangled, with great imagination and intricacy, to measure this near-imperceptible phenomenon – a series of '"happy accidents" among technical devices, human endeavours, planetary bodies, and knowledge architectures, [which] have inspired breakthroughs in what it is possible to sense, and therefore what it is possible to know' (Engelmann and Thomson 2016a).

The authors thus conclude, following Barad (2007), that sensory limitations and thresholds should not be read as the narrow consequence of absolute properties but, instead, as the product of situated constructions – contingent assemblies of human and more-than-human actors, which constitute their respective capacities of perception, action and expression. In this vein, Engelmann and Thomson enquire, hypothetically, as to whether this invites the possibility of sensory assemblies that afford 'a more genuine openness to non-human agency and aesthetics', and so resisting the anthropic exceptionalism that is both a root cause and persistent driver of present ecological challenges.

An implicit message in the above accounts is that imagination and speculation are as much a part of the practices of machine sensing as the more readily evident aspects of technology and technique. The detection and qualification of global environmental stressors is predicated on marshalling a globally dispersed array of human, machinic and material formations, whose collective operation allows for the detection of phenomena that far exceed the scale, duration and associative capacity of our unaided senses. The worrying discoveries arising demonstrate profoundly that human agents can never stand apart from the world's unfolding, with the act of sense-making, by necessity, involving a certain exploratory entanglement with the energies and materials under study. This requires a consideration of not only the always-situated nature of knowledge-making but also the creative, performative vectors that make it possible in the first instance – the role of the imaginary in contracting the assemblies that might realize a speculated state of affairs, the creative leaps involved in enacting and interpreting the experimental process itself, and how this reshapes subsequently what possible understandings are envisaged and then sought. This performative conception underpins Pickering's (1995) account of the 'mangle' of scientific practice, in which 'human and material agency are reciprocally and emergently intertwined'. For Pickering, the unpredictable agency of the material actively resists and reorients the creative intentionality of human cognition, yielding new configurations of possibility in the process of exploring and enacting the phenomena under study.

Looking across these varied standpoints, the sensory is transformed from a remote Cartesian window into an immanent assemblage. This suggests in turn the potential for developing and deploying sensory systems not in the mode of the abstractly specular, but for articulating a creative, speculative sensibility – to establish a form of sensing and sense-making that treats the observable world not as an established formation awaiting detection and discovery but as a space for actualizing new possibilities of seeing, thinking and relating.

It was in exploring these critical and creative potentials, as a response to concerns about how the world is articulated through existing 'global' sensory practices, that *Waveform* was first developed. In order to demonstrate how this broad enquiry was grounded into practical specifics, the following sections of this chapter will outline the concrete elements that constitute *Waveform* as a sensory assemblage and examine in detail the conceptual formations manifested through their functioning.

Ocean volumes

The most visually prominent characteristic of *Waveform* is its use of drone photography to capture the flowing, turbulent patterns of incoming ocean waves from a vertical vantage – as well as its subsequent efforts at demarcating these patterns from those of the shoreline using machine vision algorithms.

The drone employed is, at this juncture, a standard consumer model that is flown at an average height of 60 feet above the shoreline, although higher altitudes are selected where there is a potential risk of terrain intersection. The site depicted throughout *Waveform* is a remote Cornish beach known, somewhat sinisterly, as 'the Strangles' (a possible allusion to its dangerous currents and jutting fingers of rock stretching just beneath the ocean surface). This site was selected primarily because its remoteness ensured that few members of the public would be present during flying activities and so allowing safe operation of the drone in accordance with the parameters specified by the UK Civil Aviation Authority (CAA) Drone and Model Aircraft Code. Nevertheless, the Strangles is also a site located near a number of key maritime data infrastructures, and so resonates with the critical aims of this project in ways that will be explored further into this discussion.

Figures 3.1 and 3.2 depict two instances of the initial image capture and the outlines generated. As these figures illustrate, the boundary drawing operation is far from exact, and there can be considerable deviation and uncertainty in the demarcated line as compared to the apparent edge of the wave from the intuitions of human vision. This is partly a consequence of the encoded limitations of the algorithm itself, which relies on assuming a strong contrast between the white foam of the cresting waves versus the relative darkness of the immediate shoreline. A clutter-rejection filter is used to eliminate outliers generated by bright reflections or pronounced shadows, which could otherwise

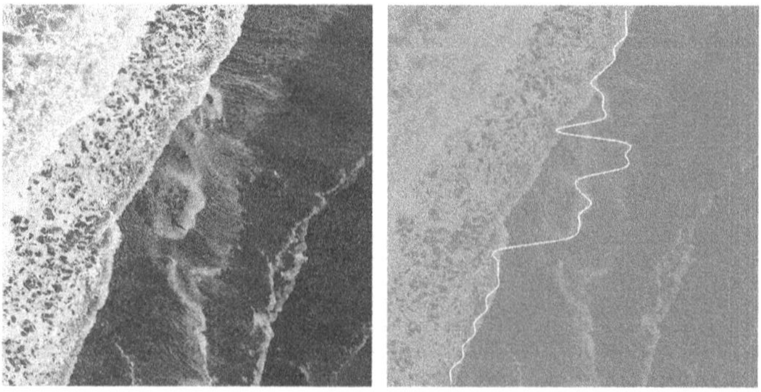

Figure 3.1 *Waveform 1*. Courtesy of Richard A. Carter.

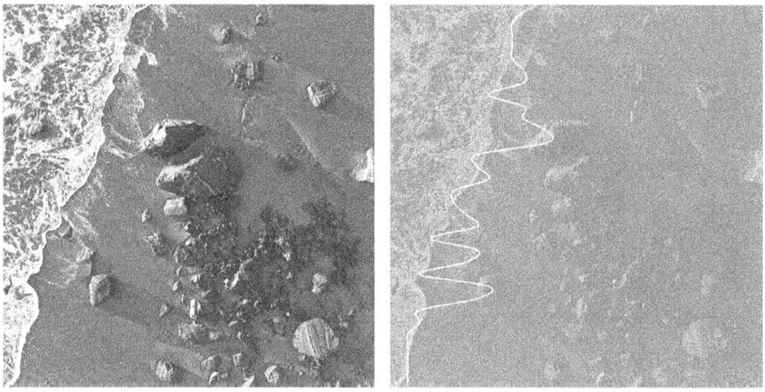

Figure 3.2 *Waveform 2*. Courtesy of Richard A. Carter.

fool the system into producing an erroneous outline. Nevertheless, across the many instances where the incoming wave front is complex, fractured and nebulous, the system invariably struggles to cope.

Two immediate questions emerge here. How does the presence of the drone itself both enable and affect the images? What might be made of an attempt (seemingly futile) at drawing a crisp line across an ever-shifting body of water? The answer to both these enquiries hinges not on treating their aspects in isolation but through understanding their embedding within the politics and modes of thinking associated with maritime cartography, and of how the latter might be reoriented through the restless, irresistible materiality of the ocean itself.

Steinberg and Peters (2015) write at length about the oceanic environment as a key site for exploring, critiquing and advancing critical thought in the contemporary world. They present the value of thinking with and through a 'wet ontology' that upends the 'static, bordered, and linear framings that typify human geographical studies of place, territory, and time' (Steinberg and Peters 2015: 1), favouring of modes that are 'indisputably voluminous, stubbornly material, and unmistakably undergoing continual re-formation' (3).

To unpack the full range of elements that constitute Steinberg and Peters' discussion is beyond the scope of this chapter, but a couple of points are worth detailing to illustrate its implications for understanding the *Waveform* project. Initially, Steinberg and Peters highlight the status of the ocean as a volumetric, dynamic formation – the full characteristics of which cannot be cleanly separated into distinctive elements, and which refute traditional axes of territorialization:

> No longer are struggles for space and resources fought on a planar level, relating to the protection of coasts through the security of flat, surface-level sea-territory. Rather contestation has depth. The source of conflict is ever moving and impacted by the movement surrounding it (be it fish, oil, silt, or water

> molecules themselves) … Even attempts at mapping vertically fail. The drawing of lines through water in an attempt to constitute levels of legal authority fails to account for the dynamic fluidity of the various elements that constitute the marine assemblage.
>
> (2015: 11)

Cartographic stratifications, their varied logics and lines, have little purchase over the churning, multiphasic mobilities of oceanic volumes. Steinberg and Peters thus identify the ocean as a model for not only the 'chaotic movement and reformation of matter' but for acknowledging how it 'enables and disrupts (or reterritorialises and deterritorialises) earthly striations' (2015: 16) – to acknowledge its entanglements with human affairs, and to read geopolitics not in the modes of the purely planar and anthropocentric but as always embedded in the volumetric materialities, mobilities and becomings of the observable world more widely. Such perspectives are of particular import for conceptualizing life in the age of the Anthropocene, which is predicated on these fundamental exchanges between intra-acting elements.

From this standpoint, the act of imaging shorelines using drone technology is evocative of the unceasing efforts by varied actors to chart the spatial parameters of the modern geopolitical environment, highlighting the vertical modes of observation, inscription and abstraction that are often intrinsic to these operations. The utility of the drone, in offering a stable platform for capturing overhead shots, is based in part on its ability to resist the exigencies of the world around it, to stay situated in the turbulent air above the shoreline, and so distilling down all such efforts to constrain the flows of the world, to impose order upon it, through technology. The subsequent act of drawing a boundary line over dynamic terrain – an idealized threshold between land and ocean – is a gesture towards those cartographic logics of zoning, knowledge construction and power projection that embed an indifference to the vibrant materialities of the world, which is treated once more as a subservient backdrop, available and amenable to human agency.

This reading initially casts *Waveform* as appropriating technologies and practices whose role, both practically and within the popular imaginary, is closely tied to the production and maintenance of scopic regimes that deliver views of a ready-to-hand world – views which are indeed closely entangled with, and implicated in producing, the conditions necessary for ecological crises to emerge. Nevertheless, in the terms described by Steinberg and Peters, such visions begin to unravel in *Waveform* through the vivid failure of the generated line to conform to the mobile terrain below. This is revealing of two key aspects: (1) the abstract grasp of a purely planar cartography and (2) the provisional thresholds by which all territorial markers are defined.

To address the first point, the boundary drawing algorithm functions by scanning the target image from left to right, one row of pixel data at a time, and has no awareness of its overall structure and patterning. Operating narrowly along two dimensions, the algorithm assumes the visual field depicts a Euclidean world of discrete points and lines. Such a world is fully commensurable to being described using linear axes, with its constituent objects moving along and across this matrix into varying configurations that define distinctive territories – such as the boundary projection of a nation's maritime frontiers or, in the case of *Waveform*, the column of points defining the meeting place between land and ocean. The frequent inability, however, of the latter to adhere to the scene below bears out Steinberg and Peters' understanding of the ocean, and the world more broadly, as 'a dynamic environment of flows and continual recomposition where, because there is no static background, "place" can be understood only in the context of mobility' – as a performance, rather than an absolute.

It is in this regard that an argument for a world-view of volumes over abstract planes, with its concomitant sensitivity towards its churning materialities, becomes especially cogent. When treated as a purely vertical projection, the images of *Waveform* suggest that the drone itself carries no further presence at all – other than affording an abstract, Apollonian overview. Nevertheless, the angles and heights by which it flies, its positioning relative to the beach, the sun and the oncoming wind, as well as the interplay of these factors with the varying sea-states below, are critical to the kinds of imagery yielded, beyond its immediate positioning in space. This dictates in turn the ultimate success or failure of the boundary drawing algorithm, as it becomes entangled with all these factors inscribed into every image.

A volumetric approach acknowledges these entanglements across space and time, the inseparability of the elements involved, as they delineate territories of perception, knowledge and, ultimately, power. Such territories are thus characterized not as discrete blocks but as being enacted (and undone) through the mobilities of their constituent actors, as they cross within and beyond particular thresholds of perception and classification – such as those supplied by the boundary drawing algorithm, separating out light and shadow according to an array of fixed values, attempting to divide land from ocean. The slippages of the latter, where image and algorithm fail to gel, thus express the contingent nature of all spatial and sensory knowledge-making, whereupon Earthly phenomena shall always far exceed their provisional framings at any given instant.

It is here that the first step towards a speculative sensory aesthetics might be established, in drawing explicit attention to the perceptual contexts and limitations of any sensory enterprise. However, continuing the emphasis on a rich, volumetric understanding of spatial enactments, this acknowledgement constitutes not a point of critical exhaustion but a catalyst for reflection on how these elements enable and inform certain possibilities of detection and interpretation – and, indeed, in the light of the work of Gabrys, Engelmann and Thomson, what new modes might yet be actualized. It is this which forms the impetus of *Waveform* as both a creative and critical endeavour, following Jessica Lehman's point that the relations between human activity and oceanic forces 'cannot be fully captured by scientific measurements' and so encouraging the assembly of alternative, speculative frameworks (quoted in Steinberg and Peters 2015).

Marking thresholds

Waveform is among many recent artistic efforts that employ oceanic data for expressing its rich contexts and varied potentials. In the work of Jill Pelto (2015), for instance, graphical charts depicting rising sea levels, temperature increases and glacial mass reductions are threaded into watercolours that depict their deleterious impacts upon landscape and wildlife. David Bowen's *tele-present water* series draws live data from scientific monitoring buoys to drive articulated wireframes depicting the detected sea surface state. In Pelto's work, the goal is to capture the material consequences of a changing climate in ways that numerical data alone cannot, whilst Bowen makes visible the scale and resolution of the 'behemoth systems' (Gabrys 2018) that measure, map and model the world for the purposes of environmental monitoring and intervention.

In the domain of electronic literature and poetry there exist several works that also incorporate the atmospheric and the oceanic as an aspect of textual expression. Cited earlier was J. R. Carpenter's *This is a Picture of the Wind* (2016), which takes a weather diary written over a period of several months and remixes this with live data from weather stations located across the UK Southwest region, ensuring the work changes between each viewing – effectively being co-authored by the atmospheric forces it describes. Mark Sample's now-deactivated Twitter bot *Station 51000* (@_LostBuoy_) (2013), like Bowen's *tele-present water*, drew oceanographic data from a monitoring buoy which it then re-articulated using the fragrant maritime vocabulary of Herman Melville's *Moby Dick* (1851), creating a work that draws connections between the idiosyncrasies of Western nautical culture and the standardized data environments governing contemporary seafaring.

The critical vectors informing the conversion of image data into generative poetry, the principal creative gesture behind *Waveform*, are manifold. Carter (2018) details one key strand that is rooted in the deep histories of electronic signal processing, digital computing and a pioneering computer artwork – a love letter generator developed by Christopher Strachey in 1952. To summarize, one early instance of electronic sensing, radar, helped pioneer the technologies and techniques that turned noisy radio waves into engineered waveforms, and so laying the groundwork for the discrete electronic signal processing necessary to realize digital computing. The latter remained bound to a military context for decades, most especially in the 1950s, and so Strachey's playful text generator would have appeared highly incongruous. Nevertheless, it demonstrated a spirit of speculative, creative engagement with different technologies, energies and materials, appropriating them for ends that diverged entirely from their origins and contexts. This is an early demonstration of the practices that can realize the alternative modes of sensing and sense-making being called for by scholars such as Gabrys. Such creativity constitutes a prerequisite for realizing a speculative sensibility, in its short-circuiting of the predominant modes by which the technologies and practices at play can be understood, and thus what their expressive capacities might ultimately be.

Going beyond this technical focus, however, is the inspiration provided by authors who have sought to enact ways of seeing and writing that are sensitive to changes that exceed a data-centric episteme. One key practitioner and theorist in this regard is J. R. Carpenter (2015), whose work on 'writing coastlines' resonates with the multilayered, multivalent thrust of Steinberg and Peters' volumetric cartographies:

> The term 'writing coastlines' may refer to writing about coastlines, but the coastlines themselves are also writing in so far as they are translating physical processes into marks and actions. Coastlines are the shifting terrains where land and water meet, always neither land nor water always both. The physical processes enacted by waves and winds may result in marks and actions associated with both erosion and accretion. Writing coastlines are edges, ledges, legible lines caught in the double bind of simultaneously writing and erasing. These in-between places are liminal spaces—points of both departure and arrival, and sites of exchange.
>
> (Carpenter 2015)

Although written outside the immediate context in which *Waveform* was first developed, Carpenter provides an evocative model here for conceptualizing the transition between the generated boundary line and the poetry it yields.

To reiterate, briefly, the technical steps involved – as these apply at the time of writing. Firstly, the line running across each target image consists of a series of coordinate values that mark the points of highest contrast on each pixel row (e.g. the bright white at the edge of the cresting wave falling upon the dark shoreline). Currently, these inputs provide a source of stochastic values for an archetypal poetry generation algorithm known as a 'Markov-chain'. Stated simply, the algorithm works by scanning the word frequencies of a source text and determining, for a given number of contiguous words ('*n*-grams'), those which are likely to occur in sequence. Selecting an arbitrary *n*-gram will thus suggest the immediate possibilities for what might follow. By making probabilistically weighted selections in this manner, it is possible to construct entirely new phrases that do not appear in the source text, but which retain some of its stylistic qualities and linguistic coherency. It is this that enables arbitrary coordinates to be parsed into poetic sequences, with the former being used to select from a range of different possibilities to assemble each link in the textual chain. Depending on the starting phrase chosen by the algorithm, each target image is capable of yielding an array of different poetic outputs, which are then curated manually on the basis of their apparent coherency and resonance with themes of coast, climate and the scientific measurement of both (for a detailed account as well as a discussion around the textual sources used to derive the final poems, see Carter 2018). Figure 3.3 illustrates some example outputs from this process, as derived from the source imagery shown previously in Figures 3.1 and 3.2.

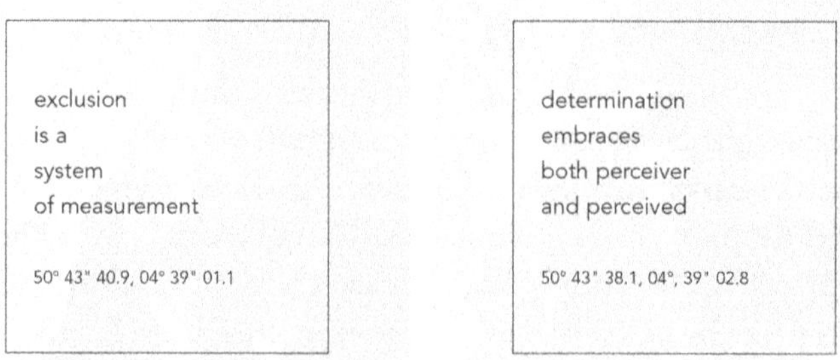

Figure 3.3 *Waveform 3*. Courtesy of Richard A. Carter.

Carpenter's description of the coastal region as a site of continual mark-making, erasure and exchange encapsulates its status as a key threshold upon which a multiplicity of material, socio-cultural, political and technical forces become entangled. The concrete processes of tide, wind and geology exert their own irresistible influences here but are shaped and structured also by the exponential material impacts of human consumption, conflict and colonization (historical or otherwise). Consequently, anthropic and mineral mark-making are always-already embedded and implicated in one another – a characteristic that is judged to be at a greater scale than ever before under the Anthropocene hypothesis.

In the case of *Waveform*, this conception means that although, in a narrowly technical sense, the wave boundary line provides only arbitrary cues for poetry generation – with there being no specified thematic or semantic relationships between image and text – it is still possible to ascribe meaning at the level of what the gesture itself represents in expressing the codefined threshold between marks of intentional communication and those inscribed by the flux of the world.

Carpenter's own work on writing coastlines draws attention to the ocean as a medium of communication between opposing shorelines – supporting mobilities of information that are carried not just through sailing expeditions, trading routes and electronic transmissions but also, for example, in the logistics of laying undersea cables or the clues of tide and current suggested by washed-up debris. To write the coast is to enter into this matrix of material and discursive exchange, and so producing resonances and meanings beyond the immediate connotations of specific texts.

One area where this becomes apparent in *Waveform* is the location featured throughout its initial outputs. The Strangles is situated on a part of the Cornish coast where key Atlantic data cables between North America and Europe come ashore. The very act of generating text out of this terrain, via generative means, is an attempt at articulating the myriad electronic messages that are relayed across this maritime frontier – as a space teeming with information exchange that nevertheless passes beyond human perceptual thresholds. The drone itself, and the software it is coupled to, are implicated also in realizing the potential messages of this infrastructure, by drawing attention to the remote, rocky shorelines that it traverses. These fragile, ever-shifting domains are exposed profoundly to the effects of a warming world, where intensifying data exchange is becoming a key driver of global energy consumption and emissions. The growing presence of violent storms, wholesale coastal erosion and rising sea levels are thus marking this milieu in ways that implicate the flood of electronic signals that cross it imperceptibly.

These transformations of coastal geographies are reciprocated in their subsequent reshaping of the sensory data gathered and the understandings it inspires. Taken in isolation, the outputs of *Waveform* resemble enigmatic reflections on oceanic agency or critical provocations concerning the very broadest contexts in which the structures of the world are measured and mapped through technology. However, their abstract, open-ended phrasing ensures these pronouncements are more inscrutable than insightful and demand work to fully actualize their expressive potential, along with any subsequent relations that might be drawn with the source imagery. The viability of any one interpretation is never a given, as other possibilities unfold continually. Indeed, the essential transience of each output encourages a focus instead on their processual origins more broadly – of what is ultimately represented by the very act of translating electronic sensory data into poetry, howsoever achieved (acknowledging that an onlooking audience is not cued into the full mechanics of these operations).

One source of inspiration for the conversion of visual data into poetry was found in the reflections of Smailbegović, who, in examining the manifold challenges of expressing the Anthropocene, describes the special power of writing:

> to act as a technology of amplification, flooding the delineated frame of the present with luminous grain of detail, in turn rendering perceptible a more variegated sense of the kinds of change that dynamically constitute the present, thereby opening the unfurling edge of this present toward the future in indeterminate ways.
>
> (2015: 95)

Smailbegović contends that understanding the concrete impacts of a rapidly changing world involves developing a sensitivity towards 'rhythms of transformation that are below the temporal sensitivity available to human perception' (2015: 96). For this end, Smailbegović advocates a 'poetics of description' for the Anthropocene that renders seemingly discrete and stable phenomena, such as concrete and glass, into 'soft' forms by shifting the temporal frame through which they are perceived, and so bringing into human awareness the material processes that continually erode and dissolve these formations over time – to open out the stabilities of the present towards indeterminate futures.

In the case of *Waveform*, this gesture towards softer, less determinate and more temporally attuned modes of textuality is performed chiefly by its generative operations, rather than through the expressive qualities of specific outcomes. In line with the critiques outlined above, concerning the datafied reduction of the world into discrete 'planar' striations and deterministic (atemporal) vectors of behaviour, the parsing of digital data into poetry is a denaturalizing manoeuvre that draws attention to the creative contingencies that characterize all acts of technically mediated sense-making – of their status as material processes in time, with the indeterminacy and possibility this entails. Likewise, by enacting a mode of representation that is strikingly removed from the standardized, often highly quantified formats associated with typical sensory readouts, *Waveform* underlines how the observable world, as detected and characterized through technical instruments, does not inherently manifest in ways that are 'transparent' to human understanding. Instead, perceptible phenomena are shown as being always articulated with and through a greater apparatus that brings them into being as measurable entities. In short, the observable is shown as being an entangled performance of intra-acting agencies, replete with different configurative possibilities of sensing and knowing, as opposed to a transparent rendering of an *a priori* object before an enquiring subject.

It is in this sense, then, that just as the generated boundary line is not intended to perfectly apprehend the incoming wave fronts, neither is the poetry yielded seeking to offer a pointed commentary on the source imagery. Instead, it mirrors the incongruity of the former – as a static line drawn across a churning body of water – in parsing exacting numerical data into indeterminate, seemingly incommensurable poetic forms. The effect is to short-circuit the stability and authority of instrumentalized sense-making – whether in the form of aerial outlooks upon the Earth, with their lingering implications of omniscience, the ostensibly 'rational' outputs of electronic measuring devices or the assumed precision of quantitative indicators. Each stage of the processes constituting *Waveform* as a sensory apparatus demands the drawing of conscious 'lines of flight' between the outputs rendered and the structures involved – of what they might represent and how they possibly contribute towards its sensory becoming. *Waveform* is ultimately an apparatus for imaging and writing the coastline that opens itself towards many different potential understandings.

Creative resistance

To summarize this discussion, *Waveform* is a speculative sensory apparatus that does not produce exacting measurements of the world, but facilitates the perception and realization of novel possibilities within it – to search for the unforeseen in the intersection of the technical, the oceanic and the textual.

The goal is to express the immanence of the observable within a deteriorating planet, as the performative realization of emergent forms and new potentialities of framing and understanding. Although such actions are not inherently progressive or reparative by default, to acknowledge them also makes clear the basic point that alternative modes of knowing and being remain possible within established sensory architectures, and that such modes, in their experimental, creative openness, can potentially serve a valuable role in negotiating the complexities of the present moment.

Another way of characterizing the role of speculative sensing and sense-making is from the standpoint of resistance. As with the emergence of any new instance of sensory technology, the development of *Waveform* was characterized by frequent breakdowns and outright failures – by the mutual resistances shown against the experimental process by the actors involved. These resistances, by virtue of their disrupting any prior creative and critical hypotheses, were often productive and insightful. In their 'stabilized' configuration, they provide in turn a resistant formation against conventional expectations and understandings of what sensory practices represent.

However, these points stated, it is worth acknowledging that the *Waveform* project, as a stand-alone enterprise, inevitably faces its own, much greater resistances. Although it may be critically and creatively provocative to entice drones to render poetry out of waves, it is quite evident that such actions, in themselves, are unable to offer a practical counter to the forces and structures implicated in the profound ecological dangers of the present moment. Ultimately, the globalized infrastructures laid down by militarism, colonialism, industrialism and capitalism – within which *Waveform* both operates and seeks to appropriate – will, in the face of such a minor intervention, continue to function unabated. An explicit note of caution should be sounded, therefore, concerning what might be achieved through such practices. At best, they can hope to inspire but not radically substitute the task of direct political engagement and reform.

However, rather than drawing this discussion to a close within the perennial debates concerning the political efficacy of artistic praxis, it is worth noting that one of the essential drivers behind all minor acts of resistance is in marking the fact they could and did take place at all. In the case of *Waveform*, it means that the story of the sensory cannot be read entirely in terms of imposition, control and the absolute, but as being contrasted through the evaluation of alternatives, which occurred in recognition of the very failings of the predominant *a priori*. The varied stories that both inspired and went into the production of *Waveform* – of wet ontologies, satellite imagery, written coastlines, airborne drones – form a patchwork of interconnected vignettes that depict a world whose richness far exceeds the embrace of any one set of framings, and, therefore, has the capacity to accommodate the smaller vectors that both prototype and provide the necessary inspiration for greater actions.

It is these endeavours, as carried through the trace of experimental enquiry and imagination, across multiple spatial and durational scales, that enact the becoming of the world more broadly. In this context, the *Waveform* project is presented as a sensory assemblage that acknowledges its role in co-producing the very signals it encounters within such an emerging world and investigates these signals not as measures of the given, or as metrics indicating their accordance with specific demands, but as a means of sensing the potentialities that come with holding an openness towards uncertainty and change.

References

Abba, T. and A. Spencer. (2021), 'Writing Ambient Literature', in J. Dovey, T. Abba and K. Pullinger, eds. *Ambient Literature: Towards a New Poetics of Situated Writing and Reading Practices*, 275–318, Cham: Palgrave Macmillan.

Barad, K. (2007), *Meeting the Universe Halfway*, Durham, NC: Duke University Press.

Carpenter, J. R. (2015), 'Writing Coastlines: Locating Narrative Resonance in Transatlantic Communications Networks', PhD diss., University of the Arts London and Falmouth University. Available online: http://ualresearchonline.arts.ac.uk/7825/ (accessed 23 November 2022).

Carpenter, J. R. (2016), 'this is a picture of the wind', J. R. Carpenter – Luckysoap & Co. Available online: https://luckysoap.com/apictureofwind/ (accessed 1 July 2023).

Carter, R. (2018), 'Waves to Waveforms: Performing the Thresholds of Sensing and Sense-Making in the Anthropocene', *Arts* 7(4). https://doi.org/10.3390/arts7040070.

Carter, R. (2023), 'Waveform', Richard A Carter. Available online: https://richardacarter.com/waveform (accessed 1 July 2023).

Cosgrove, D. (2001), *Apollo's Eye: A Cartographic Genealogy of the Earth in the Western Imagination*, Baltimore, MD: Johns Hopkins University Press.

Crutzen, P. and E. Stoermer. (2000), 'The "Anthropocene"', *IGBP Newsletter* (41), 17–18. Available online: http://www.igbp.net/download/18.316f18321323470177580001401/1376383088452/NL41.pdf (accessed 1 July 2023).

Dovey, J., T. Abba and K. Pullinger. (2021), 'Introduction', in Abba, T., J. Dovey and K. Pullinger, eds. *Ambient Literature: Towards a New Poetics of Situated Writing and Reading Practices*, 1–26, Cham: Palgrave Macmillan.

Engelmann, S. and J. Thomson. (2016a), *Perspectives*. Available online: https://www.anthropocene-curriculum.org/courses/sensing (accessed 9 June 2024).

Engelmann, S. and J. Thomson. (2016b), 'Ve Vm Vt. The Ideal Cosmic Messengers', *Technosphere Magazine*, 15 November. Available online: https://technosphere-magazine.hkw.de/p/Ve-Vm-Vt-The-Ideal-Cosmic-Messengers-gTQ3sSabgSXLhFm2Hag5ny (accessed 20 November 2022).

Gabrys, J. (2016), *Program Earth: Environmental Sensing Technology and the Making of a Computational Planet*, Minneapolis: University of Minnesota Press.

Gabrys, J. (2018), 'Becoming Planetary', e-flux Architecture, October. Available online: https://www.e-flux.com/architecture/accumulation/217051/becoming-planetary/ (accessed 10 November 2022).

Henry, H. and A. Taylor. (2009), 'Re-Thinking Apollo: Envisioning Environmentalism in Space', *The Sociological Review*, 57(1), 190–203. https://doi.org/10.1111/j.1467-954X.2009.01825.x.

Knapp, S. and W. B. Michaels. (1982), 'Against Theory', *Critical Inquiry*, 8(4), 723–42. http://www.jstor.org/stable/1343194.

Pelto, J. (2015), 'Climate Change Data'. Available online: https://www.jillpelto.com/climate-change-data (accessed 1 July 2023).

Pickering, A. (1995), *The Mangle of Practice: Time, Agency, and Science*, Chicago: University of Chicago Press.

Smailbegović, A. (2015), 'Cloud Writing: Describing Soft Architectures of Change in the Anthropocene', in H. Davis and E. Turpin, eds. *Art in the Anthropocene: Encounters Among Aesthetics, Politics, Environments and Epistemologies*, 93–108, London: Open Humanities Press.

Steinberg, P. and K. Peters. (2015), 'Wet Ontologies, Fluid Spaces: Giving Depth to Volume through Oceanic Thinking', *Environment and Planning D: Society and Space*, 33(2) 247–64.

'Stewart Brand Interview'. (2003), Massive Change Radio, 25 November. Available online: https://web.archive.org/web/20050518140354/http://www.massivechange.com/PDF/INF_StewartBrand.pdf (accessed 10 November 2022).

4

Dear reader, can I borrow your body to tell a story? On ambient interactional metalepsis, sylleptic readers and palimpsestuous embedded reading experiences of ambient stories

Agnieszka Przybyszewska

Ambient literature: Literary works that need to borrow their readers' bodies

In this chapter, I will position ambient literature in a broader research and creative context. As Ian Gadd points out, 'ambient literature demands a radical reorientation of how we understand and value reading' (Gadd 2021: 30). I will focus on ambient literature in the context of intense discussions on the evolution in our understanding of categories, such as the book (and publishing), reading, literature (and literariness).[1] One should also not ignore that the Ambient Literature Project was, in fact, a continuation of previous research conducted by Jonathan Dovey, who since 2002 has been focusing on technologically

[1] Summing up such a discussion goes beyond the scope of this paper. However, it is important to point out that the need for a holistic, interdisciplinary perspective has been strongly emphasized over recent years (e.g. Andersen, Kjerkegaard and Stougaard, Pedersen 2021). Also observable is a focus on the reader's body (thus also on the reader being understood as a corporeal, not theoretical and idealized entity). While enumerating important publications from recent years one should not forget numerous journal articles, for example, a special issue of *Poetics Today* (no. 1/2021), which focused on models of reading, or those included in *Language Sciences* no. 84/2021 (e.g. Bronwen Thomas' 'The #bookstagram: Distributed Reading in the Social Media Age') as well as book publications, for example, N. Katherine Hayles, *Postprint: Books and Becoming Computational* (2021), John B. Thompson, *Book Wars: The Digital Revolution in Publishing*, Jessica Pressman, *Bookishness: Loving Books in a Digital Age* (2021) and *Refresh the Book: On the Hybrid Nature of the Book in the Age of Electronic Publishing*, edited by Viola Hildebrand-Schat, Katarzyna Bazarnik and Christoph Benjamin Schulz (2021).

enabled, situated literary experiences, seen in the broader context of ubiquitous computing (Dovey 2016).

The term 'ambient literature' was proposed to describe 'situated writing practices in which text is able to respond to the site of reading' (Dovey, Abba and Pullinger 2021: 5) and the Ambient Literature practice-based research project aimed to look for new forms of literature that emerge when combining place-based, situated writing and new technologies. Emma Whittaker compellingly sums up the broad spectrum of the ambient literature field, arguing that 'ambient literature can be considered a frame denoting narrative practices in which the structure and story consent is intentionally integrated within the reader's physical surroundings' (2021: 233). Consequently, not only does the reader become part of the story, but also 'their environment is turned into the setting for the story events' (233).

So, the concept of ambient literature was proposed to explore what is possible in literary production and the project aimed to gather perspectives and findings for broader use and future development (Dovey, Abba and Pullinger 2021: 10). In fact, ambient literature was thought of as an umbrella term that could be used to describe past, present and future; to talk not only about works created within the Ambient Literature Project but also about works developed during a similar time but not classified as ambient by their authors or texts created before any discussion of the category began.

The term can also be applied to characterize *Dérives*,[2] a literary application that premiered in 2021, which connects reader/listener movement in space and poetry. Here, the poem that is read or listened to changes according to the walking pace of the reader/listener, who is a textual 'you'. The term can also describe Anton Ferret's *Fugue Book*, published in 2008,[3] a PC-based digital fiction that used readers' personal data from their Facebook accounts.[4] Thanks to that, the reader became one of the story's protagonists while the actual reader's Facebook friends inspired the other characters.[5]

I will discuss four examples of works of ambient literature, each representing a moment in the history of ambient writing. *Breathe* (2018) is the canonical

2 This project was created in collaboration with the poet Marine Riguet, the composer Hervé Zénouda, the author and researcher Serge Bouchardon, the researcher Erika Fülöp and a group of engineering students from the Université de technologie de Compiègne (Charles Fiers, Cécile Asselin, Antonin Guyot, Maylis de Talhouet, Augustin de Laubier).

3 The work was included in *Electronic Literature Collection*, volume 2, but it is no longer functioning.

4 Having one was a condition for experiencing the story.

5 This fictional work not only pulled the reader into the story but also blurred the borders of the real world and fiction. Real Wikipedia entries or blogs were included in the story and a large part of it took the form of personalized emails, which arrived in the reader's mailbox.

ambient work by Kate Pullinger created within the Ambient Literature Project, it tells the story of Flor who tries to contact her dead mother and receives unwanted messages from other ghosts, who begin to haunt the reader as well. In contrary, Semyon Polyakovskiy's *Maginary*,[6] published in the same year, was never described by the author as an example of ambient literature, although it is. In this story, the reader becomes one of the protagonists and needs to help another one who had been reading the book earlier but hadn't finished it and was punished by being cast into another reality (enclosed in the story). *Dzieje jednego pocisku* (2020)[7] by Marta Dziedziela and Szymon Szul is an example of a recent ambient work, it tells the story happening in the future city in which the work should be read. Also, in this case the reader becomes one of the protagonists of the story. The last example is *Her Long Black Hair* (2004), Janet Cardiff's audio walk with photographs, which reminds us of the history of such situated literary experiences. In this work, one is guided through the city while listening to the story and interacting with some pieces of evidence of it. Although almost all of these works were created for mobile devices and use the affordances of mobile phones, the term ambient literature can also describe works that are entirely digital or hybrids, for example, those that include print books as part of them, as well as fully analogue, 'completely physical, non-digital works' (Abba and Spencer 2021: 315).

In this chapter, to characterize works of ambient literature and the experience of reading them, I will examine them through the lens of three concepts; *palimpsest*, *metalepsis* and *syllepsis*.[8] What all of these concepts have in common is a paradox, that is, they each describe the impossible possibility of splicing together opposite categories. I believe that such a paradox also defines ambient literature. Then, I will interrogate the poetics of works of ambient literature, particularly the narrative form that can be useful in creating such literary experiences. I will focus on the peculiar second-person narrative, an enhanced form of what had been characterized as a *spoken monologue*, and discuss it as an emerging feature of ambient literary poetics. However, I will also argue that classic third-person narrative can be used to achieve the same goals.

6 This work is frequently classified as a game or game book, whilst it is a piece of literary art.

7 The work was created during the academic course taught at the University of Łódź in collaboration with local start-up eDialog, and the company is still working on this final publication on their platform Tropiciel.

8 Some of the proposed categories can also be used to describe literary locative narratives (Przybyszewska 2020). The complicated relationship between the field of literary locative narratives and ambient literature, described by Dovey as 'post locative but still situated' (Dovey 2016: 142), goes beyond the scope of this chapter (see Dovey, Abba and Pullinger 2021: 14–17).

The starting point for my argument is that ambient literature proposes an unusual author–reader contract, which should be also seen in a deep dialogue with evolution and changes in other than literary and word-based art. Such literary experiences are fully 'embodied readings' (Abba and Spencer 2021), not simply 'cybersomatic e-lit works' that use readers' bodies as a kind of reading tools, which are also told to work on a metaleptic level (Ensslin et al. 2020). Many works of ambient literature need their readers' bodies, understood as a part of the ambient, to tell the story. Thus, the proposed author–reader contract takes the form of a declaration: 'Dear Reader, lend me your body, and then I will show you my story.'[9] As a consequence, the reader's body is no longer 'a problem to be elided' (Dovey, Abba and Pullinger 2021: 19–20). Instead, it becomes the 'play button' for the reading experience as ambient reading requires readers' corporeal 'readiness' (Gadd 2021).

Palimpsestuous, metaleptic experiences for sylleptic protagonists

The palimpsestuous structure of palimpsestuous experiences

At the very beginning of Carlos Fuentes' *Aura*, there is a moment when Felipe Montero, the main protagonist whose name and personality is uncannily imposed on the reader, wanders, looking for the Donceles 815 Street. Various time layers, past and present, overlap in the oniric, empty city, and Felipe, also the textual 'You', sees simultaneously old and new door plates with building numbers or street names from the past mixed with the present ones as if the past is shown through the present. Fuentes' vision vividly illustrates the figure of palimpsest, which is a perfect metaphor for works of ambient literature as well as for such works' reading character.

When the reader's ambient becomes part of the story, the story world overlaps with the concrete one, and the other way around. Consequently, there are various 'layers' of reality that the reader is immersed in; and they are blended, as in Fuentes' story. The reader of ambient literature has to gather information from all the layers, including their actual surroundings, to get the whole picture. As underlined by Matt Hayler, ambient literature not only is palimpsestuous itself but also 'asks to be read palimpsestuously' (Hayler 2021: 91).

[9] This declaration can function not only in e-lit but also in many other fields of art (Górska-Olesińska and Przybyszewska 2020).

Interviews with readers of works created as part of the Ambient Literature Project show another similarity with Felipe Montero's experience. They document testimonies of being lost between the realities, of not knowing to which reality particular sounds, actions or facts belong. They depict the constant crossing of ontological borders. For example, '[I]t's really funny, but I thought I was listening to the city, and I suddenly became aware that I was listening to it on my headphones. It blended so naturally' – explained one of the interviewed readers, while another claimed: 'I actually thought that it was happening for real in the street … I could hear barking … I really jumped and looked around' (Hayler 2021: 99). These readers resembled Felipe Montero, who was lost in time and, in a metaphorical sense, between the stories and worlds.

Enhanced/ambient interactional metalepsis

Due to its palimpsestuous character, ambient literature offers readers a metaleptic experience; it blends two worlds, two ontological dimensions. Metalepsis, defined in the 1980s by Gérard Genette, is a term used to characterize different types of violations of ontological boundaries. It describes the movement between narrative levels or separate worlds (e.g. between the fictional and the actual ones). Having in mind various typologies of metalepsis, I will focus on the *ontological metalepsis* (Fludernik 2003) and on what Alice Bell and Astrid Ensslin in their most recent publication have called *convergent interactional metalepsis* (2021: 112–13), staying focused, like these researchers, on crossing boundaries between the actual world and the story world.[10]

Metalepsis has been deeply characterized in literary theory discourse, and its initially under-researched area(s) – the metalepsis in digital storytelling – has also been examined (e.g. Kukkonen 2011; Bell 2016). However, these analyses, based for example in Ryan's thesis that the cursor can be a virtual representation of the reader in the story world (Ryan 2006: 122), were mainly focused on the fact that the technology of interaction 'causes a trace of the reader [avatar, cursor, a visual imprint of haptic interaction] to appear on the screen and, thus, an imprint of them in a separate ontological domain' (Bell and Ensslin 2021: 77). In comparison with what happens whilst reading ambient literature (or,

[10] In fact, presenting an analysis of the metaleptic character of ambient literature can be seen as supplementary to the analysis of interactional metalepsis subtypes IV and V presented by Bell and Ensslin. In the same publication they describe interactional metalepsis in VR as 'ultimate' (Bell and Ensslin 2021: 104–15), and I would ask whether the one used in ambient literature isn't equally 'ultimate'.

more generally, works that use convergent interactional metalepsis, with strong emphasis also on VR experiences), this only seems a symbolic, metaphorical breaching of boundaries between the reader's world and the story world.

In the introduction to their chapter focused on interactional metalepsis, Bell and Ensslin quote the user[11] experience description (Bell and Ensslin 2021: 73). However, comparing this testimony (and its analysis) with the ones that were references for researchers within the Ambient Literature Project, one can clearly see a slight, but very important, difference. Crossing the ontological border is, in this case, still a symbolic act. 'I […] situated myself as that first person view' is interpreted by Bell and Ensslin as 'deciding to become the avatar' (73). That is because the (let's call it 'early') theory of interactional metalepsis reasonably proposed as a necessary extension of this theoretical approach in the context of digital art, is still focused on metaphorical presence in the story world, which is not connected with the real presence. In other words, as Bell and Ensslin state, the user (reader) needs to declare their will to cross the border, and the way they interact is still what in cognitive theory is called 'enacting'. It is still based on the act of imagination, although interaction 'via hardware' (73) sometimes makes a user believe that they are in the story world, as when a player 'exploring the house' is seen as 'being inside the storyworld' (73).

Entering into the story world must be linked to the act of 'stepping into someone's shoes', adopting their perspective and point of view. Of course, in the experience described by Bell and Ensslin that is also a consequence of using the first-person narrative, because there is no space for the user (reader) in the story world. To enter it, the reader needs to become someone else, someone seen as an 'automatic extension' of experiencing 'I'. But there is no 'real' connection between the reader's body and the story world. The use of the second-person narrative does not change much (Bell and Ensslin 2021). Readers' gestures and actions only permit a still symbolic presence of the reader in the story world, confirmed by perceived traces of these actions on the screen.

On the contrary, in ambient literature there is often a real space in the story world left for the reader.[12] They don't have to enact someone else in the story world or 'decide to become' someone else. The reader is still themself, with their own body, in their own ambient, which both become part of the story. And because of that, people who experienced ambient literature were

[11] Andy Cambell and Judi Alston's *Wallpaper*.

[12] A vivid metaphor of such a construction can be seen in *The Book with a Hole* by Hervé Tullet, where the reader's body and surroundings, seen through the hole, are semantically linked to the story. This book can be also seen as an example of fully analogue but highly interactive ambient literature work.

more focused on the palimpsestic structure of the word than on the fact that they could not distinguish between the actual (real) world and the story world. They did not need to think about 'situating themself' in someone's role as they played themselves. How different from the testimonial quoted by Bell and Ensslin is the one cited by Jonathan Dovey and Matthew Hayler; 'The thing that, maybe, makes it ambient storytelling is that it utilised your universe, what's surrounding you, differently than stories that absolutely ignore who you are and where you're going … it didn't impose an identity on you which sometimes happens in games […] It didn[']t tell you who you are. I think that it was immersive, but it[']s strange to be immersive but also be in the place where you are' (Dovey and Hayler 2021: 149).

Ambient literature enhances the metaleptic character of the reading experience by asking readers to interact in/with their actual world. When the story world is a type of palimpsestuous overlay for the reader's reality, the readers do not need to transport themselves in their imagination into the story world to interact; they do not see their symbolic extensions on the screen. In Kate Pullinger's *Breathe*, analysed in the last part of this chapter, when the reader moves their screen to unveil the text hidden by a ghost's message, they see it revealed. Their phone being haunted by the ghost is part of the story, but the results, as well as the reader's reaction to them and the phone itself, are part of reality. In the same work, the traces of the reader's previous locations, their movements in the actual world or images from their physical location are used in the ghosts' monologues to create the impression that they know everything about the reader, that they really 'see/saw' them. Similarly, in Semyon Polyakovskiy's *Maginary*, when the reader walks in the actual world, their steps are counted in the story world, and the story will not continue until the reader has completed 1,000 steps.[13]

Sylleptic protagonist

Characterized permission to be yourself in the story leads to the specific construction of textual 'You'. I will call it the *sylleptic 'You'*, or *sylleptic protagonist*, applying the Ryszard Nycz's term sylleptic 'I' in a new context. In ancient rhetoric, *syllepsis* was characterized as a figure of speech that permits the breaking of syntactic rules to highlight the ambiguity of the word and its ability

[13] Because we can observe here rather traces of the actual world in the story world, one could call it *descending* metalepsis. However, it is not the difference between *ascending* and *descending* metalepsis that really defines the ambient literature.

to enter two contradictory relations at the same time. In the modern age, the term found its metaphorical reinterpretation.[14] Ryszard Nycz uses this concept to build a typology of modern subjectivity, in which one of its types he called *sylleptic 'I'*. As Nycz explains, 'The sylleptic *I*, to put it most simply, is the *I* which has to be understood simultaneously in two ways: namely as true and as fictional, as empirical and as textual, as authentic and as fictional-novelic' (Nycz 1995: 386–67). Thus, this kind of 'I' is somehow fragmented, dispersed between two realities, but not self-contradictory, and that is because the relation between the real 'I' and the literary 'I' is interactive and interferential, they 'mutually affect and exchange properties' (367).

While Nycz uses the trope of syllepsis to describe textual 'I' (and a particular writing strategy) (Winiecka 2006: 7), I will apply this category to the textual 'You', which is so pivotal for ambient literature. By *sylleptic 'You'* (*addressee*), or more generally *sylleptic protagonist*, I mean 'You' that belongs to two (entangled) realities, the actual and fictional one, and which is not self-contradictory because of that.

Nycz's *sylleptic* 'I' is 'being written' (Nycz 1995: 387) and the sylleptic 'You' is being spoken to. As a 'sylleptic' entity this 'You' can belong to diverse ontological worlds at the same time and be (and act) in them in parallel. This textual 'You' is, at the same time, the reader made of flesh and blood, the addressee of the narrative and an active protagonist in the story world because – according to the concept of ambient literature – the reader and their ambient (in various modes) become part of the story world.[15]

Furthermore, in ambient literature, thanks to its palimpsestic and metaleptic character, there is a specific place created (left) in the story for this *sylleptic* 'You', for the reader. The latter is 'physically present within the work' (which responds to it 'accordingly') because 'such embodied literary experiences bring their reader into contact with a physical location as part of a narrative' (Abba and Spencer 2021: 284), what can be seen as similar to breaking the fourth wall in theatre or movie. But, as Pullinger's *Breathe* shows, it does not always mean that the reader is in a specific place during the act of reading.

[14] For Derrida, *syllepsis*, when used in a text structure, 'cancels the choice between two contradictory options' (Winiecka 2004: 139) and makes both of them, paradoxically, possible. Also, in Michael Riffaterre's interpretation *syllepsis* permits 'parallel actualization of both alternatives' (139).

[15] The proposed concept would be similar to what Bell and Ensslin term the '*mataleptic you*' (Bell and Ensslin 2021: 222) and could be also seen in the context of Hanebeck's (2017) category of *second-person metalepsis*. However, such comparison goes beyond the scope of this chapter.

Embodied spoken monologue and the reader of flesh and blood enclosed in the story

Narrative structure can help to create enhanced metaleptic character of the story and make it easier for the reader to cross the ontological borders unnoticeably and fluently to be in two worlds simultaneously. Dovey, Abba and Pullinger emphasize the role of narrative techniques for immersion in ambient literature (Dovey, Abba and Pullinger 2021: 1), underlying the usefulness of the second-person addressee in this context (14). Bell and Ensslin also appreciate the second-person narrative as a textual metaleptic device (Bell and Ensslin 2021: 212–46) and even see the textual 'you' as 'one of, if not the most powerful, linguistic-rhetorical device for digital fiction writers and developers' (245). One of the narrative structures that makes the textual 'You' an essential element of the story is a *spoken monologue* characterized by Michał Głowiński (1963).

Spoken monologue was developed in the 1950s in Europe, following a model for this narrative construction seen in *The Fall* by Albert Camus (1956), and it became popular in the 1950s and 1960s in some countries (e.g. France and Poland), especially for literature of intellectual reckoning, influenced by existentialism and philosophy of the absurd.[16] In contemporary times, along with the growing popularity of interactive storytelling and second-person narration, it is again in play. I will use this concept to characterize one of the narrative structures frequently used in ambient literature.

Spoken monologue is 'paradoxically dialogical'. Głowiński also calls it a 'one-sided dialog' (Głowiński 1963: 236, 237).[17] Although the addressee (textual 'you') cannot answer, the speaking 'I' constantly behaves as if they were there, including reacting to the 'given' responses, which are known because the speaking 'I' repeats them while commenting. Not only does the speaking 'I' address its monologue to this textual 'You', but there are also traces of this 'you' in the text because this 'you' has its role to play. The specific construction of the *spoken monologue* invites the reader to substitute the textual 'You' for themselves. Such a process is termed the 'method of invocation' by Głowiński (238).

In the 'embodied reading' practice, like in ambient literature, this substitution loses its metaphorical, symbolic character. *Spoken monologue* takes the form

[16] Wolf Schmid uses a similar term '*dialogic narrative monologue*' (2010: 87) when describing texts that lack mentioned ideological themes and the intellectual argumentation structure typical for the literature of intellectual reckoning.

[17] What Głowiński had called the 'mute partner of the conversation', Richardson (2006) later described as a *figure of interlocutor*.

of *embodied spoken monologue* in which the 'you' is substituted by the actual reader of flesh and blood. A work of ambient literature becomes a literary work in the form of the 'score' (Bogalecki 2020) in which there is a special role for the reader; it seems to resemble a kind of performance (Abba and Spencer 2021: 290). A vivid example of this can be seen in Janet Cardiff's *Her Long Black Hair*, a locative audio walk with photographs in which one can immerse themself into Central Park's nineteenth-century pathways, retracing the footsteps of a mysterious woman. The speaking 'I' in this case not only creates an imaginary relation with 'you', but also places the 'gap' for the reader in the actual reality, combining two ontological levels. It is hard to maintain that the meeting of speaking 'I' and listening-to 'you' is only fictional because if it hadn't happened, how would the reader have had the pictures in his hand? In *Her Long Black Hair* the 'gap for the reader is (re)located in the actual world; it is moved from the text to the reality (what is the nub of embodiment of *spoken monologue* structure). This allows the reader to act as a *sylleptic "you"*. In the structure of both story and narrative, the "you" is the one who acts in the actual world, who holds the photographs and looks at them, guided by the speaking "I"'.

Similarly, in *Dzieje jednego pocisku* by Marta Dziedziela and Szymon Szul (2020), analysed in the last part of this chapter, the reader-listener's phone through which they listen, read and watch the story is the element that links two ontological dimensions. It is a permanent point of reference for both the textual 'I' (or 'I-s', because there is more than one speaking 'I' in this story) and the textual 'You'. The speaking 'I' comments on how old (from his future perspective) this phone is and asks to 'acknowledge location' with it. From the story's beginning, it is clear that the mobile phone will be an instrument of communication between the reader-listener and the protagonist(s). This 'pact' is a crucial element of the story as the reader realizes through their mission. Thus, for the reader-listener, their mobile phone is the 'metaleptic machine'[18] (Ryan 2006), which converges two worlds in a similar way as did the photographs in Cardiff's work.

[18] Bell and Ensslin talk about 'acting as a conduit rather than as an ontological barrier' (Bell and Ensslin 2021: 107). While fifteen years ago, Ryan was sure that the actual world 'remains protected from metaleptic phenomena' (Ryan 2006: 209), the deeply embodied reading proposed in ambient literature shows that the overlapping and amalgamation of the actual and virtual world in a literary experience is possible. In 2006, Ryan was dreaming about the possible 'metaleptic' future of VR experiences and actual literary production, including VR literature, which has shown that the reader's whole body, as well as the reader, can become part of the story and not only be used as a reading machine, a tool or a kind of virtual extension that enables the reader's non-trivial effort needed in ergodic reading practices.

So, to sum it up, in ambient literature there is no avatar offered to a reader. Instead, the stories borrow the reader's body and provide this paradoxical (sylleptic) experience of being *here* and *there* simultaneously (Hayler 2021: 93); an experience in which – palimpsestuously – different ontological layers are entangled. As the real reader of flesh and blood to whom the textual 'I' speaks, is *conditio sine qua non* for this, I propose to call such a narrative structure an *embodied spoken monologue*.

Such a monologue is frequently used in ambient writing, however, it is not the only option, even if it is the most natural, intuitive and simple one. The palimpsestuous structure of the world, the metaleptic overlapping of real and story worlds, and the sylleptic structure of reader-protagonist can fruitfully nourish other narrative structures. Semyon Polyakovskiy's *Maginary* is a perfect example here as, despite being written as a third-person narrative, one of its protagonists is the *sylleptic* one. In this 'immersive book' described by its author as demolishing the fourth wall between the reader and their imagination (Polyakovskiy 2019), the reader helps the central protagonist, Michael. As it is a playable story, they have various tasks to accomplish.

The reader of *Maginary* discovers that in the story they are reading on their screen, a protagonist is reading the same screen.[19] And this protagonist is the one who is given the name of a proper reader, the one they had used to sign the e-book just before having entered into the story world (not only metaphorically as it seems). Polyakovskiy proposes an intriguing narrative structure in which we read about ourselves as the Other, in the third-person narrative. And at the same time, we can observe how our actual actions impact the story world (as in the example mentioned previously). We are a *sylleptic protagonist* of the story, even though we are not its addressee.

In the narrative of palimpsestic and metaleptic works of ambient literature, which I call *embodied spoken monologue*, there is a 'gap' left for the reader who becomes the *sylleptic* protagonist of the story. Because 'ambient literature seeks to make work that responds to the presence of a reader' (Abba and Spencer 2021: 278), the readers' bodies are, in this case, a kind of 'play button' for the whole experience. So, as was stated, ambient stories propose a new pact with the reader, metaphorically declaring: 'Dear Reader, lend me your body, and then I will show you my story.' And, because readers' bodies are different, works of ambient literature 'by their nature, offer unique experiences to each

[19] *Maginary* conjures up many canonical metaleptic literary texts, not only *The Continuity of Parks* by Julio Cortázar.

reader' (Marcinkowski 2021: 199). They also make it clear that 'reading is also sometimes done with the feet or the nose' (Andersen, Kjerkegaard, Stougaard Pedersen 2021: 145) and readers, instead of being perceived as 'theoretical, idealized entities' can be 'human beings with a pulse and a digestive system (not to mention hands and sensory organs)' (137).

Close-up: Embodied spoken monologue and palimpsestuous, metaleptic experiences for the sylleptic readers of *Dzieje jednego pocisku* and *Breathe*

Having characterized the theoretical background for literary experiences that use *ambient metalepsis*, *embodied spoken monologue* and the structure of *sylleptic you*, in the last part of this chapter, I will focus on two recent examples of small screen fiction in which such structures are interestingly applied to create innovative reading experiences that ask readers to lend their bodies.

Dzieje jednego pocisku

The usefulness of embodied spoken monologue form for works of ambient literature can be seen in *Dzieje jednego pocisku* by Marta Dziedziela and Szymon Szul; a small screen fiction based on the close relation between the story protagonists and the reader. There is no doubt that, when experiencing this work, the reader-listener[20] enters the palimpsestuous space in which the actual (real) and future (fictional) visions of the city of Łódź (in which the story takes place) are blended. The body of the textual 'you' is needed for the story to continue, as they have a task to accomplish in the city's space. In other words, there is a 'gap' in the story that the presence and actions of the reader-listener should fill in. One after the other, the voices of story protagonists (Leon, Kama, Weszycki and Gryziak) guide this sylleptic 'you' through the streets, explaining step by step the reader-listener's function in the story and their actual situation, as well as providing a commentary on the city. Because it is explained in the story that, for some reason, the reader-listener does not remember everything about what had happened before, such explanations are a natural and logical part of the narration. The reader-listener needs to be introduced not only to the task they have to accomplish but also – at least a little – to the world they live in.

[20] The experience is mostly based on audio narration.

The story's protagonists are constantly in contact with the reader-listener as they ceaselessly speak or write to them. The reader-listener's phone, which enables such a connection, plays the role of a *metaleptic machine* and permits a connection between the actual world and the fictional one. It functions as the real, physical phone in the actual world and as an important element in the story (thus, within the fictional world). At the beginning, the reader-listener receives instructions about how and why they should use the phone and headphones. This information is given in the extradiegetic introduction to the experience and, above all, in the story itself.

The Unknown, a protagonist who communicates with the reader through written messages that accompany the main audio narration, explains the role of the phone held by the reader in their hand, 'Nobody will speak to you normally, cameras can read the lips movements. The headphones are your messenger. They capture thoughts and transform them into sound. You must have them on. Sometimes there will be some disruptions, that is the price of using unofficial software.' The function of the phone in the story world explains the lack of verbal responses from the reader and the 'one-sidedness' of the contact. Leon, the first character met by the reader, clearly underlines that the worlds (the fictional future and the present in which the reader lives) are connected by the reader's phone, 'Did Chemist upload all important information at your banger? Stupid question. If he hadn't, you would not have been here.' The Unknown asks the reader to always 'confirm his presence' with the phone. Also, other characters who communicate with the reader-listener with audio and whose thoughts are, according to the rules of the story world, translated into the sound, frequently mention the presence of the physical phone, reminding the reader-listener about sending them messages or about using headphones.[21]

Making the reader's phone the central tool in both worlds enables the solving of some other problems that would otherwise have been disorienting for the reader. For example, various characters ironically comment on the out-of-dateness of the tool. As Leon says, 'What is it, that thing in your hand? Mobile phone? Christ, how old it is … When did they stop producing them? Ten years ago? Aren't you afraid? They are so easy to hack!' Thanks to this, all the technical problems that could possibly influence the experience (e.g. losing GPS signal, etc.[22]) are linked to the way such an 'old' mobile phone functions. As Leon

[21] Sometimes they advise the reader-listener to take them off, as when Kama admonishes them to not go through the cemetery with their headphones on.

[22] Such complication is unpredictable and frequent in case of locative narratives.

explains, 'In any case, when something screws up, it's not our fault. You should have changed to lentus.'

Fictional entities are in a constant 'one-sided dialogue' with the reader-listener, and they do a lot to establish and strengthen the contact. The protagonists ask questions that do not need to be answered (e.g. 'Have you heard, comrade, that the system is slowly resuming space travels? As for me – a whopping lie' [Weszycki]; 'Do you know that there used to be a shopping mall there? That's why it looks the best of all these buildings' [Kama]). Some other tricks are used for the strong authentication of the reader-listener and the fictional protagonists co-presence in the same (not-only-story) world. 'Sorry, I really can't stop looking at them … You know, the shoes. You have very nice shoes, comrade. They look comfortable', comments Weszycki, which suits whatever shoes the reader-listener is wearing. The clue is that the fictional character comments on the authentic shoes and so the ontological border between realities has been crossed.

Sometimes, to strengthen the sense of being in dialogue, the fictional protagonists react to the reader-listener's answers to their questions and, no matter the answer, their reaction is adequate, for example, 'What had you been doing for a living before? You have never mentioned … I used to work at the university. I was a librarian' (Kama).[23] Underlying the importance of being in contact is especially important when a new narrator's voice intercepts the story's sylleptic protagonist. For example, in the case of the last narrator, Gryziak, who introduces himself; 'Hey, hello. Haven't you heard the fucking shots?! They killed that guy. Get out. I said – better get out!!! Come on, move your ass […] You should be glad I have run into you, otherwise, they would probably have caught you. Hey, do you understand me at all?'

The metaleptic impression of the co-presence of the reader and the story's protagonists in the same reality is also created by how they describe the reader-listener's surroundings. They not only guide them through the city, which is typical for locative narratives, but also comment on what they see or hear and on the whole situation. For example, Leon warns; 'Be careful on the tram tracks, some idiot got run over there a week ago. Lots of blood […] On the crossing, you should be careful as well,' and Weszycki comments: 'This street is plainly not picturesque enough to have the name after Matejko as it has. Hedges not trimmed, everything grey and dull'. The story script had been prepared in such a way that narrative perfectly accompanies the route as, for example, the sound of

[23] In traditional forms of spoken monologue, the frequently used way to simulate the dialogue was to repeat whatever was 'told' by the textual 'you' (e.g. 'You say that it is raining?').

steps in the background is used to influence the pace of walking. Thanks to that, the sense that the voices know where the reader-listener is and what they are doing accompanies the reader-listener. This is evident, for example, when Kama introduces herself; 'It's me, don't turn around. Pretend that you are waiting for the tram. Okay, now focus. We have school behind us. If you look to the right, there is Tamka Street. You see? Go there, turn right, and I will follow right behind you. Come on!' The use of the 'you' addressee and the plural form 'we' in Kama's question, 'Do you see the cemetery in front of us? We are going to go there anyway. We will go and split up', brings out the impossible encounter between reality and fiction, and creates the strong feeling that fictional characters walk alongside the reader-listener. This is also seen in Leon's explanation, 'You know what? Wait. Let's go right, towards the Lumumby residential area.'

Thus, in the palimpsestuous *Dzieje jednego pocisku*, the gap for the sylleptic protagonist of the story (textual 'you' at the same time) is evidently put in the reader-listener's actual world. The reader-listener is not asked to metaphorically substitute the addressee but to act, that is, to do what the textual 'you' is asked for, and, for that, the real body that can act in the actual world is needed. For example, Weszycki asks to send him a code that the reader-listener needs to find at the cemetery, guided by Kama.[24] In general, the reader-listener's mission in the story is to reach a specific location and detonate the load that had been previously unconsciously put in their arm. Of course, no matter how much the fiction had been blended with reality, it would not have been possible for the reader-listener to explode at the end of the story. But this potentially restrictive logical barrier of the story world is eluded with the Unknown's words 'Sorry, I won't let you detonate yourself.' There is no need for the impossible to happen, so there is no lack of logic in the story. Unknown reminds the specific contract that has been a starting point for the whole experience: 'Are you confused? More than at the beginning? You gave me access to your phone. It's just as simple as that. Then I just listened and watched.'

And that's true, because at the beginning of the story, in one of his first messages, Unknown writes: 'You are being abused. I can help you, but you have to compromise. Otherwise, we will not be able to continue.' To continue, the reader-listener had to accept the use of their location data and give access to

[24] This is an example of the situation when the reader-listener is asked to do something in their actual world that is important for the story to continue. *Dzieje jednego pocisku* can be therefore seen in the context of other works that use such a strategy, for example, *WuWu&Co* or *Maginary*, the last one also analysed in this chapter.

their photo gallery[25] ('You won't regret it' – assured Unknown). The reader-listener's agreement to use his data has been an essential part of the proposed author–reader contract that enables this specific literary experience in which the reader-listener's 'ambient', as well as their body, becomes part of the story.

Breathe

You cannot read *Breathe* without a mobile phone, not only because it was created as a work of mobile screen fiction dedicated to 'm-reading',[26] but also because the mobile phone is a crucial element in the story world, and it plays a similar function to the photographs in Cardiff's *Her Long Back Hair* as it links different ontological dimensions. It is needed to begin the experience, as the introduction asks the reader: 'Is your phone in your hand? / Yes I am ready.'[27] The mobile phone ensures that the readers' surroundings become story settings, as the phone makes it possible to 'transform physical space into textual space' (Abba and Spencer 2021: 294). This is achieved in various ways. Firstly, the reader's data is frequently used to personalize the text and to reinforce the feeling that the text is somehow specially related to the particular reader. APIs are used in the protagonist Flo's narrative to build up a sense that the reader is in a similar situation to her, and in the ghosts' interruptions to create the feeling of being haunted by ghosts that know a lot about the reader. Moreover, a photograph of the reader's surroundings is used as the background for messages from ghosts. That way, thanks to their haunted phone, readers become part of the narration and slip into a story world (as they do in *Maginary*).

However, in *Breathe* the narrative takes a different form than in Polyakovskiy's work. It is what I call embedded spoken monologue, and such a form helps the reader feel included in the story and the story world. The narrator-protagonist addresses her speech to the textual 'you', the reader. Flo needs this 'you', their corporeal 'readiness' (Gadd 2021), and such a contact is *conditio sine qua non* for the whole story. At the beginning of the experience, she declares, 'I talk to my mother at night, but she doesn't answer me […] My mother won't speak

25 The first plan of the creators was to add the last photograph in the reader-listener's gallery into Unknown's message with commentary: 'This is the last photo you took before they intercepted you […] I got it back. If you haven't trusted me so far, now is the time to do so.' Because the producer blocked the possibility of using users' data, the generic picture of an anonymous hand was used in the final version of the work.

26 Defined by Anežka Kuzmičová, Theresa Schilhab and Michael Burke (2020) as 'smartphone-supported fiction reading for leisure'.

27 What's more, in this story, even the way the phone should be held is dictated to its readers (Gadd 2021).

to me, so I'll talk to you instead' (Pullinger 2018: 1, 3), 'I'm glad I found you. I'll tell you my stories' (6). Such a constant dialogue with the reader determines the stylistics of the text. Because Flo confesses a story to the reader, she can or needs to explain many things that would otherwise seem unnatural in a first-person narrative. She introduces herself by saying, 'You'll want to know a bit more about me first' (9) or tells Rifat's story (obviously well known to her) and explains 'Rifat is not my boyfriend' (25). She comments on the act of telling the story or asks rhetorical questions that help her and her listener to order the story.[28] Many of Flo's questions have primarily a phatic function; they maintain and strengthen contact with the reader, for example, 'And yet, something – someone? – is here tonight. I feel it. Can you feel it?' (56) and 'Who's there? It's a woman. Is it a woman?' (58). She does not receive an answer, but there's nothing strange in it as it seems natural. The spoken monologue and its embedded form are both 'one-sided dialogues'. The embodiment of such a narrative structure means that what is needed is, in fact, the real reader's body. And what Flo needs is the presence of 'you' and not their verbal activity.

At one point in the narrative, she explains, 'If you concentrate with me, surely she will appear' (Pullinger 2018: 66). This sentence is followed by the variable fragment that changes according to the time of the day in which the reader is reading the story, and the function of this fragment is to strengthen the sense of similarity between Flo and the reader's situation (such a level of use of the reader's API is often unnoticed in an analysis of *Breathe*, while – in fact – it is a key aspect of renewing the ghost story format). The last sentences just before the ghost of Rifat's mother appears are: 'I can feel someone in the room, watching me. Is it you? Is it my mother?' (68–9). Thus, Flo starts to make a space (a gap) for the reader in her story by offering them the position of active listener. Then, the variable narrative that uses the reader's APIs (time, weather, location) creates in the reader a strong sense of being close to Flo, who, moreover, constantly emphasizes her relationship with the reader. Consequently, although the question, 'Is it you?' (69) could be addressed to Flo's mother, it is more probable that the reader would think that it is directed to them. It seems another sign of Flo's need for the reader's 'presence' – real presence.

[28] Repeating (un)asked questions of the (tacit) reader-listener is one of the techniques frequently used in spoken monologue. These not only emphasize the presence of 'you' but also are used to smuggle information about the surrounding (e.g. 'It's raining, you say?'). In *Breathe* it is sometimes unclear whether rhetorical questions are repetitions of such questions (un)asked by the reader, or whether they are questions she asks herself ('His manners are – what's the word? – courtly' [24]; 'Did Rifat tell me this war story?' [32]).

Step by step, both Flo and the reader understand that the main ghost is not Flo's mother, Clair, but Rifat's mother, Nour. Flo has confused Clair and Nour because of the many similarities between them, which is gradually revealed to the reader, for example, whilst reading a favourite song, 'sung' by the ghost. Those are not the only similarities in the story; various analogies are crucial for the story world structure. One of them Flo has understood at the end of the story; she needs the reader to connect her to her mother, precisely as Rifat's mother needed Flo to connect her to her son. Flo tells the reader her story, as Rifat told her his. But it is more than simply telling or confessing, that is, Flo needs the reader of flesh and blood, not only the textual construct she can speak to. She explains, 'Nour has come to me because of Rifat. She's found a way to him through me. And I'll find a way through her to you' (Pullinger 2018: 98–9). And then she asks for real action, 'Place your hand against the wall nearest to you. I place my hand against the wall nearest me. We are connected now' (100). Flo doesn't need someone in her (fictional) world; that is why there needs to be a gap for the reader in the fictional world.

Breathe is a ghost story, thus it is a story about crossing the borders of ontological layers, and Flo needs the reader, who is in another ontological dimension. Because of this, the narrative does not take the form of a 'standard' second-person narration, in which the reader is invited to enact an intradiegetic character, but what I call an embedded spoken monologue structure is used. Leaving a gap for the reader in the story world, making them a part of the story, refreshes the concept of the ghost story. The reader unquestionably immerses themselves more deeply through the feeling that they and their phone are haunted. Being a part of the story, not as someone who enacts a character in the story world (that is in a way typical for games or game books that use second-person narrative) but as themselves, the reader has a different experience.[29]

In ambient literature, unlike other forms of digital fiction, no avatar enables the reader to act within the story world and shape the storyline.[30] Ensslin, while

[29] Such a strategy has been used also in immersive cinematic ghost stories, for example *Last Call* (2010), the 'first interactive horrible movie in theaters' by Milo (Christian Mielmann), in which spectators had to share their phone numbers while buying tickets, and later the movie's protagonist called them while running away to ask for advice. Using new technologies, the movie on the screen evolved using this dialogue with the public. It can also be seen in the customized cinema installation directed by Chris Hales' *You Who?* (2019) in which some information that the viewer has shared about oneself and their image are used to create a thriller in which someone has stolen some of the main protagonist's personality. Having returned from a conference, he observes himself being gradually 'possessed' by another conference attendee. The latter is portrayed by data from each viewer. Ironically, this work was exhibited during the conference (Electronic Literature Organisation annual conference in Cork in 2019).

[30] Such an avatar, described by Ensslin as a 'metaleptic vehicle' (Ensslin 2011), was crucial in Ryan's reflection (Ryan 2006).

describing interactional metalepsis in interactive fiction, proposes the term 'metaleptic commands' to characterize short directive speech acts by which the reader instructs their avatars and, in that way, acts in the story world (Ensslin 2011: 13). There is nothing like that in ambient literature – the reader is asked to do real, not simulated actions, to do it by themselves and not by enacting anyone's role. The difference can be perfectly seen when we analyse *Breathe* in the context of *The Breathing Wall* (2003). This early digital work by Pullinger, co-authored with Stephan Schemat and Chris Joseph, can be seen as pioneering in making readers' bodies and physiology essential in the act of reading.[31] Analysed as an example of interactional metalepsis by Bell and Ensslin, *The Breathing Wall* is also a ghost story, and there are many similarities between *Breathe* and this work.[32] The latter tells the story of Michael, who was convicted of his ex-girlfriend Lana's murder and is in prison despite being innocent. He hears Lana's voice in his dreams and tries to figure out who murdered her. The story is a multimodal narrative told in 'daydreams' that use Flash animation with sound and text, and 'nightdreams', to access which the reader needs to use a special headset, because the story responds to the reader's breath.

So, in both Pullinger's works, breathing is used as a device and metaphor to join two worlds. In *Breathe*, the act of breathing links Flo and the reader, who is part of the story, and then unites both of them with the ghosts who are, as Flo explains at the beginning of the story, 'in the air we breathe' (Pullinger 2018: 4).[33] In *The Breathing Wall*, not only does software (Hyper Trans Fiction Matrix) enable the unveiling of the story according to the reader's breath rate, but also the breathing is what links in the narrative[34] the reader[35] with the story world and with Michael (analogically as it links him and Lana). The reader is invited to perceive the world as Michael does and to 'step into his dreams', and 'follow him through his memories' through breathing. He is encouraged by the protagonist: 'Come with me / Follow me / You can move through these walls / With your eyes closed you can find my cell / And you can listen through my ears'. And it is the reader's breath, the exceptional, 'successive' breath, that permits

[31] Breathing was intended here to substitute clicking (as Pullinger never was a fan of hypertext fiction).

[32] Those two are not the only ghost stories by Pullinger. Also mentioned can be: her first digital fiction, *Branded*, co-authored with Talan Memmott, which is a kind of prelude or multimodal exercise for *The Breathing Wall*, or *Jellybone*, another smartphone story in which the main protagonist receives messages from ghosts (now not accessible, although published in 2017).

[33] Such a connection is also emphasized by the final repetition of the words 'Breathe in. Breathe out' (Pullinger 2018: 104), which earlier appeared in the context of Rifat and his mother's story as a kind of memento from her.

[34] There are multiple 'you' addresses used, as Michael is not only speaking to the reader but also to Lana who is speaking to him.

[35] It is important to remember here that this reader is, in fact, a 'breather' (Ensslin 2009).

it. As Michael explains, 'So there is your breath [...]. Your breath supports me / with your breath, you can open doors. But not everyone can enter this story'. 'It's not always easy to live in the dreams of another' (first nightdream). And it is not always easy to breathe 'right' through the story, to be relaxed enough to access all its parts.

In both *Breathe* and *The Breathing Wall*, breathing (mentioned already in the titles) emphasizes the importance of the reader's body in the act of reading. This body, through the act of breathing, is a tool that enables entering the story. For example, Michael says; 'with your breath, you can open doors', and Flo reminds 'Breathe in / Breathe out'. The eponymous 'breathing wall' is the fourth wall that is crossed with the reader breathing, and the title of Pullinger's mobile story from 2018 is an open invitation to breathing/being in the story.

In *The Breathing Wall*, the reader's breathing permits them to step into Michael's mind, memories and senses and somehow enact him, that is, feeling like him and co-focalizing with him. As aptly pointed out by Ensslin, it operates 'on the basis of phenomenological, embodied empathy with the protagonist rather than the semiotic representation of selfhood in the avatarian "other"' (Ensslin 2011: 153). So, there is a gap for the reader in the story, but it appears to be left to make it easier for him to feel what Michael and Lana feel and to understand the story. Thus, although the reader's body is engaged in the reading process, they must forget about themselves to become immersed in the story. In *Breathe*, the reader's breathing seems more like a symbol of being with your own body, in your own space and in the here and now, while at the same time being part of the story (world). That is what Flo needs from the reader.

Ensslin points out that 'as readers we categorically do not need a physical representation of our own subjectivity in the text world' (Ensslin 2011: 153). For her, this is what differentiates literature from game narratives. An implied, model reader of literary works, as characterized in all reader-response theoretical concepts, seems to be only a theoretical entity, and, because of this, body-less. Works of ambient literature, however, finish with such an approach. Firstly, they do not neglect the corporealness of readers and, instead, ask the readers to 'lend' their bodies, which become 'play buttons' for the story. Secondly, readers do not so much need a physical representation of themselves in the story world as they are not re-embodied in the story world in the form of an avatar. However, while their surroundings become part of the story, they enter the story world by themselves, as real people with real bodies,[36] as part of the experience of a

[36] We can think about a similar situation in storytelling that uses augmented reality technology, because it also creates palimpsestuous experiences.

palimpsestuous character. While in physio-cybertexts, as characterized by Ensslin, the implied reader 'can share his or her phenomenological physicality with the narrator, and/or hero of the story' (153), in ambient literature, the reader receives a unique role to play in the story and needs their own body to do so. In such a way, the double-situatedness of the reader's body results in the specific construction of the reader-protagonist, which I call the *sylleptic you*.

To sum this up, the metaleptic character of *Breathe* is multidimensional. The reader balances on the ontological border between fiction and reality, having difficulties distinguishing the actual world and the fictional one because of the palimpsestuous character of experience. The reader sees their surroundings as part of the story on the screen, as the photograph taken at the beginning of the story serves as a background for the ghosts' messages. The real phone seems haunted by fictional(!) ghosts. Some of these ghosts know a lot about the reader. In the case of two of five ghosts in the story, the text of their messages alters according to data pulled into the story via APIs, so the messages are highly personalized and dependent on user location, time and weather.[37] While the phone enables contact with ghosts, at the same time, it is the main channel of communication between Flo and the reader. The whole story is a kind of message from Flo to the reader. She, as used to communicate with entities from other ontological dimensions (ghosts), is focused on making contact with the reader, the real, not fictional, person, someone belonging to the other reality than she belongs.

Conclusions: 'Porous'[38] borders of fiction and reality, reading bodies and powerful words that fly away

In this chapter I have looked at ambient stories through lenses of embodiment of the act of reading. I was interested in a way the readers' bodies, as well as their actual actions in the world, could become an essential part of the literary experience. I also characterized narrative structures useful for such a kind of immersion, focusing on second-person narrative and *sylleptic you* (protagonist) and showing the usefulness of the form I call *embodied spoken monologue*. Palimpsestuous overlapping of layers of reality and fiction and the use of metalepsis in digital literature have been characterized in the

[37] Donna Hancox emphasizes that such a 'sense of not being able to distinguish between reality and fiction' is crucial to creating the uncanny experience of *Breathe* (Hancox 2021: 93).

[38] I am using this vivid metaphor borrowed from Spencer who applied this to characterize ambient experiences (Spencer 2021: 312–13).

context of various examples of interactive art, including interactive movies and new tendencies seen in traditional print publishing. Thanks to that, the embodiment of the act of reading typical for ambient stories could be discussed in the context of the history of reading and in deep relation to cultural changes of modern times. Ambient storytelling, when seen from such a perspective, seems a natural response to the needs of modern readers, who are step by step more used to not forgetting about their bodies while interacting with art.

On the other side, ambient literature uses technology as well as poetics, for example a particular form of narration, to link readers' bodies with the story (world) and in such a way that reminds us of the true meaning of the Latin phrase 'verba volant, scripta manent' – a maxim that is frequently misinterpreted. The original meaning of the proverb was not that the written word is better because it lasts longer. On the contrary, the spoken word was described as more powerful and having a true impact on people. In the past, the act of reading used to be more closely linked to the readers' bodies and such corporeal relation with the text is even marked in the Bible.[39] As Manguel reminds us, 'In sacred texts, where every letter and the number of letters and their order were dictated by the godhead, full comprehension required not only the eyes but also the rest of the body: swaying to the cadence of the sentences and lifting to one's lips the holy words, so that nothing of the divine could be lost in the reading' (1996: 45–6). That is why for so long people were reading aloud, to make the words 'fly away' (volant), to give them real power (Saint Augustine of Hippo was still surprised by tacit reading). And maybe ambient literature, literature which needs to borrow its readers' bodies, literature in which these bodies are a 'play button' for the stories is a way to make the literary word powerful again.

Acknowledgement

This paper has received funding from the Polish National Agency for Academic Exchange through the Bekker programme (Grant Agreement No PPN/BEK/2019/1/00264/U/00001). It is partially based on a paper presented during the Electronic Literature Organisation's annual conference in May 2021.

[39] The apostle John had to 'eat' the scroll. See Revelation 10.9.

References

Abba, T. and A. Spencer. (2021), 'Writing Ambient Literature', in T. Abba, J. Dovey and K. Pullinger, eds. *Ambient Literature: Towards a New Poetics of Situated Writing and Reading Practices*, London: Palgrave Macmillan, 275–318.

Andersen, T. J., S. Kjerkegaard and B. Stougaard Pedersen. (2021), 'Introduction: Modes of Reading', *Poetics Today*, 42(2), 131–47.

Bell, A. (2016), 'Interactional Metalepsis and Unnatural Narratology', *Narrative*, 24(3), 294–310.

Bell, A. and A. Ensslin. (2021), *Digital Fiction and the Unnatural Transmedia Narrative Theory, Method, and Analysis*, Columbus: Ohio State University Press.

Bogalecki, P. (2020), *Wiersze-partytury w poezji polskiej neoawangardy*, Kraków: Wydawnictwo Uniwersytetu Jagiellońskiego.

Cardiff, J. (2004), *Her Long Black Hair*. Available online: https://cardiffmiller.com/walks/her-long-black-hair/ (accessed 6 June 2024).

Dovey, J. (2016), 'Ambient Literature: Writing Probability', in U. Ekman, J. D. Bolter, L. Diaz and M. Søndergaard, eds. *Ubiquitous Computing, Complexity and Culture*, 141–54, New York: Routledge.

Dovey, J., T. Abba and K. Pullinger. (2021), 'Introduction', in T. Abba, J. Dovey and K. Pullinger, eds. *Ambient Literature: Towards a New Poetics of Situated Writing and Reading Practices*, 1–26, London: Palgrave Macmillan.

Dovey, J. and M. Hayler. (2021), 'Critical Ambience', in T. Abba, J. Dovey and K. Pullinger, eds. *Ambient Literature: Towards a New Poetics of Situated Writing and Reading Practices*, 141–61, London: Palgrave Macmillan.

Dziedziela, M. and S. Szul. (2020), *Dzieje jednego pocisku*.

Ensslin, A. (2009), 'Respiratory Narrative: Multimodality and Cybernetic Corporeality in "Physio-Cybertext"', in R. Page, ed. *New Perspectives on Narrative and Multimodality*, 155–65, London: London.

Ensslin, A. (2011), 'From (W)reader to Breather: Cybertextual De-intentionalisation in K. Pullinger et al's Breathing Wall', in R. Page and B. Thomas, eds. *New Narratives: Stories and Storytelling in the Digital Age*, 138–52, Lincoln: University of Nebraska Press.

Ensslin, A., C. Rice, S. Riley, C. Wilks, M. Perram, H. Fowlie, L. Munro and A. K. Bailey. (2020), 'Bodies in E-lit' *Electronic Literature as Digital Humanities: Context, Forms, and Practices*, 93–104, New York: Bloomsbury Academic.

Fludernik, M. (2003), 'Scene Shift, Metalepsis, and the Metaleptic Mode', *Style*, 37(4), 382–400.

Gadd, I. (2021), 'Reader Reader One: Recovering Reading as Ambient Practice', in T. Abba, J. Dovey and K. Pullinger, eds. *Ambient Literature: Towards a New Poetics of Situated Writing and Reading Practices*, 27–52, London: Palgrave Macmillan.

Głowiński, M. (1963), 'Narracja jako monolog wypowiedziany', in K. Budzyk, ed. *Z teorii i historii literatury*, 1–34, Wrocław: Ossolineum.

Górska-Olesińska, M. and A. Przybyszewska. (2020), 'O „wypożyczaniu" ciał odbiorców na potrzeby (nie tylko literackich) immersyjnych wędrówek po przestrzeniach pamięci', *Przegląd Kulturoznawczy* (2), viii–xxvi.

Hancox, D. (2021), *The Revolution in Transmedia Storytelling through Place: Pervasive, Ambient and Situated*, London: Routledge.

Hanebeck, J. (2017), *Understanding Metalepsis: The Hermeneutics of Narrative Transgression*, Berlin: Walter de Gruyter.

Hayler, M. (2021), 'Objects, Places, and Entanglements', in T. Abba, J. Dovey and K. Pullinger, eds. *Ambient Literature: Towards a New Poetics of Situated Writing and Reading Practices*, 77–102, London: Palgrave Macmillan.

Kukkonen, K. (2011), 'Metalepsis in Popular Culture: An Introduction', in K. Kukkonen and S. Klimek, eds. *Metalepsis in Popular Culture*, 1–21, Berlin: Walter de Gruyter.

Kuzmičová, A., T. Schilhab and M. Burke. (2020), 'm-Reading: Fiction Reading from Mobile Phones', *Convergence: The International Journal of Research into New Media Technology*, 26(2), 333–49.

Manguel, A. (1996), *A History of Reading*, London: Harper Collins.

Marcinkowski, M. (2021), 'Where I'm Coming from: Studying the Novelty of Immersive Algorithms', in T. Abba, J. Dovey and K. Pullinger, eds. *Ambient Literature: Towards a New Poetics of Situated Writing and Reading Practices*, 199–232, London: Palgrave Macmillan.

Nycz, R. (1995), 'Traces of "I": Concepts of Subjectivity in Polish Literature of the Last Century', trans. A. Nask and M. Haltof, *Canadian Slavonic Papers/Revue Canadienne Des Slavistes*, 37(3/4), 373–92.

Polyakovskiy, S. (2018), *Maginary*. Available online: https://apps.apple.com/us/app/maginary-adventure-text-book/id1291905541 (accessed 6 June 2024).

Polyakovskiy, S. (2019), 'Maginary – animated immersive book for iOS', *Medium*, 18 January. Available online: https://medium.com/@semyonpolyakovskiy/maginary-animated-immersive-book-for-ios-3aec8f5136bc (accessed 10 November 2022).

Przybyszewska, A. (2020), 'W stronę lokacyjnego monologu wypowiedzianego. O eksplorowaniu literackich ucieleśnionych przestrzeni pamięci', *Przegląd Kulturoznawczy*, 2(44), s. 1–24.

Pullinger, K. (2018), *Breathe*. Available online: https://breathe-story.com/ (accessed 6 June 2024).

Richardson, B. (2006), *Unnatural Voices: Extreme Narration in Modern and Contemporary Fiction*, Columbus: Ohio State University Press

Ryan, M. (2006), *Avatars of Story*, Minneapolis: University of Minnesota Press.

Schmidt, W. (2010), *Narratology: An Introduction*, trans. A. Starritt, Berlin: Walter de Gruyter.

Spencer, A. (2021), 'Reading Ambient Literature: Immersion, Distraction, and the Situated Reading Experience', *Poetics Today*, 42(2), 301–15.

Szul, S. and M. Dziedziela. (2020), 'Andrzej Strug's "Dzieje jednego pocisku" as an inspiration to create retrofuturistic locative-narrative', Asynchronous, Panel 1.

Available online: https://stars.library.ucf.edu/elo2020/asynchronous/panels/1/ (accessed 25 May 2024).

Whittaker, E. (2021), 'An Aesthetics of Ambient Literature: Experience, Narrative, Design', in T. Abba, J. Dovey and K. Pullinger, eds. *Ambient Literature: Towards a New Poetics of Situated Writing and Reading Practices*, 233–62, London: Palgrave Macmillan.

Winiecka, E. (2004), 'O sylleptyczności tekstu literackiego', *Pamiętnik Literacki*, 95(4), 137–57.

Winiecka, E. (2006), *Białoszewski sylleptyczny*, Poznań: Poznańskie Studia Polonistyczne.

5

At the edges: A question of audience invisibility, disappearance and failure

Joanne 'Bob' Whalley and Lee Miller

Herbert Blau suggests that to watch performance is to watch someone dying right before your eyes (Blau 1982: 134). What then, is being experienced in those exchanges designed to separate the audience and the performer, where the interaction is understood through some form of mediation? Rather than consider the generalities of performance work which attenuates the space between the maker and the receiver of work, this chapter engages with the specifics of a piece that extends affective encounters to include both real world and online exchanges. By moving beyond the representational space of the art venue and instead blending the real/fictive landscape of IRL/online encounters, Blast Theory's *Uncle Roy All Around You* opens valuable space to consider the role of failure in meaning-making in co-constitutive arts practice. Perhaps unsurprisingly, any reference to failure and performance evokes the writing of Samuel Beckett in *Worstward Ho*: 'All of old. Nothing else ever. Ever tried. Ever failed. No matter. Try again. Fail again. Fail better' (Beckett [1983] 1989: 101). Beckett positions failure as a starting point, a place from which to begin. He understands failure as a process, not an end point. This chapter seeks to hold to the idea of failure as process and consider how it informs the reading of work predicated on a success/failure binary and what subversion, however unintended, means for the audience.

Our failure

In 2001, Jay Schneider and Gerd Kortuem published 'How to Host a Pervasive Game: Supporting Face-to-Face Interactions in Live-Action Roleplaying' as a means to reflect on the development of live-action role-playing games to include readily available technologies. In their essay they reflect upon the evolution of the board game to include a range of assistive technologies, first VCR, then DVD and eventually computing technologies. From this, they developed the term 'pervasive gaming', which is one way that Blast Theory has since defined *Uncle Roy All Around You*. When considered through the lens of gaming, success and failure are necessarily central to the potential reading of the work. However, in May 2004, the term 'pervasive game' had yet to reach the kind of cultural saturation necessary to make it part of common parlance. Instead, we approached the work as a piece of site-specific performance, related to other immersive and sited acts of storytelling, a strategy that still holds twenty years later.

Our failure began before we had even begun to engage with the piece. Believing that he could keep all the information in his head, Lee failed to bring any of the venue details with us and confidently drove us to the Contact Theatre just off Manchester's Oxford Road. We walked towards the Box Office:

> 'Hi, I have some tickets booked in the name of Miller.'

After consulting the computer, Lee was informed that there was no record of him booking any tickets and was asked the name of the piece.

> 'Sorry, I can't remember – the group is Blast Theory if that's any help.'

It turned out to be a great deal of help as the person in the Box Office was able to tell us that we were at the wrong venue. We needed to be at the Cornerhouse not the Contact. Bob's supportive response to this initial error was to point out that at least Lee got the first two letters of the venue correct.

Before we had even begun, we had failed to follow a simple instruction. This kind of failure – the inability to be in the right place at the right time – is of a significantly different order than the subsequent success-failure elision that would follow. In these first moments, those that lie beyond the formal start of the work, there is no doubt that the actions of the two key players in the narrative are flawed. A failure to bring the correct information, to arrive at the right venue with enough time, these are behaviours that very nearly derailed the experience before it had the chance to properly begin. The borders of this type of failure are clear and defined; there is little room for nuance in regard of what went wrong here. Failures such as these have sharp edges, the kind that indicate the point at which something ends. In contrast, the 'failure' that follows has porous edges, and speaks more to Heidegger's boundary as a line which marks the edge of a territory, the point from which something else might begin to emerge. This understanding of failure is much more useful when considering what might be happening in the space between an audience and a performance. It is the failure of Beckett; processual, and moving constantly forward and towards an ending. It strikes us that failure of this kind might be described as ambient; quietly working in the background with an intention ultimately to move forward. Certainly, in terms of our experience of Blast Theory's *Uncle Roy All Around You*, we experienced a failure that might more comfortably be thought of as ambient than catastrophic.

This processual form of failure serves as a boundary line between what was and what could be. The experience of failure points towards the next steps but only if we are willing to follow the path: when Lisa Le Feuvre posits in her essay 'Strive to Fail': 'we can sometimes only become truly attentive when something is indeed wrong' (2010: 14). Our experience of *Uncle Roy All Around You* could have ended at the Contact Theatre. We could have decided to stop for a coffee, abandon our plans and walk to the nearby Manchester Museum or the Whitworth Art Gallery. The failure to be in the right place at the right time presented us with a boundary, the choice to cross it was ours alone. As Heidegger reminds us, '[a] boundary is not that at which something stops but, as the Greeks recognized, the boundary is that from which something begins its presencing' (Heidegger 1971: 152–3).

The idea of a boundary, a line which marks the edge of a territory, is particularly useful when considering what happens in the space between success and failure or rather when recognizing the potential to move beyond binary thinking. Heidegger's reminder that a boundary is the point from which something emerges offers a different perspective to the more commonly understood sense that a boundary indicates the point at which something ends. In performance, and particularly at the point where the audience and the performer meet, it is more helpful to think of the presencing offered by Heidegger than of more formalized demarcation of behaviours that seek to keep the audience and performer in their separate spheres of influence. Blast Theory positioned *Uncle Roy All Around You* at just such a boundary, describing the piece as the moment 'where espionage movies become interactive; where the console game breaks onto the streets. It is a game that pitches online players around the world alongside players on the streets of a real city' (Blast Theory 2003). The invocation of game structure, one that repositions audience as players, clearly opens up a discussion about power, control and hierarchy. Whilst the concept of 'play' opens up conversations around ludic interaction, the concept of 'game' invokes rules, structures and the potential for winning. The real-world environment and the potential for chaotic, ludic abandonment, sits alongside the deliberately configuring structures of an online, closed system.

Uncle Roy All Around You

Uncle Roy All Around You occupies an interesting place in performance history. First presented in collaboration with the Institute of Contemporary Arts, London in 2003, it had a further seven public presentations between 2004 and 2013. We experienced the work at the Cornerhouse, Manchester in 2004 as part of the Digital Summer event. Even twenty years later, the kind of challenge to the status quo offered by *Uncle Roy All Around You* retains a sense of novelty. By adopting a structure more familiar to MMORPG (massively multiplayer online role-playing game) participants, and blending live and online elements, *Uncle Roy All Around You* placed the audience/player in a situation that required problem-solving and cooperation to reach a conclusion. Rather than the denouement of traditional performance product, the work required adherence to a set of predetermined rules for the audience member to experience completion.

This was not our first experience of Blast Theory's game playing/performance hybrid. In 2001 we had participated in *Desert Rain*, a piece that required the successful completion of an interactive game to open up access to the subsequent installation. *Uncle Roy All Around You* developed this game structure further, and in his chapter 'Frames and Bystanders: *Uncle Roy All Around You*', Stuart Reeves describes it as a pervasive game. Reeves explains that the game is constructed for both the online and real-world players, and relies upon cooperation between the two. He notes that '[o]perating behind-the-scenes in a control room and out of sight on the streets are a team of orchestrators (described as "control room staff" and "street performers" respectively)' (Reeves 2011: 134), with 'orchestration' used as a means to keep real-world players safe and supporting their progression through the game. According to Reeves account, real-world players were given a PDA device to navigate through the city/game, which used 'self-reported positioning' rather than location tracking and allowed them to record and send short audio clips to the online players. It is somewhat dislocating to read Reeves account of the work, not simply because he, quite understandably, positions it entirely as a game but because of the clarity with which he explains how the various systems work.

Ambient failure

Maybe it's because we arrived late, already reeling from an earlier failure, but our memory of the rules and the interface lacks the clarity afforded by Reeves' description. We remember arriving and rushing up the stairs to the first floor of the Cornerhouse. We remember the staging area, where we were prepared for what would follow. Mostly we remember being separated. Being told firmly that this was an experience for one person at a time. We remember surrendering our personal belongings, emptying pockets and handing over bags. We remember being given the thing we always thought was some kind of GPS-enabled handheld computer and having its functions explained to us. Here the stickiness of failure grew snowball-like, as Ricoeur noted in his essay 'Memory and Imagination', '[t]o the mis-fit is added the erroneous grasp, the mis-take' ([2000] 2010: 71). Evidently, we didn't really understand the exchange because it wasn't a GPS at all. Apparently, it allowed self-reporting. This aspect of 'mis-take' might be important. It might make more sense of the smearing success-failure that Bob would later experience. We remember a briefing and we remember walking out of the building, separately. However, we have no memory of recording clips for online players, although we do remember text exchanges. A good friend, Tamsin, was an online player, and Lee remembers multiple exchanges with her – but in his memory these were the simple back and forth of text messages. Bob has no memory of communicating with online players at all, remembering instead the importance of location and a desperate urge to communicate with the actors responsible for the 'orchestration' of the real-world environment; 'live performers played several significant roles in the experience, ranging from planned and rehearsed performances (the initial briefing, phone call and interview in the car) to more general orchestration duties on the streets, including monitoring players' progress and occasionally improvising interactions with them (e.g., fixing technical problems as is presented below)' (Reeves 2011: 124–5).

In contrast, Lee's experience was less complex, more straightforwardly a 'failure'. Upon leaving the Cornerhouse, he turned left when he should have turned right. This wasn't from any sense of wishing to be belligerent, simply from an inability to follow a map. Lee has always been a wanderer with a propensity to turn left if he is unsure which way to go. Interestingly, there was no mechanism to catch this initial error, despite the assertion in Reeves' article. It is important to note that this is avowedly not offered as a critique of either Reeves' account or the 'orchestration' offered by the company and those providing support on the ground, it is offered only to note that there is a gap between the authorized narrative of the work and the experience of two participants. We have already considered the unreliability of memory and the potential unruliness of subsequent narratives but to suggest that this is the only reason for slippage is to miss the complexity of a large-scale ambient narrative/locative game structure and the potential for failure of both audience and the work.

The fact that Lee struggles with map-reading and initially went in the 'wrong' direction could be seen as a catastrophic failure of both the player and the game. However, the more ludic interpretation of Lee's wrong turn is that it opened him up to the experience of ambient failure, in which he was able to use the architecture of the game/performance to have encounters that would otherwise not have occurred. By failing at such an early point, too much time was lost to be able to successfully reintegrate himself into the goal-oriented structure of the work, leaving him free to embrace a version of play that does not really work in a game context. Lee's failure took him outside the structure of the game, providing him with an opportunity for a gently guided dérive through streets he knew. By drifting in this way, he remained guided by the meta-structure of the work without fully functioning as part of it. Rather than use the portable computer as a means to play the game, it served as a useful motor for social engagement, prompting conversations with strangers, real and imagined, before eventually 'timing out' and requiring him to make his way back to the starting point and wait.

And wait. The waiting came about because of Bob's experience. If we think of ambient failure as a kind of matrix, a scale of failure within which to be positioned, Lee's falls very much at the limits. Perhaps his failure creates what film theorist Deborah Linderman calls a 'limit-text'; works that 'query a boundary that is normatively repressed in other texts' (Linderman 1981–2: 200). By creating space for a ludic engagement in this way, there is little doubt that his potential to offer a stable critical analysis of *Uncle Roy All Around You* is impacted. Of course, all readings are subjective; they are a product of gendered, social and cultural construction. In this sense, analytical readings are no more accurate than those based purely upon feelings. However, to attempt to offer some kind of analysis of a text that has been so avowedly stepped outside of would be a perverse assertion of the subjective voice. There is some of Lee's experience work that remains valuable, as it speaks to the potential of accounts that sit outside the authorized version to interrogate the received wisdoms of what 'happened'. But it sits within the matrix of failure in such a way that obviates any real analysis. While not deliberate per se, Lee's failure was much closer to catastrophic than ambient. Simply put, there is little to be learnt about the audience interaction from his wrong turn, where he transformed 'into a lost object to be found' (Benford et al. 2006: 431).

In contrast, and fundamentally more interesting, was Bob's experience. She followed the clues and found her way to Uncle Roy. Or rather, the limited technology of the self-reporting location software contained within the handheld computer was certain that she has found Uncle Roy. As the clock ticked down, Bob followed the clues and made her way towards Uncle Roy. She opened the door, climbed the stairs, turned the handle and went in. But Bob had not found Uncle Roy, instead she had somehow found her way into a different building; '*Uncle Roy All Around You* invited participants to enter an office that had been rented for the occasion, but in so doing raised the possibility that they might try enter some other office' (Benford et al. 2015).

To all intents and purposes, Bob had been successful. She had followed the instructions, made her way up to the second floor and into an empty hotel room. All the prompts from the small screen in her hands were telling her that she had succeeded and there was no reason that she should think otherwise. After all, she was standing in an empty hotel room, a room that had not been locked. She had walked past the front deck unchallenged, made it up the stairs and into a room. By her reckoning, this must be part of the experience. An instruction on the screen required her to pick up the phone. She was in a hotel room. That was totally possible. She picked up the phone and all that met her was a dial tone. Somewhere, in a building nearby, a phone was possibly ringing. That phone went unanswered. Street actors who had been ghosting her footsteps were deployed to hasten the performance to its predetermined close. The performers found an empty room, yet the digital dialogue absolutely assured them that the game had been successfully completed. And the phone rang on.

It is as a result of this ambient failure that we understand Bob's experience to be much more valuable in terms of analysis. If failure is understood as a spectrum, Bob's experience lies much closer to success than Lee's but is a failure, nevertheless. The complexity, and thus the interest here, is that the game positioned Bob in terms of success. Her device was communicating completion, without her having been able to complete the necessary task. If understood in the context of a console game, Bob somehow missed the 'boss battle' (Zagal, Fernández-Vara and Mateas 2008: 189) but was still able to proceed to the next level. Except of course she couldn't. In the real world, bricks and mortar rather than pixels stood in the way of her progression.

Perhaps this exploration was informed by our experience of *Desert Rain*. Following the completion of the interactive game element:

> visitors find the exit corridor is blocked by a large pile of sand. Having climbed up the sand and down the other side they reach the final room of the installation. The walls of the final room are full scale photographs of the walls

> of an English hotel room. The room contains no objects apart from a magnetic card reader and a monitor cut into the wall exactly where the television is in the hotel room.
>
> (Blast Theory 1999)

Finding herself in an empty hotel room, Bob did not feel particularly out of place. The immediate absence of any human presence was also not especially disconcerting. Certainly, after an extended online/real-world treasure hunt, searching for clues in an empty hotel room did not present any particular anxiety. As time passed, with nothing in the room yielding any information and with no one arriving to move the dialogue forward, Bob settled into a way of being that would be familiar to an audience member of Robert Wilson's *Einstein on the Beach*. In the time Bob spent exploring the empty hotel room, she did not feel frustrated by the lack of conclusion. Seeing her quest, and eventual location in an empty hotel room, as an opportunity that wouldn't have normally been afforded in daily life, Bob's approach echoed that of Tim Ingold when he suggests that 'what matters is not the final destination, but all the interesting things that occur along the way' (2007: 170). Uncle Roy remained absent, but she enjoyed looking for his traces, sitting on the bed she thought he had recently vacated, wondering if he would knock at the door. When no-one came, and when her searches of the space yielded nothing, she was not irritated. She had Sophie Calle for company, and they were in this together. Ultimately, the certainty of the instructions on her handheld device inoculated her from the reality of the situation, and Bob found herself emboldened, happy to play within the confines that had been offered. Even if that playing was unintentionally rule resistant.

It was when Bob eventually made her way back to the Cornerhouse that the complexities of the failure really began to emerge. Because she had believed herself to be in the right place, there had been no incentive to leave the room. There was no context for 'right' or 'wrong' behaviour whilst in the room. Somehow, none of the hotel staff were aware of her presence, and so this particular interloper had triggered no alarms and the time she spent in the hotel room was entirely peaceful. It was only as she started to wonder about which room Lee might be in, and what was happening in his room that she began to think about returning. When she eventually made her way back to the Cornerhouse, she was greeted by a small-scale panic. The anxiety was that the technology had failed them, that somehow she was a long way from where they thought she was. Her return was met with relief and irritation. Perhaps there had been anxiety imagining the negative press that might have been generated by the disappearance of a participant, which is gently ironic from a company that made its name kidnapping strangers.

The spectrum of failure

None of this is offered as a slight, rather it is intended to reflect upon the tense relationship between 'game' and 'play' in the work, and how its rule-based structure obviated space of ludic exploration. As we have already discussed, our inauspicious 'way in' to *Uncle Roy All Around You* highlights failure as a continuum, with catastrophic at one end and ambient at the other. Much like the potential gap between intention and reception, the failure of Bob to reach the conclusion of the piece in the way designed by Blast Theory underscores the slippage between the two ends of the spectrum. The anxiety that Bob returned to suggests that the type of failure she experienced was unexpected and highlights the interplay and potential for schism between 'players' and the 'game'; a reminder of the game being 'both object and process' (Aarseth 2001). Media theorist Marshall McLuhan states, '[g]ames are popular art, collective, social *reactions* to the main drive or action of any culture' (1964: 235, original emphasis) and Alexander Galloway further describes the concept of game-play as a spectrum of possibilities:

> [a] game is an activity defined by rules in which players try to reach some sort of goal. Games can be whimsical and playful, or highly serious. They can be played alone or in complex social scenarios.
>
> (2006: 1)

Galloway's 'rules' are significant here; rules define the parameters of the interaction, and the prescribed guidelines for *Uncle Roy All Around You* point to expected audience conduct. The expectation, though, needs to be shared. In Bob, *Uncle Roy All Around You* was met by an expert player, albeit one operating to a set of behaviours quite distinct from those expected to be at play. As a performance-maker highly skilled in task-based and durational improvisational strategies, Bob has an ability to meet offers and to stay with an experience, perhaps beyond the point of comfort. While these may be valuable skills for an audience of and participant in a wide range of performance art practice, it is perhaps less valuable in relation to more traditionally structured game playing.

Bob's presence in the hotel room, a venue that was both wrong and right in the same moment could be thought of as a glitch, one that had not been anticipated in beta testing.

The glitch

In the context of *Uncle Roy All Around You*, it is worth interrogating the idea of the glitch, especially in relation to rules that are broken by accident or through misunderstanding. Bob being both inside and outside the game, a victor and loser in the same moment evokes the writing of Peter Krapp, who wonders about the possibilities of creating a 'ludology for losers' to open up rather than 'obscure the domain of the error' (Krapp 2011: 75). In this way, the breakdown of our understanding of the rules of the game within the performance of *Uncle Roy All Around You* could provide a contingency, what Galloway calls 'counter-gaming'. He offers this idea not as an emancipation of docile bodies, rather as a recognition of the need for 'alternative algorithms' within the labour of games (Galloway 2006: 107–26). If to 'win means to know the system' (91) then Bob's 'mistake' serves as an example of 'unexpected information' (Clark 2010: 164). Through the unintentional forcing of a glitch into the system, Bob opened up a state of circular relations in collaboration with the piece, albeit one that couldn't quite be held by the mechanics of the system in play. In his book *The Space of Encounter*, architect Daniel Libeskind offers a chapter called 'endless space(s)' in which he seeks to rediscovers space to 'materialize, create, investigate, illuminate, construct, touch, redeem' (Libeskind 2001: 65). Given the real-world location of *Uncle Roy All Around You*, the potential for an encounter that fell beyond the parameters of the game opened up the experience to the ambient failure, with all the attendant possibilities for expanded encounter and alternative types of play.

It is hard to offer a response to a piece without appearing critical of said work, especially when to do so requires discussion of the concept of failure. From this perspective hindsight is a marvellous thing, it offers a 20/20 vantage point. It is all too easy to reflect upon our experience and wonder why it wasn't fixed in advance, or better yet, why our experience wasn't mapped into the structure of the piece in the first instance. In all truth, this is not something that we are asking for. In fact, we are not particularly critical of the piece, no matter if our musings suggest otherwise. Rather, we are reflecting upon the potential for slippage in ambient narratives, and how anticipating and embracing these glitches might open up a space in which the audience can become visible.

Unreliable narrators

If thus far we have constructed a narrative that appears critical of *Uncle Roy All Around You*, it becomes equally pressing to hold to our own failures. Hopefully we have already communicated how our actions left us culpable in the subsequent failures of experiencing the work but as we return to the experience to offer this chapter there is a further failure worthy of consideration. Given that these words are being written twenty years after the event, we have to wonder how reliable we are as narrators of any experience. The majority of this account was written without recourse to contemporary reflections, relying instead on our memories and the narratives about the experience that have accrued over the years. We understand that the readings we offer are like pebbles on the shoreline – smoothed and rounded over time, the rough edges polished by the passing tides. Memory plays an interesting role in the sharing of stories, and the process of reading the description offered by Stuart Reeves does not evoke our experience, it serves only to marginalize us further, reinforcing the sense that our experience was a failure. By returning to an 'official' account of the practice, our memories are cast into doubt. Reeves is clear that a ten-strong team of actors was deployed to keep players on track, but our memories feature no such figures. Or rather, we remember no support from these figures, only that there were people who seemed to be aware of our presence in the city, ghosting our footsteps for some of the time, but absent at others.

Reading Reeves' words, we wonder if we have become 'unreliable narrators' in our own story. This term is introduced by Johanna Shapiro, writing about the role of the patient in narratives of medical practice. Rather than hold to this as a critique, Shapiro goes on to 'call for patient-centred and relationship-centred care, both of which reinstate the value of the patient's story in caring for patients' (2011: 68). The prescribed narratives or the 'truths' of any condition are for the most part within a Western biomedical understanding, controlled by the clinician. The unreliability of the patient occluding what 'should' be experienced in order that a speedy and reliable diagnosis can be made. Shapiro's work attempts to reconcile these 'unruly narratives' (69–70) by calling for humility from the listener to *all* narratives, whether fallacious or not. In so doing, she is encouraging the listener to respect the agency of the teller. In a clinical setting, the responsibility is then placed on the recipient of these stories. Of course, the stakes in this type of storytelling are high; how we are listened to and how we listen might impact upon the type of care patients are given. In contrast, the unreliable, or unruly, memory of two academics excavating their conjoined experience is of a considerably lower temperature and there is clearly no direct analogue between what Shapiro is doing and our call for the audience experience to be valued differently.

Ambient audience practices

That said, thinking through stories and thinking about how those stories are told is central to understanding the audience practices in the extended contexts of the ambient. When experience is singular, consensus becomes much more difficult to reach; each audience member goes through the process differently to the next, so it stands to reason that any subsequent reflection will differ. As Shapiro notes, '[e]very narrative is a negotiation about what reality is really like' (2011: 71). It occurs to us that the ambient narrative opens up space for the unruly in which 'failure' can be given the same status of 'success', as we all become the unreliable narrators of our experiences, the teller of our own stories. Or rather, there can never be an authoritative account of ambient storytelling. There can be intention and reception, and if the gap between the two is too big, there is no need to attempt any reconciliation, only the negotiation of realities suggested by Shapiro.

Of course, because we tend to work in binary thinking and because academic writing such as this works hard to reach 'valuable' conclusions that might contribute to the sum of knowledge, it is easier to accept the authorized account of an experience as more trustworthy, even when we know that authorized accounts occupy a hierarchically elevated status. In contrast to the secure account of the maker, we find ourselves writing from a position evoked by Elizabeth Grosz in her book *Architecture from the Outside* when she asks 'what does it mean to reflect upon a position, a relation, a place related to other places but with no place of its own – a position in-between' (2001: 90). This type of untethering feels closer to the experience of the ambient (whether this is an ambient narrative or an ambient failure), where the question of agency comes not just in the moment of exchange but also in later reflections upon the experience. The inherent mistrust of memory is endemic in much cultural discourse. Claude Lévi-Strauss refers to his memory as 'a self-destructive thief', and outlines the strategies he employed to coral it into behaving, citing the use of notes, postcards and journals:

> I get by when I work by accumulating notes – a bit about every- thing, ideas captured on the fly, summaries of what I have read, references, quotations [...] And when I want to start a project, I pull a packet of notes out of their

> pigeonhole and deal them out like a deck of cards. This kind of operation, where chance plays a role, helps me revive my failing memory.
>
> (in Eribon 1991: vii–viii)

Does our account have more weight if we include here a short extract from Bob's journal, written soon after her experience:

> As I walked away from the Cornerhouse, I reflected that the interaction was what had wrong footed me; the intention was that I should have used the online players as guides, but the gnomic text messages that wanted something from me before they would offer advice bored me. I didn't want to walk around a city with my head down. The screen intervened in an unhelpful way for me, requiring transaction rather than exchange.
>
> (Whalley 2004: unpaginated)

Does this contemporary reflection elevate our subsequent analysis, and does being able to access the responses Bob had in the days after the experience lend more credence to the detail being offered here, twenty years later? To ask this is to direct the enquiry of this chapter down a different avenue. Felicity is only part of the narrative here. There is a space between intention and reception, and similarly a space between events and experience.

Which brings us towards a tentative conclusion, one that recognizes the role of the audience in the context of ambient storytelling as quite different from the intersubjective exchange of what might be understood as more traditional performance exchanges and how the potential for shared affect is unsettled in the type of interactive media performance presented by Blast Theory. Being out in the world opens up the audience to radically different exchanges than those in the controlled environments of performance space. As Alain de Botton observes:

> [j]ourneys are the midwives of thought [...] There is almost a quaint correlation between what is in front of our eyes and the thoughts we are able to have in our head: large thoughts at times requiring large views, new thoughts new places.
>
> (2002: 57)

While Blast Theory's use of immersive environments might well have informed subsequent theatrical product, this kind of blending of real-world and immersive tactics remains a rarity. Agency and autonomy thus become interestingly vexed issues in *Uncle Roy All Around You*, especially as we ventured out into the world with only the handheld computers – no wallet, no keys, no phone, no markers that make us 'us', just a lump of technology that connects us to 'them': '"street players" are introduced to the game through a ritual briefing in which they are asked to hand over all of their personal possessions, bags, phones, money and identification in return for the PDA that they will use to play the game' (Benford et al. 2006: 428). There is something about being shorn of the usual clutter and then left to explore real-world locations with online support/clues, filtered through the meta-structure of game play that offered a *dis-locating* experience alongside the controlled interface which reported position and connection status and history. It is here we find comfort in our 'little failures' and in Ian Bogost's discussion of 'serious games', which he articulates as those designed to 'invoke, support, doubt, or debate [the] validity or desirability, or universality' of a given situation (Bogost 2007: 58). The ambient nature of our failure allows us to fail upwards, or succeed downwards, to lose ourselves in the confusion of streets and pixels.

References

Aarseth, E. (2001), 'Computer Game Studies, Year One', editorial, *Game Studies*, 1(1), July. Available online: http://gamestudies.org/0101/editorial.html (accessed 10 November 2022).

Beckett, S. ([1983] 1989), 'Worstward Ho', in *Nohow On: Company, Ill Seen Ill Said, Worstward Ho*, 100–128, London: John Calder.

Benford, S., A. Crabtree, S. Reeves, M. Flintham, A. Drozd, J. Sheridan and A. Dix. (2006), 'The Frame of the Game: Blurring the Boundary between Fiction and Reality in Mobile Experiences', conference proceedings, *CHI: Conference on Human Factors in Computing Systems*, 22–27 April, Montréal, Québec, Canada: 427–36.

Benford, S., C. Greenhalgh, B. Anderson, R. Jacobs, M. Golembewski, M. Jirotka, B. Carsten, S. J. Timmermans, G. Giannachi, M. Adams, J. R. Farr, N. Tandavanitj and K. Jennings. (2015), 'The Ethical Implications of HCI's Turn to the Cultural', *ACM Transactions on Computer-Human Interaction*, 22(5), article 24.

Blast Theory. (1999), *Desert Rain*, collaboration with the Mixed Reality Lab, University of Nottingham, premiered at the NOW 99 Festival, Nottingham. Available online: https://www.blasttheory.co.uk/projects/desert-rain/ (accessed 10 November 2022).

Blast Theory. (2003). *Uncle Roy All Around You*, premiered at the Institute of Contemporary Arts in London and at the Cornerhouse in Manchester, in collaboration with Digital Summer, 28 April–8 May, 2004. Available online: https://www.blasttheory.co.uk/projects/uncle-roy-all-around-you/ (accessed 10 November 2022).

Blau, H. (1982), *Blooded Thought: Occasions of Theatre*, New York: Performing Arts Journal Publications.

Bogost, I. (2007), *Persuasive Games: The Expressive Power of Videogames*, Cambridge, MA: MIT Press.

Clark, B. (2010), 'Information', in W. J. T. Mitchell and M. B. N. Hansen, eds. *Critical Terms for Media Studies*, 157–71, Chicago: University of Chicago Press.

De Botton, A. (2002), *The Art of Travel*, New York: Pantheon Books.

Eribon, D. (1991), *Conversations with Claude Lévi-Strauss*, Chicago: University of Chicago Press.

Galloway, A. R. (2006), *Gaming: Essays on Algorithmic Culture*, Minneapolis: University of Minnesota Press.

Grosz, E. (2001), *Architecture from the Outside: Essays on Virtual and Real Space*, Cambridge, MA: MIT Press.

Heidegger, M. (1971), *Poetry, Language, Thought*, trans. A. Hofstadter, New York: Harper and Row.

Ingold, T. (2007), *Lines: A Brief History*, London, Routledge.

Krapp, P. (2011), *Noise Channels: Glitch and Error in Digital Culture*, Minneapolis: University of Minnesota Press.

Le Feuvre, L. (2010), 'Strive to Fail', in L. Le Feuvre, ed. *Failure*, Documents of Contemporary Art, 12–21, London: Whitechapel Gallery; Cambridge, MA: MIT Press.

Libeskind, D. (2001), *The Space of Encounter*, London: Thames & Hudson.

Linderman, D. (1981–2), 'Oedipus in Chinatown', *Enclitic*, 5–6, 190–203.

McLuhan, M. (1964), *Understanding Media: The Extensions of Man*, New York: McGraw Hill.

Reeves, S. (2011), 'Frames and Bystanders: Uncle Roy All around You', in *Designing Interfaces in Public Settings: Understanding the Role of the Spectator in Human-Computer Interaction*, 123–39, London: Springer.

Ricoeur, P. ([2000] 2010), 'Memory and Imagination', in L. Le Feuvre, ed. *Failure*, Documents of Contemporary Art, 68–71, London: Whitechapel Gallery; Cambridge, MA: MIT Press.

Schneider, J. and G. Kortuem. (2001), 'How to Host as Pervasive Game: Supporting Face-to-Face Interactions in Live-Action Roleplaying', Position Paper for UbiComp 2001 Workshop on *Designing Ubiquitous Computing Games.*

Shapiro, J. (2011), 'Illness Narratives: Reliability, Authenticity and the Empathic Witness', *Medical Humanities*, 37(2), 68–72.

Whalley, J. 'B'. (2004), *Personal Journal*, July: n.p.

Wilson, R. (1976), *Einstein on the Beach*, premiered at the Festival d'Avignon, Avignon, France, 25 July. Available online: http://www.robertwilson.com/einstein-on-the-beach (accessed 10 November 2022).

Zagal, J. P., C. Fernández-Vara and M. Mateas. (2008), 'Rounds, Levels, and Waves: The Early Evolution of Gameplay Segmentation', *Games and Culture*, 3(2), 175–98.

6

Here. Now. Ours: Interrogating the use of situated augmented reality

Ben Gwalchmai

Introduction

When Walter Benjamin used the term Flaneur to mean an urban explorer, documentarian and whisperer of city streets (Benjamin 1999: 427), he could hardly have imagined the Apple Vision Pro or Meta Quest 3 headsets providing mixed reality (MR) layers to each street beyond what the average walker would see. Similar questions of what our twenty-first century's age of ambient information (McCullough 2013: 3) means for our city streets, our experience of them, and whether or not they create active citizens drove the interrogation at the heart of this chapter's study. The hypothesis being interrogated can also be formulated as the question 'Can eLit and AR increase awareness of the reader's shared public, green spaces and increase their civic will that, in turn, they act on?'

In this chapter, I will first give some brief context to how my PhD study using situated augmented reality came to be, then I will outline the core philosophical theories behind what it is before detailing, analysing and concluding with the findings of the interrogation. *Here. Now. Ours* is the case study software I created for my PhD and, in this chapter, we will walk through the why, where and what it meant. In many ways, this will be the summation and perhaps the continuation of the entirety of my PhD, a PhD focused on using augmented reality (AR) outside, completed amid a pandemic where we had to stay inside – no small feat (or feet).

Literary, play and political context

In that small wordplay we have a simple segue into how *Here. Now. Ours* began. It was as a Playable City competition entry. Before I knew the terms 'situated literature', 'Electronic Literature' (eLit), or 'ambient literature', I knew I had made a kind of literature that lived on (and in) its environment before. When I volunteered with a poetry-based charity in London, we made an event called Poetry and Architecture (2008) to celebrate the opening of *The Guardian*'s new offices – we commissioned poetry from Simon Barraclough and installed literary-based artworks projected onto moving spheres too. This memory is to give you an idea of how *Here. Now. Ours* came to be and because when making practice-based research, autoethnographic reflection is paramount in learning from our work; even in writing this chapter, I have remembered more layers than the flickering of memory allowed at the time of my PhD application; so it is that practice-based research is a series of collective endeavours, layered over one another – just as places are, just as networks are – then realized in the focus of an energetic time.

It wasn't until a Playable City competition pushed me to it that I wanted to put poetry on water. Bristol is a city of bridges; I wanted *beneath our feet, the stars* (Gwalchmai 2014) to take advantage of them and create a subtly playful installation that projected poetry in many languages on both sides of the bridges through powerful projectors, powered by piezoelectronic panels installed on the bridges. Though short-listed, this idea didn't win. As good ideas so often do, it stayed with me. In my downtime, I turned it over and over, thinking over the many iterations of what it might become; poetry, writ large but responsive and tailored to its environment, through digital means. When the opportunity to apply for a practice-based PhD came up, that was the idea and research area I submitted (minus the piezoelectronic panels), but instead of projection, the poetry would be writ large through the medium of AR. *beneath our feet, the stars* became *Here. Now. Ours.*

The idea was one thing, understanding what it would do, philosophically and politically, to the reader/user/player was entirely another. After taking a detour through much architectural theory, it became clear that the experience was moreover about relocating the scene of knowledge and understanding the agency that newly relocated agent/reader/user/player would or would not have.

Relocating the scene of knowledge

In *Literary Studies in the Digital Age*, Julia Flanders argues that:

> Digital literary study … seeks to move from explanatory narratives that apply to individuals to explanatory narratives that apply to populations. This is a move that seeks to relocate the scene of our knowledge.
>
> (Flanders 2013)

Flanders is not solely referring to eLit works here but also includes quantitative digital corpus studies that semantically examine connections and recurrences within genres, eras and even within individual works. She is making a wider point about the nature of digital humanities, arguing that digital humanities is a bridge that examines both the importance of IT's influence on the humanities and also of using humanities-related ways of thinking to analyse and inform digital studies, that is, not only using digital technology to analyse textual production, transmission, reception, and so on, but also using approaches from the humanities, for example, to discuss the ethical, human and philosophical implications of artificial intelligence (AI) sentience or sex-bots. This is borne out in the second sentence where Flanders, 'seeks to relocate the scene of our knowledge'.

In her radical and seminal work *Situated Knowledges* (1988), Donna Haraway argues for a need to relocate the scene of knowledge to a more situated, more multivariant perspective that considers individuals' connectedness and partial perspectives. These partial perspectives forge 'attention to the contemporary dissolution of boundaries between human and animal, human and machine, and physical and nonphysical', as G. L. Downey (2001) says, and we know that Haraway's own Cyborg Manifesto kick-started the question of whether or not we are cyborgs already. By relocating the scene of knowledge to AI and the contemporary dissolution of boundaries, these texts help join the distributed network of the internet (that can be made visible through AR) with agency of our everyday actions and agency with networked play, and help to connect my PhD in the City of Galway with a sense of its own location, its own location's networked connections and its own digital-humanitarian opportunities.

Core phenomenological texts have relocated the scene of our knowledge (e.g. from mind to body) before. Merleau-Ponty rearticulates the relationship between subject and object, specifically, self and world, and so attempts to dismantle Cartesian Dualism. He does so through accounts of the lived body where he argues that the significance of the body – 'the body-subject' – is often underestimated by philosophy, which tends to consider the body simply as an object that the mind controls to perform functions. In short, where Descartes says 'I think, therefore I am', Merleau-Ponty says (if I may paraphrase) 'I perceive the world through my body and therefore it is', and in doing so, he denies the detachment of subject from object, mind from body (Merleau-Ponty 2002: xii). As philosophy scholar Nick Crossley says in examining Merleau-Ponty, 'there is no meaning which is not embodied, nor any matter that is not meaningful' (Crossley 1994: 14). Merleau-Ponty argues, further, that 'every perceptual habituality is still a motor habit' (Merleau-Ponty 2002: 153). Here both Crossley and Merleau-Ponty argue that every reflective thought we have is something our body has learned through experience. For Merleau-Ponty, philosophers looking only at reflective thought ignore the paradoxical condition of all human subjectivity, that is, we are both a part of the world and limited by it, constituting a part of it but in turn also constituted by it (153). He grounds this in a simple notion: we have always had a body, so to think, to have knowledge or to experience without a body is inconceivable (91). It is a clear logic and one that resonates with my work, as augmented reality (AR) is rooted in a requirement to experience it through the movement of our bodies. My work considered how movement through a city might deepen our understanding of shared public space.

Phenomenological theories of 'touch'

Not only did Merleau-Ponty seek to relocate the scene of our knowledge to an embodied understanding based on experience and experiencing, but in rearticulating the relationship of subject and object, he also expanded the definition of touching. This expansion ties neatly with the desire inherent in *Here. Now. Ours* to dissolve digital and physical boundaries through AR and join the distributed network of the internet with agency of our everyday actions, such as walking through city streets.

Throughout the twentieth century, phenomenologists have explored the relationship between body and technology; Martin Heidegger's *Question Concerning Technology …* ([1954] 1993) did so and asked whether all extensions of our instrumentality (or desire or will) that have an end could be considered technology. This was a move on from his earlier conception of technology as *techne*, as all the tools we use (Heidegger, Macquarrie and Robinson 1962); in the *Question Concerning Technology …* Heidegger revised his conception of technology and posited that we live in a world that is *already* shaped by technology, and we, in turn, shape technology in a will to power (or 'producing' bringing things to be, or mastery) over the raw materials of the world (Heidegger [1954] 1993: 287). He also asked if *all* these extensions of our will might be a prosthesis. Merleau-Ponty followed on from Heidegger's point and argued that the simple (original Heideggerian *techne*) technology of a stick or cane is an extension of one's senses, with touch being transferred from the hand through to the end point of the cane (Merleau-Ponty 2002: 176).

This is especially important to the haptic-phenomenologists discussed later in this section and to how we use our touchscreen-led smartphones today. Each of our taps on a touchscreen is an extension into the internet and could be seen as technological prosthesis (whether of memory, of will or more). Heidegger did not celebrate modern technology, though; Heidegger thought twentieth-century technology was incredibly dangerous and was very concerned by the 'Gestell' (or the framework of how we interact with the world) driving us to only be interested in a world-model of 'numbers crunching' in which things exist and come into existence only insofar as they can be measured. From that fear, we can see a direct line to Merleau-Ponty's *Phenomenology of Perception* that wishes to explore our embodied understanding of the world to ensure we give space to the qualitative (within the production of knowledge). We will now explore the contemporary manifestations of extensions and how this process has become intertwined, intersubjectively, with our everyday experiences in the present day.

In the twenty-first century, we use 'cloud computing' and 'cloud storage' every day when we upload our photographs so we can store a memory. We outsource our memory when we ask our smartphones to 'remind us' of something; we have made a memory prosthesis of computing, as Heidegger suggested. Indeed, this behaviour is now so common, it has led to the adage 'We're all cyborgs now' (Case n.d.; Clark 2003). In 1999, Angela Carter (1999) ventured so far as to say 'Now we have machines to do our dreaming for us', and before her, in 1968, the science fiction writer Philip K. Dick asked 'Do Androids Dream of Electric Sheep?' These statements and questions serve to highlight how intertwined the human and the machine is becoming in contemporary society. Much as Donna Haraway noted in her 'Cyborg Manifesto', our memories are tied up in external items and machines. Merleau-Ponty's work on intersubjectivity and the expansion of the definition of touching helps us to better understand the implications of this.

Merleau-Ponty's expansion of the definition of touching is highly relevant to digital reading, something inherent to *Here. Now. Ours*. In expanding that definition, Merleau-Ponty emphasizes the relationship between touching and being touched, suggesting that there is a slight overlap in the phenomena. He explains this through the phenomenon of putting our hands together:

> [W]hen I press my two hands together, it is not a matter of two sensations felt together as one perceives two objects placed side by side, but an ambiguous set-up in which both hands can alternate the role of 'touching' and being 'touched'.
>
> (Merleau-Ponty 2002: 93)

When we put our hands together, it can begin to feel as though we are both touching and being touched as Merleau-Ponty says; that there is a completeness to the phenomena which dissolves the difference between the two states, unlike when we touch two objects, where the difference in sensation highlights and clarifies the distinction of subject–object separation. Merleau-Ponty also says that, 'The body tries … to touch itself while being touched and initiates a kind of reversible reflection' (Merleau-Ponty 2002: 93). It is this 'reversible reflection' which is the clearest way of describing the phenomena that dissolve the difference between the two states of touching and being touched. In his later work, *The Visible and the Invisible*, Merleau-Ponty asks us to consider how our very *awareness* of being physically touched overlaps with the experience of touching (Merleau-Ponty 1968: 147). He does so to complicate and expand our definition of touching because, like wearing clothes, we are always in a process of touching the world and being touched by it. He goes further and argues that the dualism between mind and body (247) and the self and the world (123) are not so distinct as traditional Cartesian philosophy would have them. He suggests they are interdependent. This interdependence is something he calls 'the flesh of the world' (251); he also states that 'we may say that the things pass into us, as well as we into the things' (123). In diluting the idea of the world as merely a static object, here Merleau-Ponty suggests to the philosophical field what so many narrative writers have been writing towards, namely, that the world is capable of altering us and touching us, just as we are capable of altering and touching it from afar. That is not to say that we *are* the world and the world is us – Merleau-Ponty goes to great pains to make the paradox of interdependence clear (127) – but, rather, our embodiment in the world is neither fusion to it nor absolute distance from it; we are continuously touched by and we touch the flesh of the world. For the twenty-first century where we wear the internet in our pockets, I would add to this and say we are continuously touched by and we touch the 'net'.

The interdependence of the flesh of the world is also something we see in reading when we associate with a character and an overlap develops between us and them; we are not that character and they are distant from us, but as we hold a book or digital device and we go on their narrative journey with them, we are emotionally moved – we are touched – by them. Our emotional selves overlap with the character's journey, from afar, creating an interdependence of emotion and journeying – 'the things pass into us, as well as we into the things' – and so we are affected by that reading. Feeling a part of a narrative or feeling an emotional connection to a character has always been referred to as 'touching' or 'being touched by' that narrative or character, and so it is entirely possible to expand the notion of touch into the digital and virtual through being 'touched-at-a-distance' and with 'felt-proximity' like contemporary phenomenologists do. This notion of interdependence is further expanded by contemporary haptic-phenomenologists to examine how a touchscreen device might revolutionize what touch and touching is.

In further expanding the definition of touching, Merleau-Ponty has enabled contemporary philosophers to use that expanded definition and apply it to the changes of the twenty-first century, specifically, the changes in digital technologies. In his book *The Senses of Touch* (2007), Mark Paterson does just this. Through his own work, which examines how blindness affects internal sight and touch, as well as his engagement with the work of other Merleau-Ponty scholars, Paterson explores all the types of touching available to different types of bodies, including abled and disabled, female, male and non-binary. Through the overlaps detected in Merleau-Ponty's work with other phenomenologists such as Luce Irigaray, Paterson then teases out a sense of what he calls 'haptic-phenomenology', felt-phenomenology or touch-based phenomenology, and applies that to early twenty-first-century digital technologies such as touchscreen computers and ultrasonics. 'Haptic technologies', as a term, has been used by engineering since the invention of the aeroplane and the resulting force-feedback of air-pressure on cockpits. However, though there were a few patents established in the 1970s, IT communities have only embraced the term since the 1990s, when computer-game controllers were given the ability to vibrate in response to actions in the game. Due to the popularity of the Apple iPhone and its touchscreen interface, the IT community has become progressively more interested in haptic technologies – so much so that Apple developed a '3D touch' pressure sensitive system for iPhones in 2015 (Apple 2015). There are also companies such as Ultrahaptics developing ultrasound-based touch-feedback technologies for everyday computing input (Ultrahaptics 2018). Paterson, however, highlights how a sense of feedback and touch through a technology was also defined by Aristotle centuries previously, who describes a man carrying a shield:

> If the shield is struck forcefully the blow is felt immediately, not as the successive blow of sword on shield and then of shield to man. The intermediary nature the shield received as the blow is felt, just as the intermediary of flesh is forgotten in tactile experience.
>
> (Paterson 2007: 158)

If our computer game avatar is struck and our controller vibrates, so too do we feel that we have been struck, like the man using a shield; if we click through an eLit text and it leads us to disappointment for our character, we too are disappointed. This echoes Merleau-Ponty's gestalt approach to touching and being touched – we can be emotionally touched at a distance, and we can be physically touched through an intermediary. Here, too, the scene of knowledge is relocated, and we can see it becoming distributed through our digitally networked technologies; to be 'touched at a distance' is something that Paterson discusses in an even wider sense than Merleau-Ponty; both Paterson and Merleau-Ponty discuss this so we will look at just one more of Merleau-Ponty's texts before going into more detail on Paterson. In another of his major works, *The Primacy of Perception*, Merleau-Ponty argues that one can perceive objects in the world relative to their significance to the lived body's needs and that the objects in the world 'display themselves' or, in other words, that to look at or through an object is to understand how it relates to other agents and objects in the world, and so we may also be able to inhabit or look through the objects perception (Merleau-Ponty 1964: 68). This 'looking through' connects the idea of a touch intermediary through objects to Paterson's ongoing expansion of what both the haptic and touch is in the twenty-first century. That inhabitation of 'looking through' will be familiar to anyone who makes a Skype or video call.

Paterson regularly suggests that feeling and touching is 'more usually a feeling-with' (Paterson 2007: 34) because all touching, all action, is embodied and our bodies sense proximity, and reversibility. Paterson argues this by referring to Merleau-Ponty's notion of intercorporeity as something which 'decouples "touch" from mere "sensation"'. Paterson pushes for the focus to 'remain on tactility, empathy and felt proximity'. We can use these terms, 'empathy' and 'felt proximity', interchangeably with 'being touched' and the inhabitation of 'looking through' discussed earlier. The terms 'touched at a distance', 'looking through', 'feeling-with' and 'felt proximity' are especially relevant to digital reading and eLit as explored in *Here. Now. Ours* because many studies of digital reading show that it is an embodied practice (Mackey 2002; Merchant 2015; Mangen and van der Weel 2016) and that embodiment can be expanded from the tactility of holding a book or device to a radical embodiment achieved through 'touching at a distance' and 'felt proximity' achieved by various technologies such as telepresence and touchscreens. Ontological boundaries are transcended when we feel touched by something that is not ourselves or another person. eLit, through haptic feedback and touching at a distance, expands and reshapes our notions of embodiment, radically, into the augmented and virtual digital worlds;

if, for example, you are using a device to navigate through an eLit horror text and it vibrates (gives haptic feedback) as you turn a click or tap to turn a corner in a tense environment, you could feel as scared and as alert as if you were touched (at a distance) by an arrow hitting your shield.

Relocating the scene of knowledge and expanding our sense of touch to include 'touched by' gave me some of the necessary theoretical touchstones I needed before I could apply the political elements of interaction I wanted. These political elements were, in part, made possible by all our cities' growing accumulation of data – both Open Data and Big Data – but also by a phenomenon I first noticed in Bristol's Cabot Circus: POPS.

Privately Owned Public Spaces (POPS)

Public space is for sale and under threat in the United Kingdom, America and much of the Western Anglosphere. These are appropriations of public space by private interests, facilitated by governments of the last 100 years. In his book, *The New Enclosure: The Appropriation of Public Land in Neoliberal Britain* (2018), Brett Christophers forensically exposes how roughly 10 per cent of the entire British land mass has passed from public to private ownership since 1979, worth approximately £400 billion, with a considerable amount of it disappearing from records entirely (Christophers 2018: 247–9). Christophers explicitly ties this sell-off to a neoliberal political ideology and, in the data since 2010, to a UK governmental programme of austerity. Christophers is not alone in this analysis; an investigation led by the Bureau of Investigative Journalism and aided by Huffington Post UK in 2019, found that thousands of English public spaces had been sold due to central UK government squeezing local government budgets (Davies et al. 2019); these included libraries, community centres, playgrounds and commons. Both investigations look at the numbers and monetary values of the sales, but it is the clarity of the second which truly shows us the scale of public space lost – 12,000 public spaces have been disposed of by English councils since late 2014 (Davies et al. 2019). So acute is the problem that protests began in 2016 and have continued regularly since, with some journalists dedicating their work to it (Gleave 2016; Dixon, Viles and Garrett 2018). There is a similar, though not as severe, problem in the United States. Public space is certainly under threat there, however, with Yosemite National Park having lost 30 per cent of its mass over the last 100 years (Emerson 2016). The subtlety of this atomizing, encroaching appropriation of public space is represented in a particularly telling way by the phenomena of Privately Owned Public Spaces (POPS): these are areas of urban environments that seem like the streets, thoroughfares or parks of Lefebvre's 'spatial practice' but are in fact privately owned and thus subject to private control and different laws of trespass; when private companies can patrol and privately police areas which have historically been public and still seem public, this is a clear and nefarious appropriation of public space.

Recent reports indicate that these negative practices continue today and are even expanding to feature technology as a means of regulating behaviour in public space. Recent reporting from *The Guardian* reveals just how much 'creeping privatisation of London parks' took place in 2019 (Hancox 2019), and how large, London property developers are facing a backlash against their plans for privacy-invading, facial-recognition technology on the streets near their development (Sabbagh 2019). Due to the Black Lives Matter protests in mid-2020, Amazon and IBM revoked American police department's licences to use their facial-recognition technologies (Levy and Hirsch 2020; Peters 2020) and some parts of the world are pushing back against big technology companies appropriation of space as well as their use of power and influence in the process – in late 2018, Stockholm refused Apple the planning permission for an Apple Store on one of their oldest public spaces because:

> 'Kungsträdgården is the most important park in Sweden,' says Johanna Jarméus of Nyréns Arkitektkontor, a leading architecture firm. 'It is the thread that pulls together the historical power of the monarchy with the commercial blocks of Hamngatan and the working-class districts of Södermalm. This is very important for democracy because it has to do with power, symbolically and spatially.'
>
> (Orange 2018)

When Johanna Jarméus says this decision around public space 'has to do with power, symbolically and spatially', she neatly conveys how important public spaces and their preservation are to cities, democracies and the people in them everywhere. That one sentence of Johanna Jarméus' sits underneath all the theories and questions of Lefebvre, Jacobs, de Certeau and Zuboff, as well as the question at the heart of *Here. Now. Ours*; there is great and growing resistance to the powerful, private appropriation of public space and some of those resistance movements will now be detailed.

There are diverse groups resisting the private appropriation of public space, such as academics, artists, legislators and technological wunderkinds. Newcastle University recently undertook a research project, *Wastes and Strays: The Past, Present and Future of English Urban Commons* (Hammersley and Rodgers 2019), that explored how these valuable green spaces can be protected through 'the historical and archaeological records relating to four case studies: The Town Moor, Newcastle upon Tyne; Valley Gardens, Brighton; Mousehold Heath, Norwich; and Clifton Down, Bristol' (Hammersley and Rodgers 2019). This was a joint research study between the history and legal departments of Newcastle University concluded in 2021. This culminated in the publication of *English Urban Commons: The Past, Present and Future of Green Spaces* (Hammersley et al. 2023) and has greater implications for how both communities and legislators think about public space. Indeed, in 2017, the London Assembly passed a motion that 'Privately owned public spaces need new London plan rules' (Labboun 2017) and the Mayor of London responded by drawing up a Charter to regulate London's POPS (Shenker 2017). This implies that legislators are aware of the problem, there is sufficient academic evidence to note the problem as a very serious problem and some steps are being taken to curb it, but the problem nevertheless persists. Global organizations continue their efforts to promote the importance of public space – the Project for Public Spaces (PPS) is a 'nonprofit organization dedicated to helping people create and sustain public spaces that build strong communities' (PPS 2019) – and have expanded to work in the growing field of 'placemaking', which is the process of embedding a space within its community (and vice versa) through a programme of events. These institutional efforts are commendable and ongoing but require a level of funding that not every group has, therefore individual efforts at resistance will now be discussed.

To combat the persistent problem of private appropriation of public space, activists, clubbing together, have been successful in some areas. One such example, and pertinent to illustrate the discussion here, is the #BlockSidewalk campaign. This group have seen some success, and in May 2020, Sidewalk Toronto announced they were 'no longer pursuing the Quayside project' (Doctoroff 2020). Therefore, Google in Toronto, like Apple in Stockholm before it, have been pushed to step away from being a property developer by activist pressure. And this same activist pressure has protected public space from the creep of both privatization and surveillance capitalism. Engaging the users of *Here. Now. Ours* to get involved with planning in their city was a core part of the interrogation; to test the theory of whether or not they would develop agency, it required understanding how they could take up those spaces.

In a more individual way, performance artists and soundscape artists have offered examples of 'taking up space' in differing and challenging ways (D'Avignon 2016). In her book *Walking and Mapping* (2013), Karen O'Rourke explores a series of walking/mapping projects by contemporary artists that are often digitally augmented, and through close readings of those works O'Rourke is able to relate them to well-known works of art from the past half-century. Elsewhere Christina Kubish's art-walks series of interactive soundscape performances, *Electrical Walks*, makes the electromagnetic fields all around us into something that we can hear during the performance. This is a playful revealing that aurally embodies ambient information, and that playfulness is key to understanding how best to engage citizens and encourage them to embrace their *agency and civic will*. It is this idea of playfulness which links the artistic and technological efforts of resistance.

Playing and playfulness within our public space isn't only a form of resistance employed by artists but something that can be done by the everyday smartphone user. This ties in neatly with the growth of smart cities and pervasiveness of technology because the new digital layer that smartphones can offer means a new, further and sometimes anarchic level of expression. One of the most popular, recent AR examples of this is *Pokémon Go*, an app inspired by the popular Nintendo Game Boy franchise that now has people walking around the real world to encounter AR experiences. It is as Leighton Evans and Michael Saker (2019) say, 'The playeur moves more, goes to different places, pensioners reconnect with cities, and experiences many benefits of this increased mobility and sociospatial awareness thanks to their play.' Here Evans and Saker have invented the term 'playeur' by combing the terms 'player' and the Walter Benjamin idea of a 'flaneur' (who traverses streets to enjoy and observe the experience of street life, a critic in the intricate ballet of Jane Jacobs' streets) so that we know that this new flaneur is critic, investigator, player and AR technology enthusiast. Some academics and independent researchers use *Pokémon Go* as a successful example of linking communities, play, geographies and encouraging the use of public space because of the communities it has had a positive effect on (MFour Mobile Research 2016; Riva et al. 2016; Saker and Evans 2018; Piera Jimenez and Hjorth 2019), while others have used AR to create smartphone applications of their own for more satirical purposes. It is these artist-activist purposes which are highly relevant to my work.

The academic, activist and artist Conor McGarrigle gained international attention and inspired community action in Dublin with his playful, satirical AR project *NAMAland*. *NAMAland* used the LayAR app as a platform on which to plot the secretive purchases of the Irish Government department the National Assets Management Agency (NAMA) in the wake of the 2008 financial crisis and subsequent domestic and international government bailouts to banks and big companies. Many of these properties sat empty or unavailable to the public, whose very taxes had paid for them; the NAMAland app plotted these locations and let the user see them, with a playful Monopoly man icon imposed on them, through the AR LayAR platform. In discussing the project, McGarrigle wrote:

> In considering AR art and data it is important to locate the discussion within an artistic tradition of using data (open or otherwise) as a tool of political critique within an art context. ... From the Occupy Dublin camp one day to city-sponsored seminars on Open Data and the smart economy the next, this was its ability to function as a conduit which reconnected NAMA with the space of the city, a connection which had been deliberately severed, to preserve the idea of the agency as a by-product of obscure international financial dealings. What NAMAland contributed was an opening up of previously unavailable data and a reconnecting of this data with the fabric of the city itself.
>
> (McGarrigle 2013: 108–12)

McGarrigle's own PhD was on agency in locative media (McGarrigle 2012) and NAMAland was a fitting, sharp example of increasing agency within a community; in the quote McGarrigle is detailing the artistic design of NAMAland, the response to it and some of the invitations he received to discuss it, as well as explaining how he saw the connection between the negative practices of global finance and his government illuminated by the NAMAland AR app. These responses and illuminated connections bring back into public discourse something which had been appropriated by private finance. Like McGarrigle proved, we can alert communities to when public – and especially green – spaces have had planning applications and/or are being changed from public hands to private through open data, urban informatics and AR. Just as McGarrigle has done, so too does *Here. Now. Ours* illuminate government practice through AR and a kind of play.

How *Here. Now. Ours* responds to these issues and theories

Whether or not the expansion of large internet companies into our public spaces has happened to citizens' benefit is a debate that continues, what is clear is that it *has* happened and *is* happening, like in Hangzhou, but that activists are using technology as well as democratic engagement tools to resist it – it is in using digital humanities to challenge private interests subsuming public spaces that this research sits. Due to the design of the software, the *Here. Now. Ours* smartphone app doesn't record user data, publish any route or personal data to me, or connect with any data-storage server except the local City Council server; this means the research sits at the edge of these ongoing smart city arguments and offers a case study which hopes to show an alternative of open data over big data, local over global and anonymized over surveilled. The 'different spatial logics' of hybrid space along with Lefebvre's *differential space* can provide a way to understand where it is possible to push back against space being privatized like so many POPS. Open Data and AR provide a new avenue for online activism and so *Here. Now. Ours* was created as a tool that enables agency in citizens, just as Lefebvre encouraged shattering 'the social body' and thus changing the relationships between citizen and state.

Throughout this chapter, the term 'public space' is used, and the term 'public sphere' avoided, because the latter has its own intellectual history and set of implications. The two overlap (indeed, are intertwined), but for the purposes of this research, the focus remained on 'public space' itself. This is because focusing on public space *itself* gives a quantifiable and qualitative measure of the awareness within the *Here. Now. Ours.* case study participants. An undiscovered park is easier to discover than where an undiscovered conversation sits within the wider cultural, political and social milieu. Measuring awareness of a public sphere is almost entirely qualitative but measuring footfall in a park (quantitative) and what led them there (qualitative) can give us a clear insight into what tools were used to raise the visitor's awareness to get them there. This is why *Here. Now. Ours* took a mixed-method approach to interrogate whether AR can be used as a part of *Situated AR eLit* to increase awareness in participants.

With augmented reality, the reader-player is automatically immersed and 'present on the scene of the represented events' (Ryan 2001: 122) because the game world is the same as the real world. This accomplishes the 'ludic immersion' (Thon 2008: 36) and 'deep absorption in the performance of a task' (Ryan 2015: 246) set out by Thon and Ryan, respectively, through the automatic understanding by AR reader-players that the real world *is* the game world. And yet, it only does so through AR's innovative metalepsis. One of my central arguments follows Ensslin and colleagues (2019) when they suggest that 'if interactivity is absorbing, it can help to immerse a reader-player within the digital storyworld', by testing whether absorbing interactivity in metaleptic play can increase awareness of the real world.

The notion of increasing awareness of the real world through play is not new to the twenty-first century and its digital technologies; play formed a central part of Walter Benjamin's *flaneur*, the Situationist International's (SI) *dérive* and Michel de Certeau's conception of the *Wandersmänner*. Here again we can see the importance of O'Rourke's *Walking and Mapping* and within these conceptions of play and playfulness, walking itself was both a kind of play and also a political act. Benjamin wanted the spirit of the *flaneur* to see the city anew and reimagine it by encouraging us to 'walk out your front door as if you've just arrived from a foreign country; to discover the world in which you already live' (1999: 427). There was a male gender bias and class privilege to Benjamin's conception of the *flaneur* but it has maintained a place of prominence in these discussions whilst coming under considered, deserved and increased scrutiny by figures such as Doreen Massey (1991, 2005, 2006). To the SI, the practice of the *dérive* was a kind of 'drift' that invited the practitioner to open themselves to the affecting flows and energies of the city. The SI particularly emphasized play as a part of the *dérive* to unpick the daily, capitalist-accumulation routines of those around them (Debord [1957] 2004). Finally, de Certeau's *Wandersmänner* concept was subtler and more personal in its play and politics. It saw urban space as a place created by the self along with the subjective other.

De Certeau discussed the importance of understanding the city as a shared practice:

> The ordinary practitioners of the city live 'down below,' below the thresholds at which visibility begins. They walk – an elementary form of this experience of the city; they are walkers, *Wandersmänner*, whose bodies follow the thicks and thins of an urban 'text' they write without being able to read it. These practitioners make use of spaces that cannot be seen; their knowledge of them is as blind as that of lovers in each other's arms. The paths that correspond in this intertwining, unrecognized poems in which each body is an element signed by many others, elude legibility. It is as though the practices organizing a bustling city were characterized by their blindness. The networks of these moving, intersecting writings compose a manifold story that has neither author nor spectator, shaped out of fragments of trajectories and alterations of spaces: in relation to representations, it remains daily and indefinitely other.
>
> (de Certeau 1984: 93)

The idea of a network of texts woven across a city isn't new, but de Certeau clearly wants us, as *Wandersmänner*, to experience and explore the city until we read its 'unrecognized poems'. This contestation of the everyday is a subtly playful reading of our place in the city, one that researchers and human computer interaction (HCI) labs have furthered. Crivellaro and colleagues expanded these notions with their paper 'Contesting the City: Enacting the Political Through Digitally Supported Urban Walks', where their case study was presented as 'a method for the situated discovery and articulation of issues at the intersection between the politics of place making and city planning' (Crivellaro et al. 2015).

To understand how much the participants might have felt like an *augmented Wandersmänner* or felt their *agency and civic will* being encouraged in *Here. Now. Ours*, it was necessary to ask questions which explored the phenomenological experience of how the process of testing felt to each of them. Asking deeper, more personal questions involved developing as much rapport with them as possible so that the participant feels comfortable enough to go into further detail; after all, 'doing ethnography is establishing rapport' (Geertz 1973: 6). Building rapport means that no one conversation (in debriefing and interviewing the participants) could be exactly the same but, instead, was 'felt out', it was entered into from both interviewer and interviewee as a conversation where both could ask questions that felt like they flowed and stemmed from previous talking points as much as possible. As the interviewer, I tried to ensure the conversation was as wide as it needed to be but also that it included the following questions (or questions with a similar intent to these):

1. How would you describe the poetry? Like graffiti? Sculpture?
2. How did the overall experience *feel*?
3. Did the AR make you feel *more* (?) or *less aware* of your surroundings?
4. Did the overall experience make you *more* or *less* aware of the planning applications around the city's green spaces?
5. Did the experience feel curious, intriguing and/or playful enough to keep your *attention*?
6. Did it feel rewarding?
7. Do you think it might have been better and/or more ambient with a more natural flow, with a pair of AR glasses?

Other questions and conversation topics may have followed from these, but these were the only questions in the qualitative section of the discussion that I was conscious to include. This focus on the *feel* of the experience was important in both experience-design and in how they articulate their understanding of their emotional responses, connection with their environment, and *agency and civic will*; the phenomenological focus in the questions tests the theory that walking, itself, around a city can connect a participant to their *agency and civic will* and heighten their awareness of their city.

The results of the case study can be put simply as: *in the majority, participants stated they were more aware of their city's green spaces through the use of situated AR eLit.*

Participants were *more* aware, *mostly more* aware of planning applications, they felt their *attention was held* and the experience was *mostly rewarding.* To be able to put the findings in one sentence like that is a success of the design of the study; the range of its findings show it has given enough flexibility to design and participants alike, to see where the study could be improved. The hypothesis stated that AR eLit can indeed increase awareness of a city's green spaces (but only through ensuring it is *situated*), and as most participants stated, they were more aware after the experience, we can now say that the hypothesis was correct. In both the quantitative and qualitative data collected from software and interviews, participants' experience showed a mobile, attentive and self-motivated response; when participants had used the software to the extent they wished, they returned to the start point and were debriefed. In that debrief, some of the theory behind the case study was discussed, and here it is important to state that this interrogation has been conducted with '*methodology* as the reciprocal relationship between *method* and *theory*' (Gold and Klein 2016: 155; original emphases). With that reciprocal relationship in mind, we can see in participant's responses: a sense of *ambient play* in their attention; embodied understanding in their unique, phenomenological experiences and descriptions; epistemic awareness in their interactions with and through Hybrid, Hertzian space; and an increased understanding of the importance of public space.

One PhD interrogation alone isn't enough to endorse the terms I wanted to test – ambient play, architectural literature, augmented Wandersmänner – and their relationships to *agency and civic will* but it is a start. A good start. Using Open Data and *situated* AR, I was able to direct people with no previous experience or interest in public planning policy to city governance through the playfulness of AR and the construction of an ambient, city-wide, poetic experience. There's great potential to do more.

References

Apple. (2015), '3D Touch – iOS – Apple'. Available online: https://developer.apple.com/ios/3d-touch/ (accessed 29 January 2024).

Benjamin, W. (1999), *The Arcades Project*, Cambridge. MA: Belknap Press of Harvard University Press.

Carter, A., ed. (1999), *The Old Wives' Fairy Tale Book*, New York: Pantheon.

Case, A. (n.d.), 'About – Amber Case'. Available online: http://caseorganic.com/about/ (accessed 10 November 2022).

Christophers, B. (2018), *The New Enclosure: The Appropriation of Public Land in Neoliberal Britain*, London: Verso.

Clark, A. (2003), *Natural Born Cyborgs: Minds, Technologies, and the Future of Human Intelligence*, Oxford: Oxford University Press.

Crivellaro, C., R. Comber, M. Dade-Robertson, S. J. Bowen, P. Wright and P. Olivier. (2015), 'Contesting the City: Enacting the Political through Digitally Supported Urban Walks', *CHI '15: Proceedings of the 33rd Annual ACM Conference on Human Factors in Computing Systems*, 2853–62.

Crossley, N. (1994), *The Politics of Subjectivity: Between Foucault and Merleau-Ponty*, Aldershot: Ashgate Publishing.

D'Avignon, A. (2016), 'Cities May Alienate Women, but Performance Art Points the Way to Reclaim Lost Space', How We Get to Next. Available online: https://howwegettonext.com/cities-may-alienate-women-but-hypersolitude-is-a-way-to-reclaim-lost-space-4a4e828f2bef (accessed 14 July 2023).

Davies, G., C. Boutaud, H. Sheffield and E. Youle. (2019), 'Revealed: The Thousands of Public Spaces Lost to the Council Funding Crisis', Bureau of Investigative Journalism. Available online: https://www.thebureauinvestigates.com/stories/2019-03-04/sold-from-under-you (accessed 14 July 2023).

de Certeau, M. (1984), *The Practice of Everyday Life*, Berkeley: University of California Press.

Debord, G. ([1957] 2004), 'Report in the Construction of Situations', in T. McDonough, ed. *Guy Debord and the Situationist International*, 29–50, Cambridge, MA: MIT Press.

Dixon, S. J., H. A. Viles and B. L. Garrett. (2018), 'Ozymandias in the Anthropocene: The City As an Emerging Landform', *Area*, 50(1), 117–25.

Doctoroff, D. (2020), 'Why We're No Longer Pursuing the Quayside Project — and What's Next for Sidewalk Labs', *SIDEWALK TALK*. Available online: https://medium.com/sidewalk-talk/why-were-no-longer-pursuing-the-quayside-project-and-whats-next-for-sidewalk-labs-9a61de3fee3a (accessed 14 July 2023).

Downey, G. L. (2001), 'Anthropology of Science and Technology', in *International Encyclopedia of the Social & Behavioral Sciences*, 13629–3633, Oxford: Elsevier.

Emerson, S. (2016), 'Yosemite National Park Used to Be 30 Percent Bigger', *Motherboard*. Available online: https://www.vice.com/en_us/article/ezpmww/yosemite-national-park-used-to-be-30-percent-bigger (accessed 14 July 2023).

Ensslin, A., A. Bell, J. Smith, I. Van Der Bom and L. Skains. (2019), 'Immersion, Digital Fiction, and the Switchboard Metaphor', *Participations*, 16(1), 320–42.

Evans, L. and M. Saker (2019), 'The Playeur and Pokémon Go: Examining the Effects of Locative Play on Spatiality and Sociability', *Mobile Media & Communication*, 7(2), 232–47.

Flanders, J. (2013), 'The Literary, the Humanistic, the Digital: Toward a Research Agenda for Digital Literary Studies', in K. M. Price and R. Siemens, ed. *Literary Studies in the Digital Age*, Modern Language Association of America. Available online: https://dlsanthology.mla.hcommons.org/the-literary-the-humanistic-the-digital/ (accessed 14 July 2023).

Geertz, C. (1973), *The Interpretation of Cultures: Selected Essays*, London: Routledge.

Gleave, J. (2016), 'The Evolving Battle for Urban Public Space', How We Get to Next. Available online: https://howwegettonext.com/the-evolving-battle-for-urban-public-space-8db45852c6b7#.etw6anjfy (accessed 14 July 2023).

Gold, M. and L. Klein, eds. (2016), *Debates in the Digital Humanities 2016*, Minneapolis: University of Minnesota Press.

Gwalchmai, B. (2014), '… beneath our feet, the stars …', *Playable City*. Available online: https://www.playablecity.com/projects/beneath-our-feet-the-stars/ (accessed 14 May 2023).

Hammersley, R. and C. Rodgers. (2019), 'Wastes and Strays: The Past, Present and Future of English Urban Commons', School of History, Classics and Archaeology, 20 August. Available online: https://scandalousartefacts.com/2018/08/20/wastes-and-strays-the-past-present-and-future-of-english-urban-commons/ (accessed 10 November 2022).

Hammersley, R., C. Rodgers, A. Zambelli, E. Cheatle, J. W. Clarke, S. Collins, O. Dee and S. O'Neill. (2023), *English Urban Commons: The Past, Present and Future of Green Spaces*, London: Routledge.

Hancox, D. (2019), 'Revealed: Creeping Privatisation of London Parks in Summer', *The Guardian*, 5 July. Available online: https://www.theguardian.com/cities/2019/jul/05/revealed-how-london-parks-are-partly-privatised-festivals-wireless-finsbury-park (accessed 28 June 2023).

Haraway, D. (1988), 'Situated Knowledges: The Science Question in Feminism and the Privilege of Partial Perspective', *Feminist Studies*, 14(3), 575–99.

Heidegger, M. ([1954] 1993), 'The Question Concerning Technology', in D. Krell, ed. *Basic Writings*, 307–42, London: HarperCollins.

Heidegger, M., J. Macquarrie and E. Robinson. (1962), *Being and Time*, London: Blackwell Publishing.

Labboun, S. (2017), 'Privately Owned Public Spaces Need New London Plan Rules', London Assembly. Available from: https://www.london.gov.uk/press-releases/assembly/privately-owned-public-spaces-need-new-london-plan (accessed 28 June 2023).

Levy, A. and L. Hirsch. (2020), 'Amazon Bans Police Use of Facial Recognition Technology for One Year', *CNBC*, 10 June. Available from: https://www.cnbc.com/2020/06/10/amazon-bans-police-use-of-facial-recognition-technology-for-one-year.html (accessed 28 June 2023).

MFour Mobile Research. (2016), 'Research Shows that Pokemon Go Boosts Friendships and Social Cohesion', *RW Connect*. Available online: https://rwconnect.esomar.

org/research-shows-that-pokemon-go-boosts-friendships-and-social-cohesion/ (accessed 14 March 2023).

Mackey, M. (2002), *Literacies across Media: Playing the Text*, London: Routledge.

Mangen, A. and A. van der Weel. (2016), 'The Evolution of Reading in the Age of Digitisation: An Integrative Framework for Reading Research', *Literacy*, 50(3), 116–24.

Massey, D. (1991), 'A Global Sense of Place', *Marxism Today*, 38, 24–9.

Massey, D. (2005), *For Space*, New Delhi: SAGE Publications.

Massey, D. (2006), 'London Inside-Out', *Soundings: A Journal of Politics and Culture*, 32: 62–71.

McCullough, M. (2013), *Ambient Commons*, Cambridge, MA: MIT Press.

McGarrigle, C. (2012), *The Construction of Locative Situations: The Production of Agency in Locative Media Art Practice*, Dublin: Technological University.

McGarrigle, C. (2013), 'Augmented Resistance: The Possibilities for AR and Data Driven Art', *Leonardo Electronic Almanac, Not Here Not There*, 19(1), 106–22.

Merchant, G. (2015), 'Keep Taking the Tablets: iPads, Story Apps and Early Literacy', *Australian Journal of Language & Literacy*, 38(1), 3–11.

Merleau-Ponty, M. (1968), *The Visible and the Invisible*, trans. A. Lingis. Evanston, IL: Northwestern University Press.

Merleau-Ponty, M. (1964), *Primacy of Perception*, trans. W. S. Cobb, Evanston, IL: Northwestern University Press.

Merleau-Ponty, M. (2002), *Phenomenology of Perception*, trans. C. Smith, London: Routledge.

Orange, R. (2018), 'Stockholm Says No to Apple "Town Square" in Its Oldest Park', *The Guardian*, 1 November. Available from: https://www.theguardian.com/cities/2018/nov/01/stockholm-apple-town-square-park-kings-garden-kungstradgarden (accessed 28 June 2023).

O'Rourke, K. (2016), *Walking and Mapping: Artists as Cartographers*, Cambridge, MA: MIT Press.

Paterson, M. (2007), *The Senses of Touch: Haptics, Affects and Technologies*, London: Routledge.

Peters, J. (2020), 'IBM Will No Longer Offer, Develop, or Research Facial Recognition Technology', *The Verge*, 8 June. Available online: https://www.theverge.com/2020/6/8/21284683/ibm-no-longer-general-purpose-facial-recognition-analysis-software (accessed 28 June 2023).

Piera Jimenez, J. and L. Hjorth. (2019), 'Meet Sofia: A 67-Year-Old Widow Who Uses Pokémon Go to Reconnect with Her City', *The Conversation*, 1 July. Available online: https://theconversation.com/meet-sofia-a-67-year-old-widow-who-uses-pokemon-go-to-reconnect-with-her-city-119389 (accessed 28 June 2023).

PPS. (2019), 'About – Project for Public Spaces', *Project for Public Spaces*. Available online: https://www.pps.org/about (accessed 28 June 2023).

Riva, G., R. M. Baños, C. Botella, F. Mantovani and A. Gaggioli. (2016), 'Transforming Experience: The Potential of Augmented Reality and Virtual Reality for Enhancing Personal and Clinical Change', *Frontiers in Psychiatry*, 7, 164.

Ryan, M. L. (2001), *Narrative as Virtual Reality: Immersion and Interactivity in Literature and Electronic Media*, Baltimore, MD: Johns Hopkins University Press.

Ryan, M. L. (2015), *Narrative as Virtual Reality 2: Revisiting Immersion and Interactivity in Literature and Electronic Media*, Baltimore, MD: Johns Hopkins University Press.

Sabbagh, D. (2019), 'Facial Recognition Technology Scrapped at King's Cross Site', *The Guardian*, 2 September. Available online: https://www.theguardian.com/technology/2019/sep/02/facial-recognition-technology-scrapped-at-kings-cross-development (accessed 28 June 2023).

Saker, M. and L. Evans. (2018), 'Pokémon Go Is Not Dead, It Has 5m Loyal Players and It's Changing People's Lives', *The Conversation*, 22 October. Available online: https://theconversation.com/pokemon-go-is-not-dead-it-has-5m-loyal-players-and-its-changing-peoples-lives-104095 (accessed 28 June 2023).

Shenker, J. (2017), 'London Mayor to Draw up Charter Regulating Pseudo-Public Space', *The Guardian*, 23 November. Available online: https://www.theguardian.com/cities/2017/nov/23/london-mayor-charter-pseudo-public-space-sadiq-khan (accessed 28 June 2023).

Thon, J.-N. (2008), 'Immersion Revisited: On the Value of a Contested Concept', in O. Leino, H. Wirman and A. Fernandez, eds. *Extending Experiences: Structure, Analysis and Design of Computer Game Player Experience*, 29–43, Lapland: Lapland University Press.

Ultrahaptics. (2018), 'Ultrahaptics'. Available online: https://www.ultrahaptics.com (accessed 28 June 2023).

7

Retrospect on the new epigraphy: Walking, reading and marking the city

Malcolm McCullough

While your feet tread a chosen path, the mind might wander ahead. You might mentally construct spatial connections – an axis, for instance. When the path wanders, as good ones often do, you might momentarily lose sense of this axis, only to discover it again – at a garden gate, a turn of a corner or an ascent of a stair. Contrasts in pavement texture guide without signs. Along the way, rows of trees, or perhaps regular intervals between doorways, might help you mark a rhythm and feel spatial intervals. Stairs, in particular, 'fit the feet'[1] and sharpen a sense of scale. Expressed as a verb, one *scales* a stair. In the French, the noun for stair is *escalier*. The more that you become a measure of context, the more scale can be felt relative to your own, and the more a space might seem somehow humane. For instance, to climb to a platform makes it feel like a stage, where your own sense of presence momentarily heightens as well. From there, the path might present choices. Whether a doorway admits or forbids, it brings attention to what lies beyond. To pass from a platform (or *plaza*) through a portal remains the most fundamental experience of architecture in the city. A window frames a view, which perhaps recalls an axis. A facade screens views, lights and access alike, both from outside and within. This works best not as a single taut boundary such as a sheet of glass but in layers. To walk through a series of doorways, especially through concentric layers of walls, increases the sense of passage from one set of expectations to another. Surfaces above and below reinforce such transitions. Under foot, the borders of a floor mosaic assure

1 This particular remark is nearly verbatim from, and this entire opening paragraph has been inspired by, a small design handbook from a quarter-century ago (Lyndon and Moore 1994: 50). Moore, an influential educator who once was my own architecture thesis adviser, kept a lifelong emphasis on the poetics of embodiment.

that you have arrived somewhere. Coming under a ceiling, whether a humble canopy or an elaborate dome, creates a sense of arrival at the centre. To look up physically invites you to look up metaphorically – or at least away from your mobile screen. Meanwhile, sound and light move through spaces and hours of the day too. Illuminations bathe walls. The sun falls on floors. Contrasts of light, warmth and air assist in the pursuit of comfort. Habitual experience embeds these perceptions into other receptivities and sensibilities until the variations between one place and another seem second only, as a cultural perception, to the variety amongst people themselves.

When all that is working, you might call it architecture. Ambient literature assumes an active role for architecture (Ambient Literature Project n.d.). New prospects in reading whilst walking invites a rediscovery of the built environment. As the Ambient Literature Project explained, this begins from architecture's role at setting the stage. Naturally, this works best when the narrative and spatial passages resonate, especially while walking through well-designed space, for instance, up a stair, onto a platform, through a portal, under a ceiling. This gets enacted not only through physical scale and enclosure but also through cultural framing and cueing. The context – no mere backdrop – helps us interpret words and actions, often with props and subject matter. Furthermore, some words are persistently placed within architecture itself as inscriptions. The built world is increasingly layered in these elements, and, in this, it juxtaposes ancient, everyday and newly augmented formats of communication. The more of these that exist, the less any one of them might stand out. Instead, they all blend into an ambient informational surrounding. This too expands prospects for narrative resonances. All literature is bibliographic, but ambient literature can also be epigraphic, therefore, architecture's own inscriptions deserve fresh consideration.

Back at the dawn of the handheld media boom and enabled in particular by the arrival of global positioning systems (GPS) on everyday smartphones, many new prospects arose for text in the city. Many digerati, literati, psychogeographers and urbanists, imagined some new kind of participatory notation, one name for which was 'urban markup language'.[2] Media were not only brought to street level but also sometimes affixed to it. Urban markup turns the privileged reader into an active tagger, an embodied interpreter and, at some level and with some unstudied degree of access and duration, a cultural producer. Alongside related new prospects for individual portable devices carrying book-like texts, which

[2] With origins unknown, and possibly my own, this expression was a favourite in my days at Carnegie Mellon, 1998–2000.

today is quite familiar as the Kindle, now (*c.* 2005) a more fixed, persistent form of augmentation would assume aspects of public social reading. That latter, much older form of reading has sometimes been known by a word more often associated with scholarly archaeology of such reading in ancient (pre-book) cultures, that is, 'epigraphy'. Ten years ago, it appeared as if 'new epigraphy' (McCullough 2008) might enrich place-based cultural accumulation or at least add a new layer to the city of collective memory. It would at least get people out the door for a walk.

The new epigraphy reconsidered

Technologically, the project of ambient literature belongs to a larger vision of street as platform that quickly arose with the smartphone (Russell 1999). The aughts were the heyday of this, especially the years 2003 to 2008, from the first affordable GPS-enabled mobiles to the economic crash after which digital culture so soon darkened.

Much jargon of that era still echoes: locative media, geosocial networking (think Dodgeball or Foursquare), public interactives, citizen science and, perhaps the most inclusive expression of these, *c.* 2007, urban computing. From a call for papers that year by the Institute of Electrical and Electronics Engineers (IEEE), one of the most influential research organizations in pervasive computing, here is a sampling of language: 'clicks and mortar; wireless society; street riders (car-car and car-street interactions); citizen sensors; public interaction displays and facilities; festivals, mediascapes, other new ways of experiencing the city; downtownware; urban noir; sous les pavés la plage' (Kindberg, Chalmers and Paulos 2007). The latter, which was the slogan of the soixante huitards of Paris '68, still resonates as an expression of escape from engineered and furnished meanings. Such escape remains the aim of situationalist action.

Ten years ago, when such themes were being freshly rediscovered for their relevance to handheld locative media, it seemed pertinent to rediscover situated technologies too (Kahn, Scholz and Shepard 2006–11). It seemed important to emphasize participation. The relationship between the mobile device and the augmented city would go beyond mere wayshowing. Artefacts, installations and localized inscriptions would form a vital part of this engagement. Much as the world had not disappeared through any larger desktop looking glass into what, twenty years ago, had been called cyberspace, neither would the city be dematerialized or reduced into smaller, more mobile screens. The qualities of engagement felt – for example, in ascending a stair or passing through concentric walls – would remain vital to cultural experience and so would give street-level media yet another advantage over sitting-on-a-sofa media. This engagement would be not only with space but also with particular data formations found within it, in one place and not another, and most certainly not anywhere or everywhere.

In a very general sense, the idea was this: locative sets of annotations would become a curated cultural resource. To repeat this would open a new middle ground somewhere between graffiti sprayed on the walls and decrees chiselled in stone. More specifically, and quite possibly of relevance to the project of ambient literature, something about these annotations would become a persistent part of the built environment. It would help bring that environment back into public sensibility. After all, publics tend to be inseparable from media constituencies. Similarly, good buildings represent organizations to their constituencies. And now, with the proliferation of memberships, followings and social networks as cultural filters that began to explode circa 2006, surely there would be new constituencies devoted to annotation, curation and narration of particular thematic aspects of urban place (Foth et al. 2012), for example, actual birders (ornithologists) perhaps, since ever the emblem of arbitrary interest; social justice workers of just about any stripe; historians interested in the individuals for whom streets have been named; pollution whistle-blowers; clubs of members sharing vital data about available parking spaces; performance artists; crowdsourced data installation artists; and, of course, storytellers. The question of whose narrative would be answered in countless new ways.

In a 2008 essay on the new epigraphy, it seemed as though:

> [t]here exists a new middle ground of urban markup that must become subject matter for cultural production, research, and scholarship. Neither organized 'media' as the twentieth century knew them, nor random graffiti as all the ages have witnessed, new practices of mapping, tagging, linking and sharing expand both possibilities and participation in urban inscription. These inscriptions have greater duration and access than the casual signage that must always have been a part of urban experience, for they involve distinct codes and they leave a trail. They have greater freedom and extent than the short official wordings of permanent physical inscriptions. They involve a wider or at least different population than graffiti. They serve a wider, or at least a different set of purposes than advertising or street signs. They present a new range of subject matter for cultural interpretation. They may stretch literacy in different ways than the usual tension of print versus internet. Do they form any lasting cultural body of work?
>
> (McCullough 2008: 69)

Already a new taxonomy was emerging for text in the city. This was still before the rise of the standardized wayshowing industry (such as Google Maps, Yelp and TripAdvisor). A new middle ground of unofficial, socially engaged tagging demonstrated high potential for embedded narratives. Perhaps the most influential early project, one now coming into good historic perspective, was Yellow Arrow by Brian House and Jesse Shapin (2003–07) (Johnson 2004; Todras-Whitehill 2006). As a play on familiar yellow stickies, this project affixed adhesive, arrow-shaped tags, pointing to items of interest in its pilot cities of Boston and Copenhagen. Each tag came with a unique number for sending or reading text comments, in what thus became a kind of guestbook or comment section for that particular spot. *The New York Times* called it one of the earliest instances of 'the Internet overlaid' on the physical world 'to make the city more browsable' (McCullough 2013). Other, more specifically purposeful annotation projects soon followed; and since these, too, are coming into historic perspective, another academic work might now reinterpret them; but here I will take a moment simply to mention a few genres: projection mappings on buildings, LED tags and installations, traces of waste and pollution, spatial audio installations, kiosks or cafe tables for neighbourhood lore, multiplayer GPS gaming and geocaching, historic walks and, soon enough, spatially tagged walks for all manner of specialized interests, for instance, urban botany. From within this wave of urban markup projects, Urban Tapestries (Lane 2002–05) became an important forerunner of the ambient literature project and needs no further introduction here. The point is, a rich set of prospects for smartphones were eclipsed by a flood of commercial wayshowing, in which the emblematic act became to ask your app if surely there must be some decent Thai food nearby.

Public interactive art may indeed remain the most vigorous and vital genre of the times. Working with light more often than text, and often working with activation of public plazas or projections on prominent civic buildings, public interactives get onto the streets by giving them a sense of engagement quite different from scrolling all day on their screens. The active embodiment of these works lets them communicate without messages, by way of physical and spatial resonances, often as simple as coupling an effect to an approach, where walking up to something activates it analogously. Like climbing a stair or passing through a portal, the haptic orientation of engaging these works produces cognitive and cultural resonance in ways that messages amid a message-saturated culture cannot. Moreover, some such augmentation can behave as a double, assuming the form of its architectural host. This is not the moment to interpret that genre, only to mention it, if only by naming some of its foremost practitioners, who are thus arguably some of the most eminent artists of the times: Rafael Lozano-

Hemmer, Jason Bruges, Dan Roosegarde, David Benjamin, realities:united and Random International. This is the movement preparing a larger public for a greater range of ambient art forms, all in counterpoint to the reduction of locative media into apps for commercial wayshowing. The Ambient Literature Project surely knew its place in relation to this movement but may wish to recall the importance of built public space to it all.

Text in the city

The idea of text in the city naturally goes back further than modern media (Manguel 1996) and warrants some recollection here. Information historians and media archaeologists may explain this best, and amongst those who look back furthest, there exists a discipline of 'epigraphers'. As any of these experts might explain, the basic idea that text isn't everywhere was a truism until very recently. Although any object might have had a label or a mark, most had none, and few had little more. Thus, any more elaborate inscription was itself a mark of cultural importance. Whether codex book, tablet, stele or scroll, textual objects were relatively scarce, as was literacy (at least if understood as the ability to read) (McLean 2002). When the few who could read addressed the many who wished to know, this lecture mostly occurred from rarefied objects in specialized settings. Whereas bibliographic writing and reading communicates privately, one reader at a time, this epigraphic form does so in a group, sometimes in public, for all to see. Even a book may be read in an epigraphic manner, as when glossed by one person visibly before a group. Such practice has been usual enough, whether amongst medieval scholastics or rural schoolchildren, wherever just one copy of a book was at hand or where just one person knew how to read it.

Amid such practices, physical settings often also served as communication devices themselves. Typically, they did so with mythological images to instruct a lay populace, but also sometimes with inscriptions in stone. Not only to inscribe and recite but also simply to inhabit such messages was often a devotional act in itself, and this has been an enduring basis of architectural ornament. Here the architects and literary critics find common ground. For then in an oft-told tale (and do skip ahead if this has been told once too often), most usually known by Victor Hugo's aphorism 'ceci tuera cela', mass-produced print overturned this ancient architecture practice. Not just incidentally, print enabled the long-form serial format still most associated with 'literature', the novel and, of course, a variety of other print narratives, particularly a glut of newspapers that altogether competed with, and sometimes eventually overturned, more official storylines emanating from church, state and wealth. All that seems familiar enough and has counterparts in much later internet culture, so it seems worth mentioning in any new look at ambient literature.

Meanwhile the nineteenth-century scene at street level, then, deserves fresh reconsideration today. For in comparison to the kinds of texts that literary culture has emphasized, and likewise with counterparts in digital culture today, the idea of text in the city was much more multifarious, chaotic and embodied back then, much more than literary tradition has been inclined to notice. That too was considered a glut of handheld portable media, namely, mass-produced print. In an influential study of handheld print at street level in nineteenth-century New York, historian David Henkin (1998) demonstrated the vitality, diversity and, although this word was not in use at the time, ambient experience of print in the city. Of course, a baker shuffling about the street in a sandwich-board advertisement was not at all literary. Nor was the new technology of silkscreen colour lithography, whether used for flyposting city walls or for middlebrow weekly magazines on offer in a new public fixture: the newsstand. Only a latter-day interest in social media would find textual interest in the countless calling cards left on silver platters, much less the trade cards, broadsheets and gazettes exchanged at street level. Only much later did historic perspective arise on the culture effects of standard street signs, which generally had not been introduced until the nineteenth century, or from another now standard form of wayshowing, the tourist guidebook, that also first emerged only then.

Despite this new plethora of print, buildings continued to be annotated and inscribed. New technologies of paint and screening made commercial facades and murals much more prominent. Yet more highbrow forms of text in the city also appeared, as industrial might and prosperity raised many new kinds of secular public institutions. Train stations, opera houses and grand public libraries, for instance, were elegantly inscribed in chiselled stone in the manner of the ancient Roman urbanism that inspired them. It would be difficult to imagine the architecture of the era without such proclamations.

Urban media archaeologies (Mattern 2017) extend well before and after that heyday of print and, of course, anthropologies of traditional cultures can reveal a deep connection between storytelling and spatial knowledge often enacted through walks, bearing story-related totems. In the British Isles, whose ancient traditions of lays, local legends and mythological geographies remain culturally alive, it is not so surprising, then, to have had an Ambient Literature Project.

Text in the city, as interpreted here, deserves such consideration for it may not be the most apparent heritage of ambient literature. That instead comes from twentieth-century notions, and legacy businesses, of 'media'. In that, sociologies of modern broadcast radio and television have also revealed a distinct relationship of media to urban place. Much as print might have been imagined as dematerializing architecture's communicative role, it did not do so entirely, likewise radio and television transformed, but did not eliminate, the role of architecture, the city and their inscriptions. Not just broadcast tower, not just a backdrop, the city now offered the densest variety of mediated experience, and in this it set the stage for new cultural forces. Perhaps no interpretation of media in the city remains more familiar amongst architectural urbanists and ambient literati alike than the mid-century cultural phenomena of spectacle, particularly via the street-level, critical reaction to broadcast culture. Situationist notions of *dérive*, detournement and happening seem important enough in the heritage of ambient literature to need no further explanation. Yet it is worth noting here how that was also the case in the history and theory of late twentieth-century architecture and urbanism. Many still widely held understandings of psychogeography emanated from those disciplines and, of course, from the experience of passing from plaza through portal, climbing a stair, or enjoying the play between axis and path.

Digital annotations and augmentations invite new forms of inscription in place. One difference is that not everyone will have to see them (Shepherd 2011). Choices to read a narrative, open or close filters, or follow a geocode all become part of ambient spatial reading. Portable texts with access according to positional coordinates might interweave with situated texts also made accessible through handheld narrative works. Public interactive arts, in evidence to all, may come and go and may figure in other, unanticipated readings. The embodied experience of well-built space becomes intrinsic to these forms of cultural production.

What architecture does for narrative

Thus, despite all manner of anytime anyplace entertainments, architecture and the city do not disappear from consideration. Moreover, wherever the built world remains actively incorporated into stories, whether written or implied, it does so as more than a backdrop. Well-situated narratives combine mobile text, situated inscription and wordless readings of form, configuration and scale into an active process of sense-making. As explained in an oft-cited defence of 'placing words' (Mitchell 2005: 1–20), most narratives still show up in particular physical contexts, often attached to, referring to or gaining disambiguation from their particular settings. As MIT Media lab director William Mitchell once explained, words often refer to, or take scope from, the place where they are exchanged. To shout 'Fire!' in a crowded theatre means one thing, he began, to shout 'Fire!' to a squadron of soldiers means another, to affix a 'Fire' label to a plumbing outlet is to tell firefighters where to hook up a hose, but 'if I receive the text message fire on my mobile phone, at some random moment, I can only respond with a puzzled huh?' (8). Anyone intent on narrative might understand this as '*mise-en-scène*'; a script needs a setting; objects (props and backdrops) provide orientation. Activity theory, as commonly interpreted by interaction designers or cognitive scientists, might explain this as 'scaffolding'; the objects and settings that language refers to become building blocks of action and thought. Rich metaphor depends on analogy in spatial experience (Clark 1997; Kaptelinin and Nardi 2006). 'The meaning of a local, spoken, synchronous message is a joint product of the words, the body language of the participants in the exchange, and the setting', explained Mitchell (2005: 8). Hence the resonance between stories and walks. Note how many metaphors are spatial; analogous understandings arise from embodiment.

This is not the moment to unpack a deeper explanation of embodied cognition or what is increasingly called the 'extended mind' (Clark 2008). Suffice it to say that the mind uses physical props and spatial configurations, especially habitually engaged ones, as a basis for rich tacit knowledge. As anyone skilled in a tangible craft, sport, martial art, dance or theatre might know (but remain unable to name and articulate), processes of haptic orientation let one play a situation. The quality of engagement can feel effortless. This kind of attention is not the kind one has to pay or the kind that so many unsolicited entertainments (and advertisements) attempt to steal. To anyone skilled in such practices, the quiet fascination that arises seems far preferable to the noisy entertainment that so saturates life. The difference between fascination and entertainment slowly alters sensibilities to other practices too. Encounters with literature can come from fascination with language, for example, and with the power of spatial metaphor or mise-en-scène and not from a need for entertainment. One might never need entertainment. Thus, as activity theory so well explains, you can act your way into understanding. The desire to know what is happening here depends not only on what you can do here but also what has most often been done, thought and said here. Sometimes conditions of access are enough for that; you might pass through this doorway and not that one. Sometimes scale remains the most important aspect of a space, and this is known through sound, light and strides all at once. Sometimes, like subtle traces of wear on a flight of steps, the natural data of the built world provides nameless, quietly fascinating cues. As architecture configures habitual engagements and encounters, it also unobtrusively helps make sense.

Retrospect on the new epigraphy reveals the importance of active, purposeful sense-making. What ten years ago was a new middle ground between transgressive graffiti (sprayed on the walls) and official proclamations (in expensive backlit signage if no longer so often chiselled in stone) today has become flooded with wayshowing apps and practices, most of them handheld and commercial. Prospects for nonmonetized participatory annotations and augmentations of built space do remain, not only in ambient literature but also in citizen science, urban explorations and, of course, civil dissent. These too have advanced relative to their state ten years ago but not relative to today's obsessions in handheld wayshowing and entertainments. Thus, the prospect of a new epigraphy, and perhaps also of the larger genre of ambient literature, needs new emphasis on background, embodiment, tacit knowledge, persistent spaces and ongoing fascinations. Its annotations and inscriptions need more sense from architectural form and not just geographic coordinates. Its engagements need more haptic orientation, more atmospheric effects, far less pointing and almost no dropping of tags/pins on pre-existing virtual maps. As any good situationalist could explain, the spatial mental map must be enacted, not furnished.

Done best, the new epigraphy pushes back against today's blunt practices of endless instructions, advertisements and entertainments. Ambient literature may necessarily operate amid such a numbing set of circumstances, but it does so with distinct advantage. For the more of those distractions there are in a space, the more they just blend all together into some more ambient condition and hence fail in their aim to capture attention. The greater the glut of information at street level, the more important it becomes to have your own narrative and thread. Only the ones with a story get through. Walking brings many a story to life. Resonances between narrative and spatial passages deserve to become much more a part of that again. Amid contentions of data, those with a story prevail. But then amid competitions amongst stories themselves, those sent from afar, and those about somewhere else, do tend to pale against stories being enacted right here.

References

Ambient Literature Project. (n.d.), 'Ambient Literature'. Available online: https://research.ambientlit.com/ (accessed 10 November 2022).

Clark, A. (1997), *Being There: Putting Brain, Body and World Together Again*, Cambridge, MA: MIT Press.

Clark, A. (2008), *Supersizing the Mind: Embodiment, Action, and Cognitive Extension*, Oxford: Oxford University Press.

Foth, M., L. Forlano, C. Satchell and M., Gibbs, eds. (2012), *From Social Butterfly to Engaged Citizen: Urban Informatics, Social Media, Ubiquitous Computing, and Mobile Technology to Support Citizen Engagement*, Cambridge, MA: MIT Press.

Henkin, D. (1998), *City Reading: Written Words and Public Spaces in Antebellum New York*, New York: Columbia University Press.

Johnson, C. (2004), 'Yellow Arrow Aimed at Building Art Community', *Harvard Crimson*, 19 November. Available online: https://www.thecrimson.com/article/2004/11/19/yellowarrow-aimed-at-building-art-community/ (accessed 23 November 2022).

Kahn, O., T. Scholz, and M. Shepard (2006–11), *The Situated Technologies Pamphlets Series*, New York: Architecture League of New York.

Kaptelinin, V. and B. A. Nardi. (2006), *Acting with Technology: Activity Theory and Interaction Design*, Cambridge, MA: MIT Press.

Kindberg, T., M. Chalmers and E. Paulos. (2007), 'Guest Editors' Introduction: Urban Computing', *IEEE Pervasive Computing*, 6(3), 20.

Lane, G. (aka Proboscis). (2002–05), 'Urban Tapestries'. Available online: http://research.urbantapestries.net/ (accessed 23 November 2022).

Lyndon, D. and C. W. Moore. (1994), *Chambers for a Memory Palace*, Cambridge, MA: MIT Press.

Manguel, A. (1996), *A History of Reading*, London: Harper Collins.

Mattern, S. (2017), *Code and Clay, Data and Dirt–Five Thousand Years of Urban Media*, Minneapolis: University of Minnesota Press.

McCullough, M. (2008), 'Epigraphy and the Public Library', in A. Aurigi and F. de Cindro, eds. *Augmented Urban Spaces: Articulating the Physical and Electronic City*, 61–71, Aldershot: Ashgate.

McCullough, M. (2013), *Ambient Commons: Attention in the Age of Embodied Information*, Cambridge, MA: MIT Press.

McLean, B. H. (2002), *An Introduction to Greek Epigraphy of the Hellenistic and Roman Periods from Alexander the Great until Constantine*, Ann Arbor: University of Michigan Press.

Mitchell, W. (2005), 'In the First Place', in *Placing Words: Symbols, Space, and the City*, 1–20, Cambridge, MA: MIT Press.

Russell, B. (1999), 'Headmap Manifesto – Know Your Place/Location Aware Devices', Headmap. Available online: http://www.headmap.org/ (accessed 10 November 2022).

Shepherd, M. (2011), *Sentient City: Ubiquitous Computing, Architecture, and the Future of Urban Space*, Cambridge, MA: MIT Press.

Todras-Whitehill, E. (2006), 'Making Connections Here and Now', *The New York Times*, 25 January: 3.

8

Ambient activism: Place, people and process

Donna Hancox

Introduction

Ambient storytelling is not necessarily a new form of story-making or story sharing. Its current iteration is informed by both the technological and social developments surrounding it, but its lineage can be found in tactical or guerrilla media, the work of the Situationist International and the DIY aesthetic of the 1980s and 1990s. Despite this, ambient storytelling has emerged as one of the most esoteric and least understood of the types of storytelling. It does not have the commercial understanding generated through the games industry of pervasive storytelling or the everyday use and identifiability of transmedia storytelling. The very nature of ambience is its simultaneous there and not-thereness. Ambience, particularly in ambient storytelling, is closely associated with embodiment and phenomenological understandings and experiences of place. The Manifesto created by the Ambient Literature Project neatly describes ambient literature as, 'a cluster of literary and (generalised) technological practices which actively engage the contextual and extra-textual apparatuses inherent in the meaningful function of literary works' (Marcinkowski and Hayler 2017). These contextual and extra-textual apparatuses often come in the form of digital applications. The role of technology in ambient storytelling presents as a *Catch 22*: it both enables uncanny and unexpectedly visceral experiences whilst also being constantly in danger of disrupting the experience. One significant observation that has emerged from the Ambient Literature Project is that ambience is understood as 'unstable and restless' (Dovey and Speakman 2018: 39). I would also add that it is a process rather than a phenomenon. The lasting impact of the ambient might be its ability to elevate the ordinary or everyday into something profound or to make the anonymous feel familiar.

Malcolm McCullough's (2013) book *Ambient Commons* examines the nature of ambient information and its effect on our attention. Although not focused on storytelling or activism per se, it does offer some original and thought-provoking insights into how we might consider the term 'ambient' in a phenomenological context and how embodiment might ground ambience in stories and particularly locative storytelling. Before considering embodiment, one of the interesting aspects to the ambient is the accumulative effect it has on our lives and experiences. Each small, subtle and sometimes seemingly inconsequential detail or addition builds inexorably towards an experience or awareness. The audience may not notice the getting there but they certainly know when they arrive. This feature of the ambient is present in advertising, activism, storytelling and social media; as Clive Thompson pointed out when writing about the ascent of Twitter in 2008 for *The New York Times*, the 'paradox of ambient awareness' in relationships is a specific consequence of social media. For McCullough, 'each little update – each individual bit of social information – is insignificant on its own, even supremely mundane. But taken together, over time, the little snippets coalesce into a surprisingly sophisticated portrait' (2013: 12).

The ambient as a term could be a simple way of categorizing a complex and complicated set of phenomena. It usefully conflates several noteworthy conditions found where a new attitude about attention meets a new era of information technology becoming situated in the world (McCullough 2013: 18). This intersection of attention and technology is the defining feature of ambient activism. This chapter examines the nature and elements of ambience and the ways they have shaped contemporary political and social activism. Similarly, I will propose that recent social developments have also shaped how we might understand ambient storytelling in more grounded and accessible ways. Through a series of case studies, I suggest that ambient activism can be understood as place-based, people-centred and oriented towards process and progress rather than outputs or outcomes.

From tactical to ambient

The projects explored in this chapter are examples of the ways in which ambient activism might be seen both as a dynamic set of features and processes which are part of a continuum of activism and advocacy, and as an emerging form with its own conventions and boundaries. One of the obvious precursors of and inspiration for ambient activism is tactical media. The concept comes from de Certeau's theory of strategic versus tactical ways of being in *The Practice of Everyday Life* (2011). Tactical methods fall outside the accepted and acknowledged ways of doing and being, so they are often not only sidelined but also disparaged or derided by those in power. Ambient activism invites us to attend to place, and to be aware of ourselves as we move around or to be aware of the way others might intrude on our space. As with all things ambient, 'the question of how to define or understand the concept of tactical media is a slippery one, as it is continuously re-articulated through practice' (TMF Editors 2017). The origins of tactical media are in the DIY artist and activist philosophy and aesthetic of the 1980s and 1990s. It was always an outward rather than reflective movement. In a similar way, ambient activism exists through its practices.

This emphasis on exploring the practices of the ambient rather than a critical inquiry of it avoids the possibility that the various applications or projects can be easily conflated. Ambient literature can also be created or experienced as ambient activism, or ambient activism can be construed or co-opted as ambient advertising. In her 2020 article 'How Ambient Advertising is Uniquely Placed to Make Audiences Think', Miriam Sorrentino (2020) discusses the merits of using ambient advertising to get through to cynical audiences. However, a number of examples she uses in this article as ambient advertising I would categorize as ambient activism, and much of the focus was on analogue and situated practices as an antidote to the ubiquity of technology. The blurred boundary between advertising and activism presented in this article was initially alarming, but it also illuminated the fluidity of late-stage capitalism, the ways that attention and spectacle can simultaneously be co-opted for commerce and social change, and that the concept of ambience is multifunctional. This pliability of ambience can be both a strength and a limitation. 'Ambient advertising is one of these alternative forms, deliberately placed where audiences go rather than in demarcated advertising sites. It playfully and imaginatively uses or places objects in everyday spaces to communicate a message on behalf of brands or organisations' (Sorrentino 2020). Sorrentino then goes on to outline the four characteristics of ambient advertising as creativity, unexpectedness, engagement and subtlety.

The power of tactical storytelling is in its ability to identify and optimize the practices of under-represented groups and amplify them creatively. The discussions of the Zapatista movement and the protests at Standing Rock in this chapter demonstrate how tactical storytelling can be used, and how stories can become ambient. Stories are inscriptions on our history; Malcolm McCullough contrasted the difference between 'durable' inscriptions (such as those carved into stone, on buildings or statues) and 'ephemeral' inscriptions (such as graffiti, banners and billboards). Most mobile media narratives fall along the spectrum of durable and ephemeral inscriptions. Jeremy Rifken suggests that through technology, we are brought together in an ever-closer embrace and increasingly exposed to each other in ways that are without precedent. Whilst the backlash of globalization – the xenophobia, political populism and terrorist activity – is widely reported, far less attention has been paid to the growing empathetic extension, as hundreds of millions of people encounter diverse others (Rifken 2010: 425). The development of empathy through exposure to experiences beyond our own, and that this empathy builds awareness of our own responsibility for and benefit from oppression, needs to be set aside. As Susan Sontag states 'instead we extend to others beset by war and murderous politics for a reflection on how our privileges are located on the same map as their suffering, and may – in ways we might prefer not to imagine – be linked to their suffering, as the wealth of some may imply the destitution of others, is a task for which the painful, stirring images supply only an initial spark' (2004: 102).

Ambient activism can be understood as those processes and cultures focused on illuminating hitherto overlooked aspects of a social or political issue by explicitly presenting them in the practices and sites of our everyday life. This is the unexpectedness Sorentino describes, and it creates both an off kilter and intriguing experience for audiences. Whether that be flooding social media or creative interventions, for instance, billboards or installations which initially appear to be part of the landscape but instead confront the public about social issues in the places where the contested practices occur. For example, the light installation outside Goldman Sachs stating Tax Evader or billboards about fossil fuels on freeways. Ambient activism is commonly seen as a resistant practice and can be understood as part of a series of disruptive exercises such as culture jamming, which traded in unexpected and off kilter visual experiences. However, back in 2006, Jenkins questioned whether 'the old concept of culture jamming has outlived its usefulness. The old rhetoric of opposition and co-option assumed a world where consumers had little direct power to shape the media' (2006: 225–6) and 'resistance becomes an end in and of itself rather than a tool to ensure cultural diversity and corporate responsibility' (259).

In particular, these interventions make visible the experiences of the people directly involved or directly impacted by the issue in an effort to 'create alternative media representations and express alternative political imaginaries based on an emerging network ideal' (Juris 2004: 98). This approach echoes Castells' theory of networked power and 'the re-programming of communication networks, so becoming able to convey messages that introduce new values to the minds of people and inspire hope for political change' (2009: 8). There are many ways to disrupt existing representations of issues but place-based ambient activism can be especially effective. For example, if activist activities such as culture jamming used imagination and appropriation to draw attention to problems, ambient activism has the potential to also draw attention to potential for change that can be led from within communities. This is particularly evident in the Standing Rock and Zapatista examples. One of the important aspects of these two projects is a commitment to a decentralized concept of authorship that does not privilege one voice, one part of the story or one platform over another.

Place-based

Mobile phone technology has shaped ambient activism. It has changed not only the places in which we can create projects to advocate for change but also how technology interacts with people and place to create those stories. The place-based nature of ambient activism is both its propensity for in-situ interventions and its ability to illuminate the nuances of place for audiences. We have seen a movement in interactive art and activist practices via mobile technology that is designed to defamiliarize people with places and the devices they are attached to. This can be described as creative misuse which encourages the audience/participant to reconsider their relationship to both devices and place through the intentional repurposing of either or both elements.

As an underlying philosophy of place, Malpas' declaration that 'place is integral to the very structure and possibility of experience … There is no possibility of understanding human existence – and especially human thought and experience – other than through an understanding of place' (2018: 13) is an excellent starting point. In this chapter, I position place as a defining feature of disruptive forms of ambient activism and that in these projects place is distinct from location or setting. It is used uniquely to build relationships between those whose story is being told, audiences, participants and the power structures being challenged. So, beyond the philosophical concept put forward by Malpas, what is place? It is a term and an experience that is at once familiar and vague. As human geographer, Tim Cresswell states: '[p]lace is a word that seems to speak for itself. It is also a problem as no one quite knows what they are talking about when they are talking about place. Place is not a specialised piece of academic terminology. It is a word we use daily in the English-speaking world. It is a word wrapped in common sense' (2011: 127).

Cresswell goes on to distinguish between space and place, stating that place suggests meaning and attachment, while space is more associated with abstraction and action. Similarly, Marxist human geographer, Doreen Massey (1991) makes the point that space and place sit in opposition to one another, and that whilst space might be viewed as ephemeral, place can be considered in context of positionality and 'one's place in the world'. Three things gather in place: materialities, meaning and process. These three things are crucial to ambient activism, that is, the materiality of such an ephemeral practice and the meanings that are embedded in the processes.

In 2020, place moved from an abstract concept to become more immediate and important than any of us could have imagined. We were confined to our homes and our immediate neighbourhoods for so much of the past two years, and paradoxically whilst international travel all but halted entirely, our lives were evermore connected to the events occurring across the globe.

Place is personal and for that very reason has the potential to be revolutionary. It is not a transactional feature that serves a purpose to attract audiences or to sell a product, rather it is to create connection and understanding. Place is filled with memories, traditions, smells, sounds, animals, trees, food, ancestors, hope, truth, injustices, resistance and love. If it is harder to hurt someone when you know their story, perhaps it is also easier to understand someone when you know the place that is theirs, and perhaps place is the story? When considering how differently we might treat the world and people if we thought more about place rather than a series of spaces or locations, Cresswell poignantly notes that 'cruise missiles are programmed with locations and spatial references. If they could be programmed with "place" instead, with all the understanding it implies, they might decide to ditch in the desert' (2011: 128). The notion of place in ambient activism is inextricably linked with people and their lives, and in doing so locates them within a political and social context. A sense of place, according to Cresswell, is found in the meanings associated with a place, that is, the feelings and emotions a place invokes (136).

Place-based engagement is not simply being physically present in a geographic location; it adheres to encompassing a more nuanced and expansive philosophy of place. Beyond the philosophical concept put forward by Malpas, what is place? It is a term and an experience that is at once familiar and vague. In this way place is an integral part of ambient activism, in its centrality to understanding complex issues, allowing for nuance and subtlety and for its ability to both immerse and unsettle audiences simultaneously. Each of the projects discussed in this chapter are inextricably tied to place.

It Must Have Been Dark by Then, a multimedia experience created by Duncan Speakman in 2017 for the Ambient Literature Project, is a profoundly subtle piece of ambient activism addressing the climate catastrophe we are currently living through. Speakman has a professional background as a composer and sound artist, and the ambient soundscapes are a major aspect of all of his work. *It Must Have Been Dark by Then* could be most basically described as an audio walk, but it is much more than that. Participants are given a mobile phone with a software application containing a library of audio stories, music, field recordings and interviews, as well as sound isolating headphones and a physical book. From any starting point in any city, you choose a route based on prompts, then create a digital map of your journey. Along the way you hear stories and sounds from other places, then overlay those on the streets you are walking through. In each location you are invited to make connections between the place you are in and the places in the audio stories. Effectively, you create a map of where you are walking and the disappearing places described in the audio stories, and the map you create exists at the intersection of physical and ambient environments. I had the great privilege of experiencing *It Must Have Been Dark by Then* on a hot summer's day in London in 2017. I was extremely jet lagged, it was a stifling day (even for an Australian) and I was in a city I don't really know and don't especially like, so walking around and exploring my environment was the last thing I wanted to do. Fast forward an hour and I was sitting in a tiny garden oasis in the middle of Soho weeping at the fleeting beauty of the world we live in. Such is the unexpected and subtle power of this work.

The sounds and stories presented to you are from three locations that were at the time the coal face of the climate emergency: Latvia, eastern and central Tunisia, and southern Louisiana. The personal accounts of loss and an uncertain future as a result of the effects of climate change bring together the overwhelming global issue alongside the individual and community lived experiences of natural and human-made disasters. Dovey and Speakman note that the sites themselves were initially chosen as being representative of changing or disappearing environments, exploring Latvia's rapidly shrinking population, the sinking wetlands of Louisiana and desertification in Tunisia. 'As the recorded material was compiled and reflected on through an iterative production process, the notion of disappearance moved us toward thinking of *It Must Have Been Dark By Then* as a new kind of eco-critical work of ambient activism' (Dovey and Speakman 2018: 34). There is a sharp intimacy in the work that forces the audience to hold two simultaneous thoughts in their head by creating an experience that Paula Levine describes as 'enabling place to be both local and global at the same time' (2014: 145).

As mentioned above in relation to tactical media, this collapsing of the global and local became most evident during the heights of globalization in the early 1990s, and the catchphrase 'act local, think global' could be seen on shopping bags, T-shirts and billboards. Its precise message at the time was not always clear; it was attached to everything from the environmental and recycling movement to selling products for multinational corporations. Both the sentiment and the action of acting locally and thinking globally have come full circle during the Covid-19 pandemic. We are once again powerfully reminded that what happens on the other side of the world has direct consequences on all of us, and that we affect change from within communities and those changes ripple out. Ambient activism creates spaces and actions that allow the participant to consider these thoughts together at the same time and to embody a map showing our individual paths for attending to our environments respectfully. This use of the physical environment as an active resource 'means that skills can neither be acquired nor applied nor explained without it. This is a fundamental premise of tacit knowledge' (McCullough 2013: 79). As participants, our embodiment of the journey we are guided through in *It Must Have Been Dark by Then* provides an orientation through the ongoing climate emergency.

People-centred places

In 2016, the Native American Sioux tribe of Standing Rock fought to stop the Dakota Access Pipeline that would see an oil pipeline run under their land and reservation. The pipeline would transfer oil from the Bakken oil fields in North Dakota and Montana across the Plains to Illinois. The protestors, numbering in their thousands and including hundreds of members of different tribes, argued that completing the pipeline would desecrate ancestral lands, threaten the water supply and unfairly burden the Standing Rock Sioux tribe, which would be unlikely to benefit from any economic development that accompanied the project. Through social media, often using video to livestream significant events, the resistance at Standing Rock has garnered international attention.

The protests played through real life. On the streets protests also had a lasting impact on the consciousness of people around the world through the lifting of First Nations voices, introducing many non-Indigenous people to water protectors, and through imagery of peaceful protests by people on their own land in the face of riot police who appeared armed for a military operation. Author and activist Naomi Klein says that 'although stopping the pipeline was crucial, there was something greater at work in this convergence. The camps were now a place where Indigenous and non-Indigenous people alike were learning to live in relationship and community with the land' (2017: 308). These events were amplified through digital media but were grounded in place and signalled a renewed collective power and model for social activism in North America. Although these protests did not stop the pipeline running through Standing Rock, the protests continue, and in Canada there are similar protests occurring. Justice may still seem a long way off, but continued protest and continued amplification of First Nations voices are shifting, albeit too slowly, the ways we think about place and protection over profit. The feel-good, no-effort nature of some online activism can result in quick uptake and just as quick forgetting. But, as was the case with Standing Rock, it is rarely considered to be an answer in and of itself, rather a way of broadcasting or amplifying an issue or the increasing urgency of an issue and to connect people. As Leshu Torchin notes, online connections can help overcome obstacles of space, time, income and knowledge, to share stories and information linking people to each other and the opportunities for action. That signalled an important acknowledgement: while online action alone cannot solve a problem, it can be a very useful tool to mobilize people and focus attention on a crucial issue (Torchin 2016).

The pervasiveness of the campaign at Standing Rock, in what could be considered a very niche or local issue, garnered attention and support around the world. The impact of this campaign is in its capacity to make us feel and to incite those not affected by the issue to take action, and it does this through powerful symbolism. There are two examples of these moments that are imbued with symbolism and connection, and that can reach far beyond people already interested or involved in the Standing Rock protests. The first is a video of the Chief forgiving a group of military veterans who sat in front of him to acknowledge the centuries of state violence suffered by Native American people, including the violence during the Standing Rock protests. The video is an extraordinary example of a transcendent moment that was the culmination of a range of activities, stories, immersions and a celebration of place as a site of healing and revolution. For Schandorf and Karatzogianni, '[t]he Standing Rock apologia where authorship and authority are as multiple and complex as the multi-modalities of production and consumption' (2018: 149). The sophistication, complexity or connection of the technology is only as interesting as the people and purposes it is being used by and for. This centring of place allows for new, and almost completely unexplored, ways of resisting, protesting, coming together, sharing, informing and also locating this otherwise ephemeral or abstract activity in the world with humans and non-human actors to anchor the hope and the hurt in something tangible and important. It is harder to dismiss or forget about an issue when it is tied to something or someone we can see and hear.

As an example of ambient activism, the Standing Rock protests had the effect of being everywhere – across all social media platforms, in graffiti in San Francisco and part of the zeitgeist in popular culture – with multiple avenues for participation both in real life and virtually. Despite the ubiquity of the Standing Rock protests, the First Nations owners of the land have continued to keep the place and the people at the centre of all discussions, reminding supporters that the issue is rooted in the land and its Traditional Owners. By connecting people and culture to place, the 'organizers' of the protests also inform, educate and radicalize individuals who have no vested interest in this particular issue. The scale of the interest in Standing Rock was clear at one of the key moments during the protest when 1 million people checked in at Standing Rock using Facebook to disrupt and overwhelm police attempts to monitor activity at the site. Whilst this specific act of disruption and protest was seen as a pivotal moment, perhaps due to the scale of interaction and the overwhelming presence of non-Indigenous actors in that form of protest, it is by no means the most influential or important aspect of the long-running protests as Standing Rock. Whilst well intentioned, the checking in on Facebook as an act of solidarity perpetuated some of the most persistent criticisms of digital and ambient activism, and generated a fair amount of scepticism about the usefulness of the online activity associated with the Standing Rock protests. 'On Tuesday, the hashtag #DAPL trended nationwide for a little while, and then was eclipsed by chatter about the Academy Awards nominations. If social media and live streaming enabled Standing Rock Sioux to amplify their protest for clean water, its speed and ceaseless flow also allowed the world to forget about them' (Dreyfuss 2017).

It would be simple from the outside to consider the protest that occurred at Standing Rock through the lens of purely social media and to dismiss it as a way for people to feel good about themselves with very little action or in a way that is purely performative. This critique would fail to see or value the intentions of the First Nations people protecting their land and water at Standing Rock to make visible an issue that is continually overlooked in mainstream media. This 'making visible' is a key aspect of ambient activism, the ephemeral and persistent nature of the protests serves to illuminate and encourage the public to explore the issue further, whilst also ensuring that there is a foundation to the protests 'in real life'. While the Dakota Pipeline has still not been resolved, the Biden administration appointed First Nations woman Deb Haaland as the Secretary of the Interior in 2021. During the hearings prior to her appointment, Secretary Haaland was open about her opposition to the Dakota Pipeline and is committed to working to have the existing legislation from the Trump administration overturned. This focus on raising awareness through the authentic voices of those most impacted and led by the most under-represented was also a feature of the Zapatista movement which will be discussed further below.

Creating ambient soundscapes and audio experiences that are able to confront the enormity of climate change and to simultaneously encourage the audience to engage with rather than retreat from our natural environment is powerful and difficult. Any entrenched social challenge that is either not immediately apparent or only affect an already marginalized cohort requires a particular brand of creativity to encourage people to engage enough to create change. Place-based ambient works seek not only to make the audience aware of their surroundings but also to be embodied in those surroundings in a way that allows for a new understanding of that place, and the people who inhabit it. Dovey and Speakman's (2018) article 'Anthropocene Elegy and GeoSpatial Presence' explores *It Must Have Been Dark By Then* and the role of sound in creating a geospatial presence to affect a critical awareness of a broad planetary presence that we must attend to. Another project that makes use of sound in exciting and profound ways is the Australian project *Listening to Country*. The aim of *Listening to Country* was to explore the value of acoustic ecology in promoting cultural connection, maintenance and well-being among Aboriginal and Torres Strait Islander women in prison.

In early 2019, an interdisciplinary team of researchers worked with women in Brisbane Women's Correctional Centre (BWCC) to produce eighty-seven immersive audio works based on field recordings of natural environments (of country) for the purpose of stress relief and relaxation. This project responded to a direct request from a group of Aboriginal women at BWCC to create a culturally appropriate sound recording for the purpose of reducing stress and connecting to natural environments and to country. The project team consisted of two Indigenous and two non-Indigenous researchers working in collaboration: Dr Vicki Saunders (Gunggari), Dr Bianca Beetson (Gubbi Gubbi/Kabi Kabi), Dr Sarah Woodland and Dr Leah Barclay. As with *It Must Have Been Dark By Then Listening to Country* uses sound as a means through which to be in and connect to place, with the underlying belief that our lives and our planet depend on this connection.

Acoustic ecology is the study of the relationship, mediated through sound, between human beings and their environment, and has an academic history associated with 'Steven Feld's "acoustomology" with sound as a distinctive medium for knowing the world and Pauline Oliveros' "deep listening" where sound facilitates expanded consciousness and healing with transformational changes in the body and mind' (Woodland et al. 2019: 41). However, this academic history is superseded by the Indigenous practice and research perspective of 'dadirri – listening to the world around us, the Country' (42). Whilst *It Must Have Been Dark By Then* encourages us to listen to the voices of the people living through extreme climate events and to the landscape to consider how we live on this planet and the protests at Standing Rock, listening to Country provides agency and benefits for the participants through the process of creating and listening to the sound recordings. For the audience of the research, the recording and the findings force us to consider what the isolation and acoustic grimness of incarceration must be like and the ways First Nations people, women especially, are detached from their Country, families and children when imprisoned, then to think about the staggering over-representation of First Nations people in prison in Australia and how this is connected to our history of taking them from their Country and family through a series of government policies since invasion. The sound of Country and the story of the project forces the audience to confront all these things with subtlety, inviting us into the experience and connecting us to incarcerated women, whilst also revealing the deep connection to Country that First Nations people have.

Both the protests at Standing Rock and *Listening to Country* centre around place, not as an experience or location but as an opportunity to learn from First Nations people about connection to Country and how this intersects with ways of addressing systemic racism, racial and environmental justice. By immersing audiences in place, the creators are able to close the distance generally felt between Indigenous and non-Indigenous people to encourage a shared human experience.

Process over output

The Standing Rock protests had a great deal in common with the Zapatista movement and uprising in Mexico in the 1990s. The Zapatista Army of National Liberation (EZLN) was an Indigenous movement demanding 'work, land, housing, food, health, education, independence, liberty, democracy, justice and peace'. This bold set of demands came from Indigenous farmers based in the state of Chiapas, which is the wealthiest state in Mexico due to rich natural resources; however, half of the Indigenous population report making no income at all and 70 per cent suffer from high levels of malnutrition. Whilst at first the demands may seem abstract, they were, in fact, grounded in struggles over self-determination, in particular the North American Free Trade Agreement (NAFTA) in the early 1990s, which would see Indigenous Mexicans even further marginalized and locked out from farming their land. Through a series of protests, including occupying municipal buildings in the tourist town of San Cristobal de las Casas on New Year's Eve 1994 and reading out a manifesto from the balcony, the Zapatistas exploded onto the global stage. Throughout the 1990s and early 2000s, there was international interest and support of the Zapatistas, so much so that it inspired me to travel from Brisbane, Australia to San Cristobal to visit a Zapatista community in 2001. That is another story.

The Zapatistas made use of the internet in its early days to publish lengthy and detailed communiques which used poetic and evocative language to inspire activists outside Chiapas. Uniquely, they demonstrated a commitment to mobilizing locally, whilst being willing to expand out their calls for justice to represent the 'voice of voicelessness for many of Mexico's poor … and to communicate a vision of justice so universal that people all over the world felt included in their struggle' (Klein 2017). The spokesperson for the Zapatistas Subcomandante Marcos once famously stated:

> We are you. Marcos is a gay in San Francisco, black in South Africa, an Asian in Europe, a Chicano in San Ysidro, an anarchist in Spain, a Palestinian in Israel, a Mayan Indian in the streets of San Cristobal, a Jew in Germany, a Gypsy in Poland, a Mohawk in Quebec, a pacifist in Bosnia, a single woman on the Metro at 10pm, a peasant without land, a gang member in the slums, an unemployed worker, an unhappy student, and of course a Zapatista in the mountains.

Even within their own movement they centred the voices of women and young people, which was radical in a Latin American revolutionary movement. Doing this demonstrated their determination to walk their talk around justice and to ensure the next generation of activists. What the Zapatistas understood was that to generate interest in forgotten unloved places and empathy for unknown and unheard voices you need to demonstrate authenticity and create a sense of connection for people not affected by those concerns.

The northwest of Tasmania is one of the lowest socio-economic electorates in the poorest state in Australia, and the suburb of Shorewell Park is one of the most under-served and marginalized communities in this area. It was established in the 1970s as a social housing estate and continues to face stigma in Burnie. Peak Tasmanian biennial arts festival, Ten Days on the Island (https://www.tendays.org.au/), commissioned Sydney-based theatre company Urban Theatre Projects (UTP) to develop a community-led project in Burnie for their 2019 festival programme. The community and UTP knew they wanted to deliver a quality event, which made the people and place visible and challenged some of the views that had stigmatized Shorewell Park since its development. UTP co-created with Burnie Community House and the Shorewell Park community an outdoor community dinner in the park beside the community house. Selected guests (twenty-five from Shorewell Park and twenty-five from the rest of Burnie) co-mingled in a gala-style, ambient setting of fairy lights, good food, live entertainment and with card prompts as conversation starters. The concept of the dinner party was driven by the community and takes a performative approach to bringing Burnie to Shorewell Park, whereby primarily controlling their own representation and identity narrative. This event's success cemented the community's affiliation and trust with UTP, and led to a large-scale public art project representing the hopes and strengths of the Shorewell Park community.

During an eight-week community engagement process asking the community how they would like to be seen and what they would like to say to the broader Burnie community a series of public billboards were created titled *The Gallery of Hopes and Dreams*. The billboards are visually striking with bright paintings of local birds with slogans such as 'We Are Better Together'. The billboards were placed throughout the community and created a positive ambient backdrop to otherwise unremarkable spaces. The most important aspect of the project was the process that supported the community to have complete ownership over the project and that the images and words were inclusive of everyone, including children and young people. This meant the choice of phrases used was a participatory, deeply thoughtful process, and the community gave careful consideration, over a seven-week process, to the design and wording. When individuals and communities are supported to respond to questions about who they are, the place they inhabit and how they see their futures with the freedom to choose what they want to communicate and how they want to represent themselves, we see very different approaches and insights.

As our human experiences change and evolve it is not surprising that why we need to tell stories, who gets to tell stories and how we share them also changes and evolves. This can be a disruptive and challenging, as well as affirming, process. Robert McFarlane states 'old forms of representation are experiencing drastic new pressures and being tasked with daunting new responsibilities' (2016: 6). Both these new responsibilities and the previously unheard voices that are seeking to be heard need new forms to be able to advocate and educate about the issues that impact them.

The similarities between the water protectors and protestors at Standing Rock and the Zapatistas go beyond their concerns over land and their opposition to multinational companies exploiting the resources of land or the interest by celebrities. The connection is that the success and longevity of the movements are based in years of protest that understand there are no easy or fast answers to ongoing colonization; philosophies and demands about justice; sustainability and self-determination that are both localized and universal; and the use of a range of media, communications and activities that reflect the protestors rather than seek to grab an audience. Klein points out that there are many lessons for social movements from the Zapatistas: they offered viable examples of alternatives to global capitalism through local cooperatives that valued community well-being above profit, and they saw that whilst there are distinct experiences of injustice across the world, it is important to collectivize and communicate 'as a reference point in terms of knowing that it is possible to change things at their root' (Klein 2017) and to share local solutions to global oppression.

This inclusivity – in intentions, people, place, language and action – means that achieving justice or equality for all these groups cannot realistically be an indicator of success. Rather, the aim must be to progress a series of ideas around social justice and to create a network of activists who are able to see the interconnected nature of inequality. Essentially, an ambient movement capable of being creative, intimate, personal, identifiable, sweeping and specific.

The Zapatistas did not name their enemy as the Mexican state but as a set of economic policies known as 'neoliberalism'. This idea of an amorphous 'enemy' is increasingly common in contemporary activism and social change. When the 'enemy' is fluid, disguised as an unbeatable system, baked into every part of our lives through legislation or culture, the avenues of fighting need to be evermore creative, simultaneously invisible and bold, hidden in plain sight. In other words: ambient. It is not only the activism that has evolved as ambient, the circumstances it is fighting can also be understood as ambient.

In the same way community focus of *The Gallery of Hopes and Dreams* and the immersion in Country and Culture of *Listening to Country* have understood that to penetrate indifference, ignorance or injustice that seems all pervasive we need to be willing to recreate and redefine the places we inhabit and invite people to experience. The true powers of ambient activism are its attendance to place as integral to every experience, its ability to centre marginalized voices in unexpected places and the richness of process which supersedes outputs. This combination offers uniquely personalized, global stories and experiences to affect social change.

References

Castells, M. (2009), *Communicative Power*, New York: Oxford University Press.

Cresswell, T. (2011), 'Defining Place', in M. Himley and A. Fitzsimmons, eds. *Critical Encounters with Texts: Finding a Place to Stand*, 7th edn, 127–36, Boston: Pearson.

De Certeau, M. (2011), *The Practice of Everyday Life*, Berkeley: University of California Press.

Dovey, J. and D. Speakman. (2018), 'Anthropocene Elegy and Geospatial Presence', *Media Theory*, 2(1), 32–56.

Dreyfuss, E. (2017), 'Social Media Made the World Care about Standing Rock – and Helped it Forget', *Wired*, 24 January. Available online: www.wired.com/2017/01/social-media-made-world-carestanding-rock-helped-forget/ (accessed 10 November 2022).

Jenkins, H. (2006), *Convergence Culture*, New York: Routledge.

Juris, J. (2004), Networked Social Movements: Global Movements for Global Justice', in C. Manuel, ed. *The Network Society: A Cross-cultural Perspective*, 341–61, Northampton: Edward Edgar.

Klein, N. (2017), *No Is Not Enough: Defeating the New Shock Politics*, New York: Penguin Books.

Levine, P. (2014), 'On Common Ground: Here As There', in J. Farman, ed. *The Mobile Story: Narrative Practices with Locative Technologies*, 143–58, London: Routledge.

Malpas, J. (2018), *Place and Experience: A Philosophical Topography*, 2nd edn, Abingdon: Routledge.

Marcinkowski, M. and M. Hayler. (2017), 'Manifesto', Ambient Literature, May. Available online: https://research.ambientlit.com/wp-content/uploads/2017/05/ambient-literature-definition.pdf (accessed 10 November 2022).

Massey, D. (1991), 'A Global Sense of Place', *Marxism Today* (June): 24–9.

McCullough, M. (2013), *Ambient Commons: Attention in the Age of Embodied Information,* Cambridge, MA: Massachusetts Institute of Technology Press.

McFarlane, R. (2016), 'Generation Anthropocene: How Humans Have Altered the Planet Forever', *The Guardian*, 1 April. Available online: https://www.theguardian.com/books/2016/apr/01/generation-anthropocene-altered-planet-for-ever (accessed 27 May 2024).

Rifken, J. (2010), *The Empathic Civilization: The Race to Global Consciousness in a World in Crisis*, Cambridge: Polity Press.
Schandorf, M. and A. Karatzogianni. (2018), '#NODAPL: Distributed Rhetorical Praxis at Standing Rock,' in J. Alexander and J. Rhodes, eds. *Routledge Handbook of Digital Rhetoric and Writing*, 142–52, New York: Routledge.
Sontag, S. (2004), *On Regarding the Pain of Others*, New York: Penguin Books.
Sorrentino, M. (2020), 'How Ambient Advertising is Uniquely Placed to Make Audiences Think', *Westminster Papers in Communication and Culture*, 15(2), 95–111.
TMF Editors. (2017), 'The Concept of Tactical Media', Tactical Media Files, 7 March. Available online: http://www.tacticalmediafiles.net/articles/44999 (accessed 10 November 2022).
Thompson, C. (2008), 'Brave New World of Digital Intimacy', *The New York Times*, 7 September. Available online: www.nytimes.com/2008/09/07/magazine/07awareness-t.html (accessed 10 November 2022).
Torchin, L. (2016), 'What Can the Mass "Check-in" at Standing Rock Tell Us about Online Advocacy?', *The Conversation*, 5 November. Available online: https://theconversation.com/what-can-the-masscheck-in-at-standing-rock-tell-us-about-online-advocacy-68276 (accessed 10 November 2022).
Woodland, S., L. Barclay, V. Saunders and B. Beetson. (2019), 'Listening to Country: Exploring the Value of Acoustic Ecology with Aboriginal and Torres Strait Islander Women in Prison', *Soundscape: The Journal of Acoustic Ecology*, 17, 41–4.

9

Ambient writing in a terrain of threatened subjectivity: Unfolding codes, tainted models and holey spaces

Phil Smith

In 2011, I set out to walk the putative route of W. G. Sebald's apparently autobiographical prose work *The Rings of Saturn* (1995). To me it was an unfamiliar road. Sebald's text was my map and guide; a book that is openly but inconsistently unreliable about places, distances and landmarks (a quality which was a part of my reasons for attempting to follow it). It transplants Eccles Church Tower to the beach at Dunwich and messes with the patina of authenticity given it by the dog-eared monochrome illustrations that pepper its pages. To the ambiguous writing of *The Rings of Saturn*, somewhere between stream of consciousness and historiography, I had added my own unreliable memory of the text: realizing (re-reading as I walked) that, according to the narrative, Sebald had not recuperated from a nervous breakdown by taking this journey but was precipitated into it after the walk. This rather changed the dynamic of my re-enactment (Smith 2014).

Near Lowestoft, I followed Sebald's route into the gardens of Somerleyton Hall. A country house, formerly the home of Norman gentry, its present house built for Morton Peto, a nineteenth-century entrepreneur who provided railways for British military adventures. At Norwich Station I had noticed Peto's bust, perched high up above the station concourse on a stone ledge and had spontaneously sought to find where I needed to place myself to look directly into its brass eyes. In the Somerleyton gardens, I attempted the same task but with the statue of Atlanta; a mythic persona abandoned at birth for being a girl, raised by bears and refused a place amongst the Argonauts on the grounds that her beauty would destabilize an all-male crew. At Somerleyton she is depicted, naked, in the middle of a race to avoid marriage but distracted by apples dropped by Aphrodite. The sculptor, Gustav Natorp, shows Atlanta holding an apple in one hand and stooping to pick up a second so that the viewers' gaze is drawn from one apple to the other, up and down and across the model's breasts.

Adopting the same tactic for Atlanta as I had for Peto, I could swerve the sculptor's objectifying intentions and look directly into the subject's eyes. Unlike in Norwich Station, where I had to walk some considerable distance before I could meet the magnate's lofty gaze, in the gardens the task brought me to my knees, steadying myself with a hand on the plinth. To my walking companion and to passers-by, I became, momentarily, part of the sculpture's spectacle; I had introduced a second line of gaze along my own back and neck, through the sculpture's empty hand and reaching arm, up to its metal eyes.

I added this meeting of the gazes of statues and other representations to a growing toolkit of actions, from which, over the years, I have published selections (Smith 2010; Crab Man 2012). It was, like many of those assembled, a transferable tactic. It could also serve as a component of a more complex fictional or associational quest; part of a syntax for weaving invented narratives around official heritage or touristic discourses, engaging the multiple layers of site and routes, and challenging dominant or homogenizing themes there. Such oblique and self-deprecating tactics can lure bullying narratives onto a poetic-comedic terrain; for example, framing the absurdity of a sign that offers tourists the chance to 'View History, Beauty & Wildlife at speeds of up to 60mph', whilst proposing its critique as part of a quest every bit as engaging and reflexive as a proposal about speed boats.

Unfolding codes

Another way I found to 'write' such a quest was to (re)interpret found ciphers, signage, objects and symbols as sets of unfolding codes; these might include paint splashes on pavements, the collage effects created where multiple layers of posters have been torn through to reveal their stratigraphy or the spray-painted symbols and words left by inspectors as instructions to repair workers. Or I might recruit things as my co-writers; picking up an object that had attracted my attention and walking with it, allowing it to influence or even determine my route, engagements with it and internal monologue about it, until a new partner-object would make itself known, picking that up and leaving the first object in its place, then repeating the process. One such walk included my accompanying of red soil, a plastic seal, a stick and then a visit to a junk shop where I bought (cheaply) two framed objects: one, a small painting of a beach that I took to a beach and collaged with cuttlefish bones, the other a reproduction woodcut of a 'wanderer' (made, I discovered later, by a German artist who went on to make propaganda images for the Nazis) that I hid in brambles.

None of these tactics, nor many of the similar ones I have invented, tried and gathered, required any technologically sophisticated instrumentation (though all of them could be recorded and their images distributed digitally). Nevertheless, and despite the fact that similar tactics had been enacted prior to mass digitization and had turned out substantially the same as now, these tactics share qualities that are characteristic of the uses of information technology: entanglement and bilocation, sensual immersion, action across fields, multiplicity, sampling and mashing up, rapid access to popular cultural cross-referencing and so on. Just as with an ambient literature, or a sonic artist's adding an extra layer of sound to an audio recording, these predigital actions could run alongside the lines of a performance trajectory, shadowing the dispersal of its representations. They are testimony (enacted through a torque-like snagging and irritation) to the way that a transformation of technology may not always facilitate an entirely new cultural content, but instead enable more efficiently or more powerfully parts of an existing, if marginal, one.

Uneven technologies

Neither the illusions nor the realities of 'technological revolution' are smooth; there is unevenness even within its contradictions. Responding to the accelerated digitization and pixilation of information, a mixture of extremes of progressivist enthusiasm and apocalyptic paranoia, producing its own hybrids such as accelerationism (Mackay and Avanessian 2014), has, at times, threatened contemporary discourse with a narrative every bit as determinist as the famous assertion by Marx and Engels, buoyed up on the horrified euphoria of an earlier wave of acceleration, that 'slavery cannot be abolished without the steam engine' (1970: 61). Evading such crude technological determinism, wherever it falls along a continuum from overexcited optimism to pessimism, may mark only the beginning of a valid critical response, still far from an effective praxis, but I will attempt to use such an evasion as, at least, a useful catalyst.

So, rather than looking for opportunities amongst increased velocities and densities to discuss the latest technological capabilities, I will instead try to take advantage of odd wrinkles in rates of accumulation and changes of quality in information and sensoria; focusing on rumples and puckers that have arisen in the general smoothness, particularly where older discourses are re-emerging (or where new discourses are now imagined in elderly terms). A generation ago, Erik Davis detected a general hypermodern but dualist ideology that was coming from cyber-enthusiasts and pioneers; 'a Gnostic flight from the heaviness and torpor of the material earth, a transition from the labouring body into the symbol-processing mind' (1998: 115), who, despite their futurism, often relied upon anachronistic tropes of 'imagineering' and pseudo-medieval narratives of revenge (costumed Gothic-lite) through which to pitch themselves against a world of treacherous and limping matter.

Whilst much of the styling may have changed in the last two decades, these dramaturgical structures and assumptions have been remarkably resilient. My intention here is to turn them on their head; retaining the anachronistic qualities, stripping them of their costuming and attending to the material world as a positive ecology and an agentive partner rather than as an untrustworthy lower order of things to be transcended by digital gnosis. I will not be drawing directly on my experiences of making ambient literature, but continue in the way I have begun, by taking a sideways step away from the process of development and approach its productions more obliquely, by drawing ideas, tactics and techniques from clunky ambulatory arts and performance. I will draw some lessons for ambient literature's future from the methodology of *dérives*, the destination-less wandering, guided by attention to atmospheres rather than directions, devised by the activists of the International Letterists in Paris in the late 1950s, from analogue clumsiness, embodied presence, hyper-sensitization (particularly to spatial ambience) and the cultivation of the 'edge of chaos' in the performance of everyday life. All this through the 'prism' of a situated reader; considered not as a neutral or discrete figure, but as one who is necessarily embattled, invaded and abject in the city of the spectacle, at the mercy, whether connected or not, of a digital curiosity about her inner life of preferences and predilections.

Situated readers

When considering how work might be made for and with such a situated reader, it is necessary to break from the idea that she is best considered as a passive consumer or an active interpreter but rather that she has an agency equivalent to that of the ambulatory artist. In that sense ambient literature should seek to apply its ambient qualities – an ablative mobility comparable 'to the side' of a certain kind of live art, connectedness, the displacement from the centre to the local environment, a tendency to prioritize mood or atmosphere – to the means and forces of literary production, looking to relational aesthetics before literary criticism. At the same time, it should not dissolve its 'reader'/listener in the ecstasy of writing but address her need for support and for the tools necessary to make her own protected reading, by which she can not only resist but also asymmetrically turn around to her own ends the spectacular economy's algorithmic and visual invasions. Such a situated and supported reader not only listens, looks and contemplates, but also can entangle with enchanted and vibrant things, explore and be explored by her sites. She is an actor and an agent, immersed in the materiality of ambience, identifying what the malevolent gazes seek; protecting and enjoying those targeted things, whilst disrupting other gazes by her own readerly critical presence.

Such a reader, in older guises, has been heavily surveyed and theorized. Through two centuries of flâneuserie (Elkin 2016) and flâneurie (White 2001), through recent site-specific art and performance practices (Kastner 1998; Pearson and Shanks 2001; Pearson 2009), psychogeography (Richardson 2015) and increasingly hybrid forms (Smith 2010; Papadimitriou 2012), a variety of strategies for an agentive and performative presence (mostly urban, mostly ambulatory) has been formulated and contextualized within narratives of cultural geography, avant-garde art, ethnography, activism and (secular and occult) pilgrimage. One strain within such narratives, though often inflected by theory, has favoured the instructional handbook as its most appropriate expression: examples have included Tim Brennan's *Guidebook: Three Manoeuvres* (1999), Simon Pope's *London Walking: A Handbook for Survival* (2000), Anna Best's *Occasional Sights – A London Guidebook of Missed Opportunities and Things that Aren't Always There* (2003), Wrights & Sites' *A Mis-Guide to Anywhere* (2006) and *The Architect-Walker* (2018), Carl Lavery's 'Teaching Performance Studies: 25 Instructions for Performance in Cities' (2005), *Manual for Marginal Places* by Close and Remote (Sophie Mellor and Simon Poulter) (2011), Brandon LaBelle's *Handbook for the Itinerant* (2012) and Bryan Sonderman's *Walking Games* (2012).

Rather than a brash technicism, these handbooks represent the idea that critical reflection and the engagement of immersed presence for walking artists, and, I suggest, now for situated readers, should be entangled in a self-reflexive and meatworld practice. Just as a revenant of theatricality persists in the walking arts (sometimes as a stowaway within live art, returning to thing-ness, via the 'dematerialisation of the art object' [Lippard 1973], through the body), so, by the reverse process, there were prefigurations (even premonitions) of a mobile digital arts – awareness of the sensorium, invocation of a crude noosphere, synchronic entanglement across multiple fields – in the meatworld of walking arts. That part of disrupted and performative walking's roots that are in a psychogeographical 'science' of atmospheres, that is about navigating according to the presence of *genii loci* (dispersing the Roman idea of identifiable and nameable place spirits into moods and affects), was always as ambient as it was ambulant. There is, however, nothing inevitable about this return of repressed materiality.

Its precarious potential is evident in Grafton Tanner's recent discussion, as relevant to literature as to music, of the emergence of vaporwave: 'an Internet-born electronic-music microgene … with its singularly strange aesthetic and guerrilla methods … its roots in avant-garde electronic pioneers … critical of Western culture's preoccupation with the past' (2016: x–xi). Tanner places vaporwave within recent critical discourses around the uncanny and the ghostly, including those of Jacques Derrida (2006) and Mark Fisher (2016). On the one hand, he detects a contextual strain, drawing from Derrida, in which ghosts 'empty "reality" of meaning … speak the nothingness, the death, of the things they name', and, on the other hand, he describes 'a line connecting vaporwave to the fairly recent artistic and philosophical trends … in favour of … what philosopher Graham Harman calls an "object-oriented philosophy"' (Badley 1995, cited in Tanner 2016: 5–6).

In other words, the context for the emergence of an ambient literature (just as for vaporwave), whilst decentring the human subject from the seat of discrete agency, need not disperse materiality, but by 'tak[ing] seriously the vitality of (nonhuman) bodies … the capacity of things … not only to impede or block the will of humans but also to act as quasi agents or forces with trajectories … of their own' (Bennett 2010: viii) the reader returns as one more thing with power and agency in the landscape. Thus, the ambulatory tactics of the walking arts, because of rather than despite the anachronism of walking, already prefigure the possibilities of a digitally enhanced ambient literature whose realization they can now facilitate. Not by playing the role of a programme, or a necessary line of progress, but as resolutely fragmentary catalysts for changing each other into something else.

Many of these tactics are very simple, and amenable to adaptation. They generally require little, if any, preparation; which means that a writer of ambient literature, once having learned the simple techniques, can deploy them spontaneously as opportunities arise. Despite their simplicity, they can constitute working methods for the production of complex ends. Because of their simplicity they can be deployed anywhere along the continuum of a creative process. For example, both readers and writers of ambient literature can use a tactic like 'walking with a character'.

For my book, *Anywhere* (2017), I walked in relation to the unfolding narrative of a fictional researcher called 'Cecile Oak'. I was not imitating or pretending to be 'Cecile', not even trying to imagine her feelings, but walking with her narrative in mind. This was a similar process to one I have described elsewhere (Smith 2015) as 'zombie walking', where a walker is not impersonating either a zombie or a survivor but walks with the zombie mythos in mind, interpreting the immediate terrain (their ambience) through a spectral imagining, or ghosting, of the terrains of zombie narratives. So, for example, the mythos can be used as a springboard to sudden changes of pace or direction (precipitating the subject into unexpected and barely chosen spaces), to create abrupt heightenings of sensitization and equally sudden dispersals of focus.

Optic flows

The eye resolutely frames our vision; and although our brain mostly edits them out, the edges of our nose and eyebrows are constants in what we see (even if not recognized). Encouraged by certain traditional aesthetic assumptions, ignoring the moments in 1911 when the Futurist Umberto Bocconi introduced a piece of a real window into a painting or in 1924 when Max Ernst's painting *Culture Mechanism: The Robing of the Bride* (1924) escaped from its frame, it is easy to assume that a camera image or a painting must always be framed, and that the frame is an unchallengeable 'how things are'. That with each message comes its medium. In Wrights & Sites' site-specific portmanteau performance *Pilot Navigation* (1998), Cathy Turner gave empty wooden frames to the audience, who were seated in a ferry boat moving gently along the Exeter Ship Canal.

Turner's use of frames overtly referenced painting; encouraging the audience to use the frames reflexively to imagine representations of an electricity pylon standing close to the banks of the canal, whilst the spoken reflections of a fictional painter played over the ferry boat's Tannoy. In turn, this narrative was turned inside out by the audience, who used their frames to enclose and outline other parts of the terrain and other dramas on the banks. Once the physical frame has been used, it can also be imagined without the physical object; a recognition of the enclosures that we may unconsciously be projecting onto the visual array.

An actual or an imagined frame, with their associations to both screens and pages, can help to set to work the two cities of locative literature, sliding the mirage or blueprint of the ideal, spectral or pixelated city across the labyrinth of its physical materials. Walking out of a small Devon town, accompanying the ornithologist and composer Tony Whitehead, as part of the preparation for *Anywhere*, our imaginary frame was a 'found footage' horror movie filmed in a deconsecrated church in a nearby village. On the margins of the town, in a small industrial estate, we found a stonemason's yard piled with heavy polished-stone baths and the recovered fragments of memorials and statues, including a plinth with broken feet. The narrative frame of threatened bodies and souls in the horror movie was now stretched across the ambiguous stones in the yard, representations of fixed corporeal wholeness broken by chance or violence, overwhelmed by excessive instruments of cleansing and immersion.

Such a doubleness can *itself* become a character in ambient fictions. As in the John Carpenter movie *They Live* (1988) where the doubleness of the central character, homeless building worker John Nada ('John Nothing'), both marginalized and central to the economy, opens up a paranoid interwoven world of advertising and skull-faced aliens, manipulated surfaces and minimalist messages. By such paranoid framing fictions can recruit everything and everybody as props or bit part players in their narrative; just as the coach tour PA commentary performed by Forced Entertainment for their 'Nights in this City' (1995) or the recorded footsteps heard in the opening part of Janet Cardiff's audio walk 'The Missing Voice (Case Study B)' (1999) in London's Whitechapel Library recruited passers-by as unknowing characters in their semi-fictions.

Doppelgangers

The ambient terrain provides its own doubleness. Cities, particularly, are full of, often rarely acknowledged, reflective surfaces, available for use as temporary screens. Where they are clean and flat, they reassure a reader that what is represented there is maybe really there, yet explicit about their shiny shallowness; when they are filthy or deranged the effect is of a more diffracted and entangled surface, more immediate in its assault upon a sensorium. This disturbance can also be distancing, when the reader responds by mentally stepping back in an attempt to reframe the whole. If she catches a glimpse of herself in the reflection, she is now placed outside herself and in the terrain of the story, as well as within its flow of letters or sounds.

This kind of doubled and redoubled shift can be recruited to a binocular looking. When an ambient writer asks a reader to imagine 'the world', she will often picture it as a distant globe, imagined from a place far away, adopting a viewpoint something like that of a satellite in orbit. From such a position what shows up below is as likely to be trajectories through space as boundaries. Another kind of knowing, to which the ambient writer can invite her audience is obsessively close to hand, going in layer by layer. What then gets emphasized are levels, layers, textures and the identification of constituent materials, evidence, back story and motives. If reader-writer can put the two together, or oscillate between them, then they can have a displaced reading of narrative space, a repeated shifting from surface to plane and on to something more topological; a reading that maybe gets (beyond any routinized tearing or gluing) to a field that is more totalized. This is ambient terrain where shifting features can entangle with and contest those circling points of malevolent viewing that engage upon a locative reader: surveillance cameras, the glance of a passer-by who turns an ambient explorer into a performer, the gaze of 'big others' (those feelings of being obliged to behave in certain ways in accordance with invisible authorities).

An ambient literature, a walking in fiction, can serve to turn on these gazes and expose their presence and their intents. During the Cold War, my father was stationed at RAF Geilenkirchen close to the western border of what was then West Germany. In his later years, he recounted flying on missions towards East German military positions, not to engage or invite their response, but to light up and expose their radar and make its positions and capacities readable. An abject reader, if they forefront their abjection, can become a resistant one, in a double movement that not only draws the gaze of the malign and inquisitive terrain, but also disrupts its orientation to the instructions and privileges of literature. By avoiding the words marching across plaza-like pages; by dipping the shoulder and making a feint away from subjectivities gathered on the edge of the master's square in clubs with restrictive door policies; by sidestepping Modernism's old problem of elitism.

Making players or characters of the layers of a terrain is to remove the minotaur and hollow out the labyrinth. It is one way of creating space that is 'place minus one' (Deleuze and Guattari 1987: 23); using an ambient fiction to subtract from space. Taking away an authority, an identity or a dominant narrative and inviting a more affordant agency into the narrative routes of the literature.

These 'places minus one' have their own dynamics and agency, and they come in numerous forms. They might be 'fake sacred' such as modern stone circles erected by town planners in town centres or they might be artistic simulacra such as Rod Dickinson's realization of 'The Air Loom', a delusion of a human-influencing machine drawn in detail by James Tilly Matthews in 1810, whilst incarcerated in the Bedlam Hospital (Jay 2003). They may be giveaways, tells, blurts out and overspeakings, like the advert for speedboats described above, or the tinny sword sunk in a concrete block outside the prefabricated hut of 'Excalibur Fabrications' on a Sunderland industrial estate, or excessive policing and guiding that overwhelms and demeans the things they mean to protect or narrate. They may be places of competing apocalypses; I remember a screen in Times Square displaying giant explosions from an action movie trailer above the large 'golden arch' logo of McDonalds and the tension between exterminations by terror or obesity. Or street viscera, when the tubes and pipes of the city street are like a body turned inside out, and hauntological remnants of past attempts to imagine the future, such as flying cars on carousels.

There is no escape, as such, from privilege, either through literature or geography, because different readers have different permissions in different spaces, but both disciplines, when they put ambience first, can make their privileges evident, difficult and questionable, and put them into play. When Albert Speer, the Nazi architect, was incarcerated after the Second World War, he walked across the world in his head, whilst circumambulating his prison yard, he remained toxic and invasive in both mind and action. The Swiss-born Dominican Felix Fabri wrote a guidebook for taking virtual pilgrimages, *Sionpilger* (1492), so that the enclosed order of nuns under his guidance could make a virtual prayer walk to Jerusalem without leaving their convent walls or even their cells.

The ambient writer can use such tainted models; so that the walk in place is always a walk dis-placed. It is always a noble retreat or an ecstatic flight from the algorithmic attention its connectedness is sure to draw to its 'here' and 'now', to its sitedness and to its specificity. Against such intrusions, a responsible locative literature will seek a 'there' and a 'to come'; not simply in place and narrative, but in texts that slip out of their own vocabularies, in engraved letters that fill up with moss, in signs that slide away or decay into new meanings, when the 'D' falls off 'DANGER', or when signposts collapse and directions and destinations are put in doubt. Through such interruptions of the flow of words (the accidental addition of a space in a New York window display changing PSYCHIC to PSY CHIC) or the upset of solemnity (an exclamation mark inside a red triangle placed in a cemetery), the ambulatory arts return to an early source in the 'Lettrisme' of Isidore Isou and a challenge to the authoritarianism of the Roman alphabet, a culture forged by global war renewed through the remaking of the most basic components of representation.

In tune with a 'thing-power' (Bennett 2010: 2) that is not a spiritual supplement or 'life force … not a vitalism in the traditional sense … [but] a vitality intrinsic to materiality as such' (xiii), the street generates its own art forms, its involuntary paintings (the rusting of metal surfaces that spill and shape simulacra of figures and landscapes), its portraiture in those pedestrian figures that infringe the limits of their stencils and take on new back stories by a spill of blood or the dropping of a toy. Locative literature can find its drives in these surpluses; it can carve its reader into the niches, verges and shop windows of the present and the here, because there is always a ghost there to hide behind.

Spectres of marks

I recently experienced a vivid encounter with such a spectral presence, whilst navigating a public footpath, climbing through trees, just outside Totnes in Devon. I turned a corner, and the landscape was 'a picture', the shaping of the trees and the fall of the land felt painterly; although I did not know it at the time, my response was far from accidental, for the terrain had been shaped by an eighteenth-century landscape designer to look like the artist's painting that I found myself suddenly channelling. There is always such a 'then' in the 'here', and it is very often a fabricated one.

In the case of my experience at Totnes, the two elements of representation and material were welded, but where they have come apart, they create a gap, a void or an affordance. The black 2D cut-outs of the shapes of dogs in a Minnesota park, ignored by the flocks of giant geese they had long ago failed to scare away, were tiny examples of what, by industrial derelictions and financial crashes, can become a landscape of voids that Francesco Careri proposes as the realization of the New Babylon of the situationist architect Constant Niewenhuis (cited in Koivu 2015: 348–59). Not as a fixed physical structure, but – bypassing the contradiction jamming Niewenhuis' signal vision, long ago appropriated for automobile cities – as a mystery motherboard of missing parts and affordances, which a walk or a literature – at full speed – can light up in sequences.

This can be achieved by writing and performing a score, as much about movement as text, spinning out syntax in the form of a progress across an ambient terrain. Indeed, literature might have much to learn, in this respect, from other disciplines such as site dance (see Kloetzel and Pavlik 2010), particular with a view to creating new space (see Smith 2018). I will, however, finish by returning to something I am more qualified to describe – the making of *Anywhere*. I will draw out a little more from that project to recount in greater detail how an ambient writer can immerse herself in multiple layers of space and meaning for the purposes of creating, first, a new text and, second, a new space.

One of the things I did for *Anywhere* was to take a walk with another book. Called *The Scoriton Mystery*, it was written by Eileen Buckle in 1967. The book describes what it supposes was the first alien-human encounter in the United Kingdom in the age of modern post-1947 'flying saucery'; an event that took place on the edge of Dartmoor, near the small village of Scoriton. In the company of Tony Whitehead, I walked with the book in the places it describes; for a while it became for us a meta-text, an unfolding structure that set a whole orrery of narratives, spaces, recordings, tamperings, techno-magics, charged objects and both real and impersonated characters into distorted orbits around each other. As these gravitational attractions reached a certain intensity, the orbiting meanings began to pull at our own orbits and a new narrative began to emerge in which we, now as both readers and writers, were both characters and authors, and compromised and incorporated on both accounts.

Enigmatic artefacts guided us. These included photographs of 'debris' collected by the contactee, Arthur Bryant, a local handyman and caretaker; these included mechanical fragments that Bryant said he had found in a field close to his home and in the lane beside it, along with a glass 'phial' containing silver sand along with a fragment of paper on which, written in classical Greek, were the words 'Adelphos Adelpho' or 'brother to brother'. These photographs had provoked us, early on in our walk, to call in at a workshop of devout organ builders we discovered, to ask them if they thought the aliens had, perhaps, left a musical instrument; one of the objects in the photographs looked similar to a musical pipe. Surrounded by rows of their newly fashioned giant wooden organ pipes, the organ makers downed tools; they were polite and passionate; their answer was 'no' and the other mechanical objects looked like car parts. Over the years, the artefacts left behind by aliens fell into the clutches of various journalists, impostors and youthful ufologists; some of the objects were destroyed, any record of the location of the others was lost. This impregnated our story's expanding terrain; making every loft we passed suspect.

Our confidence in the photographs in Buckle's book as a touchstone to the mystery was shaken when we attempted to use one of them, of Bryant and Buckle at the site of his second encounter, to orient ourselves and identify the exacts spots in the field where the various incidents had occurred. Fifty years of rebuilding, growth and tree-felling had radically altered the look of things; only our discovery of a large drain cover under a considerable bush (in the photograph the drain was in the open) helped us to fit the image to the field. In the process we had, book in hand, danced a short score around the field, watched by resident sheep.

On learning, from the account of one of Buckle's rival ufologists, that Arthur Bryant's wife had first heard the account of the encounters from him in the form of a proposed sci-fi novel, we had to rethink ourselves as readers of, and even characters in, Bryant's own ambient literature. His unwritten novel now being completed, in the fields of his imagined contacts, by us. His testimony-fiction became biological, pathological even, when we then read in Buckle's account of how Bryant's death, shortly after telling his story, was caused by a brain tumour. Had his tumour been like that of Brian O'Blivion's in David Cronenberg's 1983 movie *Videodrome*, that is, a tumour that did not cause visions but rather was caused by visions? Was the saucer-narrative – strong enough to have us dancing in a choreography in a field half a century on – one that transformed brains?

When we finally found Bryant's original contact site, a field on the very edge of the moor, we oriented ourselves by Bryant's descriptions of the date, time and the place (once again we performed the choreography that Bucket and he had left for us). Looking across the field above which Bryant recounted seeing a hovering craft, we realized that the narrow, green and grassy top of the hill we were facing across the small valley, which, at the time and season described in the book, would have been struck by the light of a golden hour sun was saucer-shaped. The ambience of the isolated path, on the very edge between grazing fields, saucer hill and wild moor, was author of Bryant's imagined fiction, which in its turn was authoring and choreographing us.

Similarly, Bryant's 'indentikit' impression of the leading alien's appearance, drawn up with help from a police artist, had somehow manifested itself in a carved stone head on a Scoriton village gatepost. There was a kind of joy, comparable to a readerly immersion in a fictional world, to walking in the gaps of Bryant and Buckle's meta-text, wrapped in and around the numerous hoaxes and fabricated soundscapes of others caught up in the narrative; including an intervention by the astronomer Patrick Moore as 'Cedric Allingham', the pseudonymous author of the mirage hoax text *Flying Saucer from Mars*, fabricated tapes made by Eileen Buckle's infatuated co-investigator, and later rival, and an appearance by Desmond Leslie, an electronic composer infamous for punching Bernard Levin on live TV, who appeared to Bryant in the dual form of 'Des/Les'.

Holey spaces

When a walker-reader is coiling around doppelganger texts such as these, or going off in search of narrative clues to the whereabouts of their wandering objects, she enters a kind of holey space, in which everyday objects are continually falling into fiction. A literary holey space that is doubly voided, doubly inauthentic, full of portable and probable potential. She gains entry to a shallow, wide and under-populated field, with occasional spectres, disguises, decoys and false trails; and these are the 'places-minus-one', where the ambient reader can explore distraction, and yet stay under the radar, too trivial to draw surveillance. This is the kind of space where ambient writers might in the future find ways to allow words to make their own arrangements, where swiping a page will be like opening a door, between the things and their voids.

These are spaces where earphones can be elsewhere; walkways through clouds and webs of information, ways of navigating fictions about discrete and ethereal versions of 'cyberspace', a making your way by disconnection through returning aether and something older, more colonial, more orientalist than anyone is daring to mention. It is a sign that something good is coming sooner than anyone is daring to believe. Bad things are putting themselves up on display: and the short-circuits that make us strangers in our own cells are turning out to be, and are being turned to become, tunnels where we can protect an inner darkness by becoming strangers under our own suns, by becoming reader-pilgrims across ordinariness and making it odd.

Ambient literature is an invitation to wear our fictions like ill-fitting clothes, walking with a stutter, skirting those race tracks where Bifo Berardi has seen 'signs produce signs without any longer passing through flesh' (2012: 17), and where, instead, we can take the shortcut, via spectral fictions, and back through flesh again.

References

Badley, L. (1995), *Film, Horror and the Body Fantastic*, Westport, CT: Greenwood.

Bennett, J. (2010), *Vibrant Matter*, Durham, NC: Duke University Press.

Berardi, F. (2012), *The Uprising*, Cambridge, MA: MIT Press.

Best, A. (2003), *Occasional Sights – A London Guidebook of Missed Opportunities and Things that Aren't Always There*, London: The Photographers' Gallery.

Brennan, T. (1999), *Guidebook: Three Manoeuvres in London E1/E2*, vol. 2, London: Camerawords.

Close and Remote (Sophie Mellor and Simon Poulter). (2011), *Manual for Marginal Places*, Close and Remote.
Crab Man. (2012), *Counter-Tourism: The Handbook*, Axminster: Triarchy Press.
Davis, E. (1998), *TechGnosis*, London: Serpent's Tail.
Deleuze, G. and F. Guattari. (1987), *A Thousand Plateaus*, London: Continuum.
Derrida, J. (2006), *Spectres of Marx*, London: Routledge.
Elkin, L. (2016), *Flâneuse*, London: Chatto & Windus.
Fisher, M. (2016), *The Weird and the Eerie*, London: Repeater.
Jay, M. (2003), *The Air Loom Gang*, London: Bantam Press.
Kastner, J., ed. (1998), *Land and Environmental Art*, London: Phaidon Press.
Kloetzel, M. and C. Pavlik, eds. (2010), *Site Dance: Choreographers and the Lure of Alternative Spaces*, Gainesville: University Press of Florida.
Koivu, A., ed. (2015), *The Walking Society*, Zurich: Lars Muller Publishers.
LaBelle, B. (2012), *Handbook for the Itinerant*, Cambridge, MA: MIT Press.
Lavery, C. (2005), 'Teaching Performance Studies: 25 Instructions for Performance in Cities', *Studies in Theatre and Performance*, 35(3), 229–38.
Lippard, L. R. (1973), *Six Years: The Dematerialisation of the Art Object from 1966 to 1972*, New York: Praeger.
Mackay, R. and A. Avanessian, eds. (2014), *#Accelerate: The Accelerationist Reader*, Falmouth: Urbanomic.
Marx, K. and F. Engels. (1970), *The German Ideology (Part One)*, New York: International Publishers.
Papadimitriou, N. (2012), *Scarp*, London: Hodder & Stoughton.
Pearson, M. (2009), *Site-Specific Performance*, Basingstoke: Palgrave Macmillan.
Pearson, M. and M. Shanks. (2001), *Theatre/Archaeology*, London: Routledge.
Pope, S. (2000), *London Walking: A Handbook for Survival*, London: Batsford.
Richardson, T., ed. (2015), *Walking Inside Out*, London: Rowman & Littlefield.
Sebald, W. G. (1995), *The Rings of Saturn*, London: The Harvill Press.
Sonderman, B. (2012), 'Walking Games Database', Now, Here, 24 May'. Available online: http://bryan-sonderman.blogspot.com/2012/05/walking-games-database.html (accessed 12 November 2022).
Smith, P. (2010), *Mythogeography*, Axminster: Triarchy Press.
Smith, P. (2014), *On Walking*, Axminster: Triarchy Press.
Smith, P. (2015), *The Footbook of Zombie Walking*, Axminster: Triarchy Press.
Smith, P. (2017), *Anywhere: A Mythogeography of South Devon*, Axminster: Triarchy Press.
Smith, P. (2018), *Making Site-Specific Theatre and Performance*, Basingstoke: Palgrave Macmillan.
Tanner, G. (2016), *Babbling Corpse*, Winchester: Zero Books.
White, E. (2001), *The Flâneur*, London: Thorndike Press.
Wrights & Sites. (2006), *A Mis-Guide to Anywhere*, Exeter: Wrights & Sites.
Wrights & Sites. (2018), *The Architect-Walker*, Axminster: Triarchy Press.

Bibliography

Aarseth, Espen. 'Computer Game Studies, Year One', editorial, *Game Studies*, 1(1), July, 2001. Available online: http://gamestudies.org/0101/editorial.html (accessed 10 November 2022).

Abba, Tom. *From Bitter Ground*, 2023. Available online: https://people.uwe.ac.uk/Person/TomAbba.

Abba, Tom. *Words We Never Wrote*, 2018. Available online: https://people.uwe.ac.uk/Person/TomAbba.

Abba, Tom. *Yesterday You're Still Dreaming*, 2017. Available online: https://people.uwe.ac.uk/Person/TomAbba.

Abba, Tom and Amy Spencer. 'Writing Ambient Literature', in Tom Abba, Jonathan Dovey and Kate Pullinger, eds. *Ambient Literature: Towards a New Poetics of Situated Writing and Reading Practices*, 275–318. London: Palgrave Macmillan, 2021.

Abba, Tom, Jonathan Dovey and Kate Pullinger. 'Introduction', in Tom Abba, Jonathan Dovey and Kate Pullinger, eds. *Ambient Literature: Towards a New Poetics of Situated Writing and Reading Practices*, 1–26. London: Palgrave Macmillan, 2021.

Abba, Tom, Duncan Speakman, and Emilie Grenier. *These Pages Fall Like Ash*, 2013/2020. Available online: www.wearecircumstance.com (accessed 6 June 2024).

Abram, Davis. *The Spell of the Sensuous*. New York: Vintage, 2017.

Alderman, Naomi. 'Naomi Alderman's Podcast, Listeners Walk into the Story'. North Country Public Radio, 2018. Available online: https://www.northcountrypublicradio.org/news/npr/596443185/in-naomi-alderman-s-podcast-listeners-walk-into-the-story (accessed 12 November 2022).

Alderman, Naomi and Six to Start. *The Walk*, 2013. Available online: https://play.google.com/store/apps/details?id=com.sixtostart.thewalk2 (accessed 10 November 2022).

Almond, David. *Skellig: 15th Anniversary Edition*. London: Hodder Children's Books, 2013.

Alston, Adam. 'Politics in the Dark: Risk Perception, Affect and Emotion in Lundahl and Seitl's Rotating in a Room of Images', in Nicola Shaughnessy, ed. *Affective Performance and Cognitive Science: Body, Brain and Being*, 217–28, London: Methuen, 2013.

Ambient Literature Project. 'Ambient Literature', n.d. Available online: https://research.ambientlit.com/ (accessed 10 November 2022).

Andersen, Tore Rye, Stefan Kjerkegaard and Birgitte Stougaard Pedersen. 'Introduction: Modes of Reading', *Poetics Today*, 42(2), 131–47, 2021.

Antony, Rachael and Joël Henry. *The Lonely Planet Guide to Experimental Travel*. Footscray: Lonely Planet Publications, 2005.

Apple. '3D Touch – iOS – Apple', 2015. Available online: https://developer.apple.com/ios/3d-touch/ (accessed 29 January 2024).

Aragon, Louis. *Paris Peasant*. Boston: Exact Change, 1994.

Attlee, James. *The Cartographer's Confession*, 2017. Available online: https://research.ambientlit.com/cartographersconfession (accessed 6 June 2024).

Attlee, James. 'Towards Anarchitecture: Gordon Matta-Clark and Le Corbusier', *Tate Papers*, 2007. Available online: https://www.tate.org.uk/research/tate-papers/07/towards-anarchitecture-gordon-matta-clark-and-le-corbusier (accessed 12 November 2023).

Auster, Paul. *The Invention of Solitude*. London: Faber and Faber, 1989.

Badley, Linda. *Film, Horror and the Body Fantastic*. Westport, CT: Greenwood, 1995.

Barad, Karen. *Meeting the Universe Halfway*. Durham, NC: Duke University Press, 2007.

Barthes, Roland. *The Pleasure of the Text*. New York: Hill and Wang, 1975.

Beckett, Samuel. *Molloy, Malone Dies, The Unnamable*. New York: Chelsea House Publishers, 1988.

Beckett, Samuel. 'Worstward Ho', in *Nohow On: Company, Ill Seen Ill Said, Worstward Ho*, 100–128. London: John Calder, [1983] 1989.

Bell, Alice. 'Interactional Metalepsis and Unnatural Narratology', *Narrative*, 24(3), 294–310, 2016.

Bell, Alice and Astrid Ensslin. *Digital Fiction and the Unnatural Transmedia Narrative Theory, Method, and Analysis*. Columbus: Ohio State University Press, 2021.

Benford, Steve, Andy Crabtree, Stuart Reeves, Martin Flintham, Adam Drozd, Jennifer Sheridan and Alan Dix. 'The Frame of the Game: Blurring the Boundary between Fiction and Reality in Mobile Experiences', conference proceedings, *CHI: Conference on Human Factors in Computing Systems*, 22–27 April 2006, Montréal, Québec, Canada.

Benford, Steve, Chris Greenhalgh, Bob Anderson, Rachel Jacobs, Michael Golembewski, Marina Jirotka, Bernd Stahl, Job Timmermans, Gabriella Giannachi, Matt Adams, Ju Row Farr, Nick Tandavanitj and Kirsty Jennings. 'The Ethical Implications of HCI's Turn to the Cultural'. *ACM Transactions on Computer-Human Interaction*, 22(5), 1–37, 2015.

Benjamin, Walter. *The Arcades Project*. Cambridge, MA: Belknap Press of Harvard University Press, 1999.

Bennett, Jane. *Vibrant Matter*. Durham, NC: Duke University Press, 2010.

Berardi, Franco. *The Uprising*. Cambridge, MA: MIT Press, 2012.

Best, Anna. *Occasional Sights – A London Guidebook of Missed Opportunities and Things that Aren't Always There*. London: The Photographers' Gallery, 2003.

Blast Theory. *Desert Rain*, collaboration with the Mixed Reality Lab, University of Nottingham, premiered at the NOW 99 Festival, Nottingham, 1999. Available online: https://www.blasttheory.co.uk/projects/desert-rain/ (accessed 10 November 2022).

Blast Theory. *Uncle Roy All Around You*, premiered at the Institute of Contemporary Arts in London and at the Cornerhouse in Manchester, in collaboration with Digital Summer, 28 April–8 May 2004. Available online: https://www.blasttheory.co.uk/projects/uncle-roy-all-around-you/ (accessed 10 November 2022).

Blau, Herbert. *Blooded Thought: Occasions of Theatre*. New York: Performing Arts Journal Publications, 1982.

Bogalecki, Piotr. *Wiersze-partytury w poezji polskiej neoawangardy*. Kraków: Wydawnictwo Uniwersytetu Jagiellońskiego, 2020.

Bogost, Ian. *Persuasive Games: The Expressive Power of Videogames*. Cambridge, MA: MIT Press, 2007.

Brennan, Tim. *Guidebook: Three Manoeuvres in London E1/E2*, vol. 2. London: Camerawords, 1999.

Calvino, Italo. *If on a Winter's Night a Traveller*. London: Everyman, 1981.

Cardiff, J. *Her Long Black Hair*, 2004. Available online: https://cardiffmiller.com/walks/her-long-black-hair/ (accessed 6 June 2024).

Carpenter, J. R. 'Writing Coastlines: Locating Narrative Resonance in Transatlantic Communications Networks', PhD diss., 2015. Available online: http://ualresearchonline.arts.ac.uk/7825/ (accessed 23 November 2022).

Carter, Angela. *The Old Wives' Fairy Tale Book*. New York: Pantheon, 1999.

Carter, Richard. 'Waves to Waveforms: Performing the Thresholds of Sensing and Sense-Making in the Anthropocene', *Arts*, 7(4), 70, 2018.

Case, Amber. 'About – Amber Case', n.d. Available online: http://caseorganic.com/about/ (accessed 10 November 2022).

Castells, Manuel. *Communicative Power*. New York: Oxford University Press, 2009.

Chabon, Michael. *Maps and Legends*. San Francisco: McSweeney's, 2008.

Chatzichristodoulou, Maria and Rachel Zerihan, eds. *Intimacy across Visceral and Digital Performance*. Basingstoke: Palgrave Macmillan, 2012.

Christophers, Brett. *The New Enclosure: The Appropriation of Public Land in Neoliberal Britain*. London: Verso, 2018.

Circumstance. *A Hollow Body*, 2014. Available online: https://duncanspeakman.net/projects/ahb/ (accessed 6 June 2024).

Clark, Andy. *Being There: Putting Brain, Body and World Together Again*. Cambridge, MA: MIT Press, 1997.

Clark, Andy. *Natural Born Cyborgs: Minds, Technologies, and the Future of Human Intelligence*. Oxford: Oxford University Press, 2003.

Clark, Andy. *Supersizing the Mind: Embodiment, Action, and Cognitive Extension*. Oxford: Oxford University Press, 2008.

Clark, Bruce. 'Information', in W. J. T. Mitchell and Mark B. N. Hansen, eds. *Critical Terms for Media Studies*, 157–71. Chicago: University of Chicago Press, 2010.

Clarke, Helen and Sharon Kivland, eds. *The Lost Diagrams of Walter Benjamin*. London: Ma Bibliothèque, 2017.

Close and Remote (Sophie Mellor and Simon Poulter). *Manual for Marginal Places*. Close and Remote, 2011.

Clute, John. *The Darkening Garden*. Cauheegan: Payseur & Schmidt, 2006.

Cosgrove, Denis. *Apollo's Eye: A Cartographic Genealogy of the Earth in the Western Imagination*. Baltimore, MD: Johns Hopkins University Press, 2001.

Coverley, Merlin. *The Act of Wandering*. Harpenden: Oldcastle Book, 2022.

Crab Man. *Counter-Tourism: The Handbook*. Axminster: Triarchy Press, 2013.

Cresswell, Tim. 'Defining Place', in Margaret Himley and Anne Fitzsimmons, eds. *Critical Encounters with Texts: Finding a Place to Stand*, 7th edn, 127–36. Boston: Pearson, 2011.

Crivellaro, Clara, Rob Comber, Martyn Dade-Robertson, Simon J. Bowen, Peter C. Wright and Patrick Oliver. 'Contesting the City: Enacting the Political through Digitally Supported Urban Walks', *CHI '15: Proceedings of the 33rd Annual ACM Conference on Human Factors in Computing Systems*, 2853–862, 2015.

Crossley, Nick. *The Politics of Subjectivity: Between Foucault and Merleau-Ponty*. Aldershot: Ashgate Publishing, 1994.

Crutzen, Paul and Eugene Stoermer. 'The "Anthropocene"', *IGBP Global Change* (41), 17–18, 2000.

D'Avignon, Angella. 'Cities May Alienate Women, but Performance Art Points the Way to Reclaim Lost Space'. How We Get to Next, 30 April 2016. Available online: https://www.howwegettonext.com/cities-may-alienate-women-but-performance-art-points-the-way-to-reclaim-lost-space/ (accessed 27 May 2024).

Davies, Gareth, Charles Boutaud, Hazel Sheffield and Emma Youle. 'Revealed: The Thousands of Public Spaces Lost to the Council Funding Crisis', Bureau of Investigative Journalism, 4 March 2019. Available online: https://www.thebureauinvestigates.com/stories/2019-03-04/sold-from-under-you (accessed 14 July 2023).

Davis, Erik. *TechGnosis*. London: Serpent's Tail, 1998.

Debord, Guy. 'Report in the Construction of Situations', in Tom McDonough, ed. *Guy Debord and the Situationist International*, 29–50. Cambridge, MA: MIT Press, [1957] 2004.

De Botton, Alain. *The Art of Travel*. New York: Pantheon Books, 2002.

De Certeau, Michel. *The Practice of Everyday Life*. Berkeley: University of California Press, 1988.

Deleuze, Gilles and Felix Guattari. *A Thousand Plateaus*. London: Continuum, 1987.

Derrida, Jacques. *Spectres of Marx*. London: Routledge, 2006.

de Souza e Silva, Adriana. 'From Cyber to Hybrid: Mobile Technologies as Interfaces of Hybrid Spaces', *Space and Culture*, 9(3), 261–78, 2006.

Dickens, Charles. *Night Walks*. London: Penguin, 2010.

Dixon, Simon, Heather Viles and Bradley Garrett. 'Ozymandias in the Anthropocene: The City as an Emerging Landform', *Area*, 50(1), 117–25, 2018.

Doctoroff, Daniel. 'Why We're No Longer Pursuing the Quayside Project — and What's Next for Sidewalk Labs', *Medium*, 7 May 2020. Available online: https://medium.com/sidewalk-talk/why-were-no-longer-pursuing-the-quayside-project-and-what-s-next-for-sidewalk-labs-9a61de3fee3a (accessed 14 July 2023).

Dovey, Jonathan. 'Ambient Literature: Writing Probability', in Ulrik Ekman, Jay David Bolter, Lily Diaz and Morten Søndergaard, eds. *Ubiquitous Computing, Complexity and Culture*, 141–54. New York: Routledge, 2016.

Dovey, Jonathan and Matt Hayler. 'Critical Ambience', in Tom Abba, Jonathan Dovey and Kate Pullinger, eds. *Ambient Literature: Towards a New Poetics of Situated Writing and Reading Practice*, 141–61. London: Palgrave Macmillan, 2021.

Dovey, Jonathan and Duncan Speakman. 'Anthropocene Elegy and Geospatial Presence', *Media Theory*, 2(1), 32–56, 2018.

Downey, Gary Lee. 'Anthropology of Science and Technology', in *International Encyclopedia of the Social & Behavioral Sciences*, 13629–3633. Oxford: Elsevier, 2001.

Downing, Christine, ed. *The Long Journey Home: Re-visioning the Myth of Demeter and Persephone for Our Time*. Boston: Shambhala, 1994.

Dreyfuss, Emily. 'Social Media Made the World Care about Standing Rock – and Helped It Forget', *Wired*, 24 January 2017. Available online: www.wired.com/2017/01/social-media-made-world-carestanding-rock-helped-forget/ (accessed 10 November 2022).

Eco, Umberto. *Reflections on the Name of the Rose*. London: Secker & Warburg, 1985.

Elkin, Lauren. *Flâneuse*. London: Chatto & Windus, 2016.

Emerson, Sarah. 'Yosemite National Park Used to Be 30 Percent Bigger', *Vice*, 25 August 2016. Available online: https://www.vice.com/en_us/article/ezpmww/yosemite-national-park-used-to-be-30-percent-bigger (accessed 14 July 2023).

Engelmann, Sasha and Jol Thomson. *Perspectives*, 2016. Available online: https://www.anthropocene-curriculum.org/courses/sensing (accessed 9 June 2024).

Engelmann, Sasha and Jol Thomson. 'Ve Vm Vt. The Ideal Cosmic Messengers', *Technosphere Magazine*, 15 November 2016. Available online: https://technosphere-magazine.hkw.de/p/Ve-Vm-Vt-The-Ideal-Cosmic-Messengers-gTQ3sSabgSXLhFm2Hag5ny (accessed November 2022).

Eno, Brian. 'Music for Airports Liner Notes / Ambient 1', PVC, 1978. Available online: http://music.hyperreal.org/artists/brian_eno/MFA-txt.html (accessed 10 November 2022).

Ensslin, Astrid. 'From (W)reader to Breather: Cybertextual De-intentionalisation in Kate Pullinger et al.'s Breathing Wall', in Ruth Page and Bronwen Thomas, eds. *New Narratives: Stories and Storytelling in the Digital Age*, 138–52. Lincoln: University of Nebraska Press, 2011.

Ensslin, Astrid. *Literary Gaming*. Cambridge, MA: MIT Press, 2014.

Ensslin, Astrid. 'Respiratory Narrative: Multimodality and Cybernetic Corporeality in "Physio-Cybertext"', in Ruth Page, ed. *New Perspectives on Narrative and Multimodality*, 155–65. London: London, 2009.

Ensslin, Astrid and Alice Bell. '"Click = Kill": Textual You in Ludic Digital Fiction', *StoryWorlds: A Journal of Narrative Studies*, 4, 49–73, 2012.

Ensslin, Astrid, Alice Bell, Jen Smith, Isabelle Van Der Bom, and Lyle Skains. 'Immersion, Digital Fiction, and the Switchboard Metaphor', *Participations*, 16(1), 320–42, 2019.

Ensslin, Astrid, Caarla Rice, Sarah Riley, Christine, Wilks, Megan Perram, Hannah Fowlie, Lauren Munro and Alysee K. Bailey. 'Bodies in E-lit', in Dene Grigar and

James O'Sullivan, eds, *Electronic Literature as Digital Humanities: Context, Forms, and Practices*. New York: Bloomsbury Academic, 2020.

Eribon, Didier. *Conversations with Claude Lévi-Strauss*. Chicago: University of Chicago Press, 1991.

Evans, Leighton and Michael Saker. 'The Playeur and Pokémon Go: Examining the Effects of Locative Play on Spatiality and Sociability', *Mobile Media & Communication*, 7(2), 232–47, 2019.

Farman, Jason. 'The Materiality of Locative Media: On the Invisible Infrastructure of Mobile Metworks', in Andrew Herman, Jan Hadlaw and Thom Swiss, eds. *Theories of the Mobile Internet: Materialities and Imaginaries*, 45–59. New York: Routledge Press, 2005.

Fisher, Mark. *The Weird and the Eerie*. London: Repeater, 2016.

Flanders, Julia. 'The Literary, the Humanistic, the Digital: Toward a Research Agenda for Digital Literary Studies', in Kenneth M. Price and Ray Siemens, ed. *Literary Studies in the Digital Age*. Modern Language Association of America, 2013. Available online: https://dlsanthology.mla.hcommons.org/the-literary-the-humanistic-the-digital/ (accessed 14 July 2023).

Fludernik, Monika. 'Scene Shift, Metalepsis, and the Metaleptic Mode', *Style*, 37(4), 382–400, 2003.

Foth, Marcus, Laura Forlano, Christine Satchell and Martin Gibbs, eds. *From Social Butterfly to Engaged Citizen: Urban Informatics, Social Media, Ubiquitous Computing, and Mobile Technology to Support Citizen Engagement*. Cambridge, MA: MIT Press, 2012.

Gabrys, Jennifer. 'Becoming Planetary', e-flux Architecture, October 2018. Available online: https://www.e-flux.com/architecture/accumulation/217051/becoming-planetary/ (accessed 10 November 2022).

Gabrys, Jennifer. *Program Earth: Environmental Sensing Technology and the Making of a Computational Planet*. Minneapolis: University of Minnesota Press, 2016.

Galloway, Alexander R. *Gaming: Essays on Algorithmic Culture*. Minneapolis: University of Minnesota Press, 2006.

Geertz, Clifford. *The Interpretation of Cultures: Selected Essays*. London: Routledge, 1973.

Genette, Gérard. *Narrative Discourse*, trans. Jane E. Lewin. Oxford: Basil Blackwell, 1980.

Gleave, James. 'The Evolving Battle for Urban Public Space', How We Get to Next, 2016. Available online: https://howwegettonext.com/the-evolving-battle-for-urban-public-space-8db45852c6b7#.etw6anjfy (accessed 14 July 2023).

Głowiński, Michał. 'Narracja jako monolog wypowiedziany', in Karol Budzyk, ed. *Z teorii i historii literatury*, 1–34. Wrocław: Ossolineum, 1963.

Gold, Matthew and Lauren F. Klein, eds. *Debates in the Digital Humanities 2016*. Minneapolis: University of Minnesota Press, 2016.

Górska-Olesińska, Monika and Agnieszka Przybyszewska. 'O „wypożyczaniu" ciał odbiorców na potrzeby (nie tylko literackich) immersyjnych wędrówek po przestrzeniach pamięci', *Przegląd Kulturoznawczy* (2), s. 1–1, 2020.

Grosz, Elizabeth. *Architecture from the Outside: Essays on Virtual and Real Space*. Cambridge, MA: MIT Press, 2001.

Gwalchmai, Ben. '… beneath our feet, the stars …', Playable City, 2014. Available online: https://www.playablecity.com/projects/beneath-our-feet-the-stars/ (accessed 14 May 2023).

Halberg, Claus. 'The Tangible Invisible: Irigaray's Phenomenological Critique of Merleau-Ponty's Notion of the Flesh', in Ane Faugstad Aaro and Johannes Servan, eds. *Environment, Embodiment and Gender*, 107–31. Bergen: Hermes, 2011.

Hammersley, Rachel and Chris Rodgers. 'Wastes and Strays: The Past, Present and Future of English Urban Commons', School of History, Classics and Archaeology, 20 August 2019. Available online: https://scandalousartefacts.com/2018/08/20/wastes-and-strays-the-past-present-and-future-of-english-urban-commons/ (accessed 10 November 2022).

Hammersley, Richard, Chris Rodgers, Allesandro Zambelli, Emma Cheatle, John Wedgewood Clarke, Sarah Collins, Olivia Dee and Siobhan O'Neill. *English Urban Commons: The Past, Present and Future of Green Spaces*. London: Routledge, 2023.

Hancox, Dan. 'Revealed: Creeping Privatisation of London Parks in Summer', *The Guardian*, 5 July 2019. Available online: https://www.theguardian.com/cities/2019/jul/05/revealed-how-london-parks-are-partly-privatised-festivals-wireless-finsbury-park (accessed 28 June 2023).

Hancox, Donna. *The Revolution in Transmedia Storytelling through Place: Pervasive, Ambient and Situated*. London: Routledge, 2021.

Hanebeck, Julian. *Understanding Metalepsis: The Hermeneutics of Narrative Transgression*. Berlin: Walter de Gruyter, 2017.

Haraway, Donna. *Modest_Witness@Second_Millennium.FemaleMan_Meets_OncoMouse: Feminism and Technoscience*. London: Routledge, 1997.

Haraway, Donna. 'Situated Knowledges: The Science Question in Feminism and the Privilege of Partial Perspective', *Feminist Studies*, 14(3), 575–99, 1988.

Haraway, Donna. *Staying with the Trouble*. Durham, NC: Duke University Press, 2016.

Hayler, Matt. 'Objects, Places, and Entanglements', in Tom Abba, Jonathan Dovey and Kate Pullinger, eds. *Ambient Literature: Towards a New Poetics of Situated Writing and Reading Practices*, 77–102. London: Palgrave Macmillan, 2021.

Hayles, N. Katherine. *Writing Machines*. Cambridge, MA: MIT Press, 2002.

Heidegger, Martin. *Poetry, Language, Thought*, trans. Albert Hofstadter. New York: Harper and Row, 1971.

Heidegger, Martin. 'The Question Concerning Technology', in D. Krell, ed. *Basic Writings*, 307–42. San Francisco: Harper Collins, [1954] 1993.

Heidegger, Martin, John Macquarrie and Edward Robinson. *Being and Time*. London: Blackwell Publishing, 1962.

Henkin, David. *City Reading: Written Words and Public Spaces in Antebellum New York*. New York: Columbia University Press, 1998.

Henry, Holly and Amanda Taylor. 'Re-Thinking Apollo: Envisioning Environmentalism in Space'. *The Sociological Review*, 57(1), 190–203, 2009.

Hight, Jeremy. 'Locative Narrative, Literature and Form', in Jörgen Schäfer and Peter Gendolla, eds. *Beyond the Screen: Transformations of Literary Structures, Interfaces and Genres*, 317–30. Piscataway, NJ: Transactions Publishers, 2010.

Hight, Jeremy. 'Views from Above: Locative Narrative and the Landscape', *Leonardo*, 14(7–8), 2006. Available online: https://www.leoalmanac.org/wp-content/uploads/2012/09/09_JHight.pdf (accessed 10 November 2022).

Hill, Leslie and Helen Paris. *Performing Proximity: Curious Intimacies*. Basingstoke: Palgrave Macmillan, 2014.

Ingold, Tim. *Being Alive: Essays on Movement, Knowledge and Description*. Abingdon: Routledge, 2011.

Ingold, Tim. *Lines*. Abingdon: Routledge, 2016.

Ingold, Tim. *Lines: A Brief History*. London: Routledge, 2007.

Jay, Mike. *The Air Loom Gang*. London: Bantam Press, 2003.

Jenkins, Henry. *Convergence Culture*. New York: Routledge, 2006.

Jimenez, Piera Jordi and Larissa Hjorth. 'Meet Sofia: A 67-Year-Old Widow Who Uses Pokémon Go to Reconnect with Her City', *The Conversation*, 1 July 2019. Available online: https://theconversation.com/meet-sofia-a-67-year-old-widow-who-uses-pokemon-go-to-reconnect-with-her-city-119389 (accessed 10 November 2022).

Johnson, Camille. 'Yellow Arrow Aimed at Building Art Community', *Harvard Crimson*, 19 November 2004. Available online: https://www.thecrimson.com/article/2004/11/19/yellowarrow-aimed-at-building-art-community/ (accessed 23 November 2022).

Juris, Jeffrey. 'Networked Social Movements: Global Movements for Global Justice', in Manuel Castells, ed. *The Network Society: A Cross-cultural Perspective*, 341–61. Northampton, MA: Edward Edgar, 2004.

Kahn, Omar, Trevor Scholz and Mark Shepard. *The Situated Technologies Pamphlets Series*. New York: Architecture League of New York, 2006–11.

Kaptelinin, Victor and Bonnie Nardi. *Acting with Technology: Activity Theory and Interaction Design*. Cambridge, MA: MIT Press, 2005.

Kastner, Jeffrey, ed. *Land and Environmental Art*. London: Phaidon Press, 1998.

King, Stephen. *Danse Macabre*. New York: Berkley Publishing, 1983.

Kindberg, Tim, Matthew Chalmers and Eric Paulos. 'Guest Editors' Introduction: Urban Computing', *IEEE Pervasive Computing*, 6(3), 18–20, 2007.

Klein, Naomi. *No is Not Enough: Defeating the New Shock Politics*. New York: Penguin Books, 2017.

Kloetzel, Melanie and Carolyn Pavlik, eds. *Site Dance: Choreographers and the Lure of Alternative Spaces*. Gainesville: University Press of Florida, 2010.

Knapp, Steven and Walter Benn Michaels. 'Against Theory', *Critical Inquiry*, 8(4), 723–42, 1982. Available online: http://www.jstor.org/stable/1343194 (accessed 10 July 2023).

Koivu, Anniina, ed. *The Walking Society*. Zurich: Lars Muller Publishers, 2015.

Krapp, Peter. *Noise Channels: Glitch and Error in Digital Culture*. Minneapolis: University of Minnesota Press, 2011.

Kukkonen, Karin. 'Metalepsis in Popular Culture: An Introduction', in Karin Kukkonen and Sonia Klimek Sonia, eds. *Metalepsis in Popular Culture*, 1–21. Berlin: Walter de Gruyter, 2011.

Kuzmičová, Anežka, Theresa Schilhab and Michael Burke. 'm-Reading: Fiction Reading from Mobile Phones', *Convergence: The International Journal of Research into New Media Technology*, 26(2), 333–49, 2020.

Labboun, Sonia. 'Privately Owned Public Spaces Need New London Plan Rules', London Assembly, 2017. Available online: https://www.london.gov.uk/press-releases/assembly/privately-owned-public-spaces-need-new-london-plan (accessed 28 June 2023).

LaBelle, Brandon. *Handbook for the Itinerant*. Cambridge, MA: MIT Press, 2012.

Lane, Giles (aka Proboscis). 'Research', Urban Tapestries, 2002–05. Available online: http://research.urbantapestries.net/ (accessed 23 November 2022).

Lavery, Carl. 'Teaching Performance Studies: 25 Instructions for Performance in Cities', *Studies in Theatre and Performance*, 25(3), 229–38, 2005.

Le Feuvre, Lisa. 'Strive to Fail', in Lisa Le Feuvre, ed. *Failure*, Documents of Contemporary Art, 12–21. London: Whitechapel Gallery; Cambridge, MA: MIT Press, 2010.

Levine, Paula. 'On Common Ground: Here as There', in Jason Farman, ed. *The Mobile Story: Narrative Practices with Locative Technologies*, 143–58. London: Routledge, 2014.

Levy, Ari and Lauren Hirsch. 'Amazon Bans Police Use of Facial Recognition Technology for One Year', *CNBC*, 10 June 2020. Available online: https://www.cnbc.com/2020/06/10/amazon-bans-police-use-of-facial-recognition-technology-for-one-year.html (accessed 28 June 2023).

Libeskind, Daniel. *The Space of Encounter*. London: Thames & Hudson, 2001.

Linderman, Deborah. 'Oedipus in Chinatown', *Enclitic*, 5–6, 190–203, 1981–2.

Lippard, Lucy R. *Six Years: The Dematerialisation of the Art Object from 1966 to 1972*. New York: Praeger, 1973.

Lyndon, Donlyn and Charles W. Moore. *Chambers for a Memory Palace*. Cambridge, MA: MIT Press, 1994.

MFour Mobile Research. 'Research Shows That Pokemon Go Boosts Friendships and Social Cohesion', *RW Connect*, 2016. Available online: https://rwconnect.esomar.org/research-shows-that-pokemon-go-boosts-friendships-and-social-cohesion/ (accessed 10 November 2022).

Mackay, Robin and Armen Avanessian, eds. *#Accelerate: The Accelerationist Reader*. Falmouth: Urbanomic, 2014.

Mackey, Margaret. *Literacies across Media: Playing the Text*. London: Routledge, 2002.

Machon, Josephine. *Immersive Theatres: Intimacy and Immediacy in Contemporary Performance*. Basingstoke: Palgrave Macmillan, 2013.

Maitland, Sara. *Gossip from the Forest: The Tangled Roots of Our Forests and Fairy Tales*. London: Granta, 2012.

Malpas, Jeff. *Place and Experience: A Philosophical Topography*, 2nd edn. Abingdon: Routledge, 2018.

Mangen, Anne and Adriaan van der Weel. 'The Evolution of Reading in the Age of Digitisation: An Integrative Framework for Reading Research', *Literacy*, 50(3), 116–24, 2016.

Manguel, Alberto. *A History of Reading*. London: Harper Collins, 1996.

Manning, Erin and Brian Massumi. *Thought in the Act: Passages in the Ecology of Experience*. Minneapolis: University of Minnesota Press, 2014.

Marcinkowski, Michael. 'Where I'm Coming from: Studying the Novelty of Immersive Algorithms', in Tom Abba, Jonathan Dovey and Kate Pullinger, eds. *Ambient Literature: Towards a New Poetics of Situated Writing and Reading Practices*, 199–232. London: Palgrave Macmillan, 2021.

Marcinkowski, Michael and Matthew Hayler. *A Manifesto for Ambient Literature*. Ambient Literature, May 2017. Available online: https://research.ambientlit.com/wp-content/uploads/2017/05/ambient-literature-definition.pdf; https://research.ambientlit.com/wp-content/uploads/2017/05/22-footnotes-for-ambient-literature.pdf (accessed 10 November 2022).

Marx, Karl and Friedrich Engels. *The German Ideology (Part One)*. New York: International Publishers, 1970.

Massey, Doreen. *For Space*. New Delhi: SAGE Publications, 2005.

Massey, Doreen. 'A Global Sense of Place', *Marxism Today* (June), 1991: 24–9.

Massey, Doreen. 'London Inside-Out', *Soundings: A Journal of Politics and Culture*, 32, 62–71, 2006.

Massive Change Radio. 'Stewart Brand Interview', 25 November, 2003. Available online: https://web.archive.org/web/20050518140354/http://www.massivechange.com/PDF/INF_StewartBrand.pdf (accessed 10 November 2022).

Mattern, Shannon. *Code and Clay, Data and Dirt–Five Thousand Years of Urban Media*. Minneapolis: University of Minnesota Press, 2017.

McCullough, Malcolm. *Ambient Commons: Attention in the Age of Embodied Information*. Cambridge, MA: Massachusetts Institute of Technology Press, 2013.

McCullough, Malcolm. 'Epigraphy and the Public Library', in Allesandro Aurigi and Fiorella de Cindro, eds. *Augmented Urban Spaces–Articulating the Physical and Electronic City*, 61–71. Aldershot: Ashgate, 2008.

McDonough, Tom, ed. *The Situationists and the City*. London: Verso, 2009.

McGarrigle, Conor. 'Augmented Resistance: The Possibilities for AR and Data Driven Art', *Leonardo Electronic Almanac, Not Here Not There*, 19(1), 106–21, 2013.

McGarrigle, Conor. 'The Construction of Locative Situations: The Production of Agency in Locative Media Art Practice', PhD diss., Technological University Dublin, 2012.

McLean, Bradley H. *An Introduction to Greek Epigraphy of the Hellenistic and Roman Periods from Alexander the Great until Constantine*. Ann Arbor: University of Michigan Press, 2002.

McLuhan, Marshall. *Understanding Media: The Extensions of Man*. New York: McGraw Hill, 1964.

Merchant, Guy. 'Keep Taking the Tablets: iPads, Story Apps and Early Literacy', *Australian Journal of Language & Literacy*, 38(1), 3–11, 2015.

Merleau-Ponty, Maurice. *Phenomenology of Perception*, trans. Colin Smith. London: Routledge Classics, 2002.

Merleau-Ponty, Maurice. *Primacy of Perception*, trans. W. S. Cobb. Evanston, IL: Northwestern University Press, 1964.

Merleau-Ponty, Maurice. *The Visible and the Invisible*, trans. Alphonso Lingis, ed. Claude Lefort. Evanston, IL: Northwestern University Press, 1968.

Miall, David S. and Don Kuiken. 'The Form of Reading: Empirical Studies of Literariness', *Poetics*, 25(6), 327–41, 1998.

Mitchell, David. 'Enter the Maze', *The Guardian*, 22 May 2004. Available online: https://www.theguardian.com/books/2004/may/22/fiction.italocalvino (accessed 1 December 2022).

Mitchell, William. 'In the First Place', in *Placing Words–Symbols, Space, and the City*, 1–20. Cambridge, MA: MIT Press, 2005.

Moure, Gloria, ed. *Gordon Matta-Clark: Works and Collected Writings*. Barcelona: Ediciones Poligrafa/Museo Nacional Centro de Arte Reina Sofia, 2006.

Nycz, Ryszard. 'Traces of "I": Concepts of Subjectivity in Polish Literature of the Last Century', trans. Alice Nask and Marek Haltof, *Canadian Slavonic Papers/Revue Canadienne Des Slavistes*, 37(3/4), 373–92, 1995.

Olson, Charles. *Projective Verse*. New York: Totem Press, 1959.

Ong, Walter. *Orality and Literacy*. London: Routledge, 2002.

Online Etymological Dictionary. s.v. 'read', n.d. Available online: https://www.etymonline.com/word/read (accessed 10 November 2022).

Orange, Richard. 'Stockholm Says No to Apple "Town Square" in Its Oldest Park', *The Guardian*, 1 November 2018. Available online: https://www.theguardian.com/cities/2018/nov/01/stockholm-apple-town-square-park-kings-garden-kungstradgarden (accessed 28 June 2023).

O'Rourke, Karen. *Walking and Mapping: Artists as Cartographers*. Cambridge, MA: MIT Press, 2013 and 2016.

Papadimitriou, Nick. *Scarp*. London: Hodder & Stoughton, 2012.

Paterson, Mark. *The Senses of Touch*. London: Routledge, 2007.

Pearson, Mike. *Site-Specific Performance*. Basingstoke: Palgrave Macmillan, 2009.

Pearson, Mike and Michael Shanks. *Theatre/Archaeology*. London: Routledge, 2001.

Pelto, Mauri. *Climate Change Data*, 2015. Available online: https://www.jillpelto.com/climate-change-data (accessed 10 June 2024).

Peters, Jay. 'IBM Will No Longer Offer, Develop, or Research Facial Recognition Technology', *The Verge*, 8 June 2020. Available from: https://www.theverge.com/2020/6/8/21284683/ibm-no-longer-general-purpose-facial-recognition-analysis-software (accessed 28 June 2023).

Pickering, Andrew. *The Mangle of Practice: Time, Agency, and Science*. Chicago, IL: University of Chicago Press, 1995.

Piera Jimenez, Jordi and Larissa Hjorth. 'Meet Sofia: A 67-Year-Old Widow Who Uses Pokémon Go to Reconnect with Her City', *The Conversation*, 1 July 2019. Available online: https://theconversation.com/meet-sofia-a-67-year-old-widow-who-uses-pokemon-go-to-reconnect-with-her-city-119389 (accessed 28 June 2023).

Polyakovskiy, Semyon. *Maginary*, 2018. Available online: https://apps.apple.com/us/app/maginary-adventure-text-book/id1291905541 (accessed 6 June 2024).

Polyakovskiy, Semyon. 'Maginary – Animated Immersive Book for iOS', *Medium*, 18 January 2019. Available online: https://medium.com/@semyonpolyakovskiy/maginary-animated-immersive-book-for-ios-3aec8f5136bc (accessed 10 November 2022).

Pope, Simon. *London Walking: A Handbook for Survival*. London: Batsford, 2000.

Project for Public Spaces (PPS). 'About – Project for Public Spaces', 2019. Available online: https://www.pps.org/about (accessed 28 June 2023).

Pullinger, Kate. *Breathe*. 2018. Available online: https://breathe-story.com/ (accessed 6 June 2024).

Pullinger, Kate. 'Introducing the Next Generation of Ambient Literature', *The Bookseller*, 2016. Available online: https://www.thebookseller.com/futurebook/introducing-next-generation-ambient-literature-338141 (accessed 12 November 2022).

Przybyszewska, Agnieszka. 'W stronę lokacyjnego monologu wypowiedzianego. O eksplorowaniu literackich ucieleśnionych przestrzeni pamięci', *Przegląd Kulturoznawczy*, 2(44), s. 1–24, 2020.

Reeves, Stuart. 'Frames and Bystanders: Uncle Roy All around You', in *Designing Interfaces in Public Settings: Understanding the Role of the Spectator in Human-Computer Interaction*, 123–39. London: Springer, 2011.

Reinfurt, Dexter. *This Stands as a Sketch for the Future*, 28 October 2007. Available online: http://www.dextersinister.org/MEDIA/PDF/Thisstandsasasketchforthefuture.pdf (accessed 1 October 2022).

Richardson, Brian. *Unnatural Voices: Extreme Narration in Modern and Contemporary Fiction*. Columbus: Ohio State University Press, 2006.

Richardson, Tina, ed. *Walking Inside Out*. London: Rowman & Littlefield, 2015.

Ricoeur, Paul. 'Memory and Imagination', in Lisa Le Feuvre, ed. *Failure*. Documents of Contemporary Art. London: Whitechapel Gallery; Cambridge, MA: MIT Press, [2000] 2010.

Rifken, Jeremy. *The Empathic Civilization: The Race to Global Consciousness in a World in Crisis*. Cambridge: Polity Press, 2010.

Riva, Giuseppe, Rosa M. Baños, Cristina Botella, Fabrizia Mantovani and Andrea Gaggioli. 'Transforming Experience: The Potential of Augmented Reality and Virtual Reality for Enhancing Personal and Clinical Change', *Frontiers in Psychiatry*, 7, 164, 2016.

Roquet, Paul. *Ambient Media: Japanese Atmospheres of Self*. Minneapolis: University of Minnesota Press, 2016.

Russell, Ben. 'Headmap Manifesto – Know Your Place/Location Aware Devices', Headmap, 1999. Available online: http://www.headmap.org/ (accessed 10 November 2022).

Ryan, Marie-Laure. *Avatars of Story*. Minneapolis: University of Minnesota Press, 2006.

Ryan, Marie-Laure. *Narrative as Virtual Reality: Immersion and Interactivity in Literature and Electronic Media*. Baltimore, MD: Johns Hopkins University Press, 2001.

Ryan, Marie-Laure. *Narrative as Virtual Reality 2: Revisiting Immersion and Interactivity in Literature and Electronic Media*. Baltimore, MD: Johns Hopkins University Press, 2015.

Sabbagh, Dan. 'Facial Recognition Technology Scrapped at King's Cross Site', *The Guardian*, 2 September 2019. Available online: https://www.theguardian.com/technology/2019/sep/02/facial-recognition-technology-scrapped-at-kings-cross-development (accessed 28 June 2023).

Saker, Michael and Leighton Evans. 'Pokémon Go Is Not Dead, It Has 5m Loyal Players and It's Changing People's Lives', *The Conversation*, 22 October 2018. Available online: https://theconversation.com/pokemon-go-is-not-dead-it-has-5m-loyal-players-and-its-changing-peoples-lives-104095 (accessed 28 June 2023).

Schandorf, Michael and Athina Karatzogianni. '#NODAPL: Distributed Rhetorical Praxis at Standing Rock', in Jonathan Alexander and Jacqueline Rhodes, eds. *Routledge Handbook of Digital Rhetoric and Writing*, 142–52. New York: Routledge, 2018.

Schaub, Mirjam. *Janet Cardiff: The Walk Book*. Vienna: Thyssen-Bornemisza Art Contemporary, 2005.

Schmidt, Ulrik. 'Ambience and Ubiquity', in Ulrik Ekman, ed. *Throughout: Art and Culture Emerging with Ubiquitous Computing*, 175–87. Cambridge, MA: MIT Press, 2013.

Schmidt, Wolf. *Narratology: An Introduction*, trans. Alexander Starritt. Berlin: Walter de Gruyter, 2010.

Schneider, Jay and Gerd Kortuem. 'How to Host as Pervasive Game: Supporting Face-to-Face Interactions in Live-Action Roleplaying', Position Paper for UbiComp 2001 Workshop on Designing Ubiquitous Computing Games, 2001.

Scott, Clive. *Literary Translation and the Rediscovery of Reading*. Cambridge: Cambridge University Press, 2012.

Sebald, W. G. *The Rings of Saturn*. London: The Harvill Press, 1995.

Shapiro, Johanna. 'Illness Narratives: Reliability, Authenticity and the Empathic Witness', *Medical Humanities*, 37(2), 68–72, 2011.

Shenker, Jack. 'London Mayor to Draw Up Charter Regulating Pseudo-Public Space', *The Guardian*, 23 November 2017. Available online: https://www.theguardian.

com/cities/2017/nov/23/london-mayor-charter-pseudo-public-space-sadiq-khan (accessed 28 June 2023).

Shepherd, Mark. *Sentient City: Ubiquitous Computing, Architecture, and the Future of Urban Space*. Cambridge, MA: MIT Press, 2011.

Sicart, Miguel. *Beyond Choices: The Design of Ethical Gameplay*. Cambridge, MA: MIT Press, 2013.

Sing London. 'Talking Statues', 2014–17. Available online: http://www.talkingstatues.co.uk (accessed 12 November 2022).

Smailbegović, Ada. 'Cloud Writing: Describing Soft Architectures of Change in the Anthropocene', in Heather Davis and Etienne Turpin, eds. *Art in the Anthropocene: Encounters Among Aesthetics, Politics, Environments and Epistemologies*, 93–108. London: Open Humanities Press, 2015.

Smith, Phil. *Anywhere: A Mythogeography of South Devon*. Axminster: Triarchy Press, 2017.

Smith, Phil. *The Footbook of Zombie Walking*. Axminster: Triarchy Press, 2015.

Smith, Phil. *Making Site-Specific Theatre and Performance*. Basingstoke: Palgrave Macmillan, 2018.

Smith, Phil. *Mythogeography*. Axminster: Triarchy Press, 2010.

Smith, Phil. *On Walking*. Axminster: Triarchy Press, 2014.

Solnit, Rebecca. *Wanderlust*. London: Granta, 2014.

Sonderman, Bryan. 'Walking Games Database', Now, Here, 24 May 2012. Available online: http://bryan-sonderman.blogspot.com/2012/05/walking-games-database.html (accessed 12 November 2022).

Sontag, Susan. *On Regarding the Pain of Others*. New York: Penguin Books, 2004.

Sorrentino, Miriam. 'How Ambient Advertising is Uniquely Placed to Make Audiences Think', *Westminster Papers in Communication and Culture*, 15(2), 95–111, 2020.

Speakman, Duncan. *It Must Have Been Dark by Then*. 2017. Available online: https://research.ambientlit.com/index.php/it-must-have-been-dark-by-then/ (accessed 6 June 2024).

Steinberg, Philip and Kimberly Peters. 'Wet Ontologies, Fluid Spaces: Giving Depth to Volume through Oceanic Thinking', *Environment and Planning D: Society and Space*, 33(2), 247–64, 2015.

Szul, Szymon and Marta Dziedziela. 'Andrzej Strug's "Dzieje jednego pocisku" as an inspiration to create retrofuturistic locative-narrative', Conference Talk – Panel, University of Łódź, 1 July 2020. Available online: https://stars.library.ucf.edu/elo2020/asynchronous/panels/1/ (accessed 28 May 2024).

Tanner, Grafton. *Babbling Corpse*. Winchester: Zero Books, 2016.

Thompson, Clive. 'Brave New World of Digital Intimacy', *The New York Times*, 7 September 2008. Available online: www.nytimes.com/2008/09/07/magazine/07awareness-t.html (accessed 10 November 2022).

Thon, Jan-Noël. 'Immersion Revisited: On the Value of a Contested Concept', in Olli Leino, Hanna Wirman and Amyris Fernandez, eds. *Extending Experiences: Structure,*

Analysis and Design of Computer Game Player Experience, 29–43, Lapland: Lapland University Press, 2008.

TMF Editors. 'The Concept of Tactical Media', Tactical Media Files, 7 March 2017. Available online: http://www.tacticalmediafiles.net/articles/44999 (accessed 10 November 2022).

Todras-Whitehill, Ethan. 'Making Connections Here and Now', *The New York Times*, 25 January 2006: 3.

Torchin, Leshu. 'What Can the Mass "Check-In" at Standing Rock Tell Us about Online Advocacy?', *The Conversation*, 5 November 2016. Available online: https://theconversation.com/what-can-the-masscheck-in-at-standing-rock-tell-us-about-online-advocacy-68276 (accessed 10 November 2022).

Tullet, Barrie. 'Electro-Library Dreams', *Eye Magazine*, 16 June 2010. Available online: http://www.eyemagazine.com/blog/post/electro-library-dreams (accessed 10 November 2022).

Ultrahaptics. 'Ultrahaptics', 2018. Available online: https://www.ultrahaptics.com/ (accessed 28 June 2023).

Umbarila, Juan Álvarez Umbarila. 'Breathe: The Spatial Triangulation of Everyday Literary Experiences in Ambient Literature and m-Reading', *Perífrasis. Revista de Literatura, Teoría y Crítica*, 13(26), 123–41, 2022.

Welton, Martin. *Feeling Theatre*. Basingstoke: Palgrave Macmillan, 2011.

Whalley, Joanne 'Bob'. *Personal Journal*, July 2004.

White, Edmund. *The Flâneur*. London: Thorndike Press, 2001.

White, Gareth. *Audience Participation in Theatre: Aesthetics of the Invitation*. Basingstoke: Palgrave Macmillan, 2013.

Whittaker, Emma. 'An Aesthetics of Ambient Literature; Experience, Narrative, Design', in Tom Abba, Jonathan Dovey and Kate Pullinger, eds. *Ambient Literature: Towards a New Poetics of Situated Writing and Reading Practices*, 233–62. London: Palgrave Macmillan, 2021.

Wilson, Robert. *Einstein on the Beach*, premiered at the Festival d'Avignon, Avignon, France, 25 July 1976. Available online: http://www.robertwilson.com/einstein-on-the-beach (accessed 10 November 2022).

Winiecka, Elżbieta. *Białoszewski sylleptyczny*. Poznań: Poznańskie Studia Polonistyczne, 2006.

Winiecka, Elżbieta. 'O sylleptyczności tekstu literackiego', *Pamiętnik Literacki*, 95(4), 137–57, 2004.

Woolf, Virginia. *Street Haunting*. London: Penguin, 2005.

Wrights & Sites. *The Architect-Walker*. Axminster: Triarchy Press, 2018.

Wrights & Sites. *A Mis-Guide to Anywhere*. Exeter: Wrights & Sites, 2006.

Zagal, José P., Clara Fernández-Vara and Michael Mateas. 'Rounds, Levels, and Waves: The Early Evolution of Gameplay Segmentation', *Games and Culture*, 3(2), 175–98, 2008.

Zipes, Jack. *The Irresistible Fairy Tale*. Princeton, NJ: Princeton University Press, 2012.

Index

www.ingramcontent.com/pod-product-compliance
Ingram Content Group UK Ltd.
Pitfield, Milton Keynes, MK11 3LW, UK
UKHW020816290926
15470UKWH00003B/1197

9 781350 234130